Masterin
LLM Applications with LangChain and Hugging Face

Practical insights into LLM deployment and use cases

Hunaidkhan Pathan
Nayankumar Gajjar

www.bpbonline.com

First Edition 2025

Copyright © BPB Publications, India

ISBN: 978-93-65891-041

LIMITS OF LIABILITY AND DISCLAIMER OF WARRANTY

To View Complete
BPB Publications Catalogue
Scan the QR Code:

Dedicated to

I dedicate this book to my treasured parents, my beloved wife,
*my wonderful kids, and my esteemed mentor, **Mr. Amit Saraswat**.*
Your unwavering support and guidance have been
the cornerstone of my journey.

— Hunaidkhan Pathan

*Almighty, **Dr. Amit Saraswat**, and My Family*

— Nayankumar Gajjar

About the Authors

- **Hunaidkhan Pathan** currently serves as a Data Science Lead for a leading consulting firm with over a decade of experience in the field. Specializing in machine learning and artificial intelligence, he brings a wealth of expertise to his role. Hunaidkhan holds a PGDM in Data Science from Shanti Business School in Ahmedabad and a degree in Electronics and Communication Engineering from Gujarat Technological University.

  He has significantly contributed to the data science community, with his research papers selected and presented at the prestigious SAS Analytics Conference 2013 in Orlando. The titles of his papers include "Marketing Mix Modeling" as an author and "Predicting market uncertainty with Kalman filter" as a co-author. He was also a LinkedIn Top Voice for Data Science and Artificial Intelligence in 2023. He posts regularly on LinkedIn about Generative AI.

  Hunaidkhan is an acknowledged **Subject Matter Expert (SME)** in Generative AI and Natural Language Processing. His diverse experience spans various LLM services such as OpenAI, Nvidia Nemo, Anthropic, GCP Generative AI, and AWS Bedrock, in addition to numerous open-source LLMs. His broad experience and profound knowledge make him a valuable contributor in the domain of data science.

- **Nayankumar Gajjar**, has a rich background in Data Science, Machine Learning and Generative AI fields with 9 years of extensive experience as a Data Scientist, Machine Learning Engineer, and Python Developer. Over the years, he has made significant contributions to various high-impact projects, showcasing his expertise in statistical modeling, Generative AI, MLOps, and Cloud Computing. This diverse skill set makes him a versatile and highly skilled professional in the Data Science and Machine Learning domains. He holds a master's degree in Decision Science, further solidifying his deep understanding of the field. In addition to his professional work, he is a YouTuber and a blogger who shares his experiences and knowledge, offering a complete understanding of statistics and providing detailed coding tutorials. His commitment to education extends to his role as a visiting faculty member, where he has taught Python, SQL, Data Science, and NLP courses. He also co-authored a research paper titled "Thiessen Polygon, A GIS approach for Retail Industry in SAS," which was presented at the prestigious SAS Analytics Conference 2013 in Orlando.

About the Reviewer

Vijender Singh is a multi-cloud professional with over six years of expertise, currently working in Luxembourg. He holds an MSc with distinction from Liverpool John Moores University, where his research centered on keyphrase extraction. Vijender boasts an impressive collection of cloud certifications, including Google MLPE, five Azure certifications, two AWS certifications, and TensorFlow certification. His role as a technical reviewer for numerous books reflects his commitment to improving the future.

Acknowledgements

We would like to express our sincere gratitude to all those who contributed to the completion of this book.

First and foremost, we extend our heartfelt appreciation to our mentor, Dr. Amit Saraswat, our family and friends for their unwavering support and encouragement throughout this journey. Their love and encouragement have been a constant source of motivation.

We are immensely grateful to BPB Publications for their guidance and expertise in bringing this book to fruition. Their support and assistance were invaluable in navigating the complexities of the publishing process.

We would also like to acknowledge the reviewers, technical experts, and editors who provided valuable feedback and contributed to the refinement of this manuscript. Their insights and suggestions have significantly enhanced the quality of the book.

Last but not least, we want to express our gratitude to the readers who have shown interest in our book. Your support and encouragement have been deeply appreciated.

Thank you to everyone who has played a part in making this book a reality.

Preface

In earlier days, when AI was in its beginning phase, we used to work with statical modeling, which contains statistical models like regression, random forest, decision tree, etc. At that time, we used to work with numerical data only, and we did not have much to gain from textual data. Gradually, we got a way under the umbrella of **Bag of Words** (**BoW**) through which we can work with textual data. The main logic was converting textual data to numerical data. For this, we have a few methods, like count vectors and TF-IDF vectors. These methods create a matrix that shows the occurrence of a word in the given document. Again, these methods were not helping ML models get the context or intent of what had been said in the text. These techniques were helping us to do sentiment analysis and other prediction-based tasks using the above mentioned algorithms.

Fast forward to this time, where we have some advanced techniques like transformers having an underlying architecture of neural networks, due to which ML models are able to get the context as well as the intent of what has been said in the text. This has opened up new opportunities and possibilities in the world of **Natural Language Processing** (**NLP**) and **Natural Language Generation** (**NLG**).

Both NLP and NLG are very important fields in the current era of AI. These fields give machines the power to understand and generate texts like human beings. Some of the readers must have heard the term "ChatGPT," one of the well-known chatbot platforms from OpenAI. If you have ever used ChatGPT, you must have an idea that it can write code for you, provide medical advice as well, do future prediction as well, and again, here you can chat with ChatGPT, similar to talking to a person and the person answering your questions.

As time passes, these text generation and understanding models become more advanced and able to perform and understand almost all text related tasks. To create such an advancement in the NLP and NLG areas, we will definitely need people who not only know but also have a better understanding of all the terminologies and concepts of NLP and NLG. Also, they should be aware of the steps and phases of the development and deployment of ML models to be served to end users. As we [authors] are interacting with different people in our day-to-day lives, we have found that there is no one step solution that can provide readers with all the above-mentioned things in one place. If readers get terminologies and concepts, then they will not get steps. If they get steps, then there is no practical exposure. If readers have practical exposure, then how to deploy on the cloud is another question. This book comes into the picture in such scenarios.

This book has been written for beginners or people who are stuck at the different stages mentioned in the previous paragraph and do not know about the next steps. This can be divided into three parts. In the first part, you can consider the first three chapters, where we have shown the installation of Python, running Python scripts in different ways, the basic concepts of Python, the installation of editors, and the usage and importance of the virtual environment. In the second part, you can consider chapters 4 and 5, which show the basic and important concepts of NLP and NLG. From chapters 6 to 11, we have shown the usage of important packages like LangChain and Hugging Face. Then we have shown how you can create a chatbot with custom data and integrate it with an application like Telegram. At last, we have shown deployment to an AWS cloud environment. The rest of the chapters are related to future direction and include some useful tips and references.

In this book, we have not only discussed the theoretical approach, but we have also implemented and provided practical exposure as well. In the practical implementation, you will learn all the required steps to be performed to make things work.

We hope that this book will be helpful to any individual who is looking forward to starting their journey in the NLP and NLG fields. We also hope that this book will provide complete guidance and help readers to the required understanding with practical exposure.

Chapter 1: Introduction to Python and Code Editors – In this chapter, readers will learn about Python as a programming language and its history. Readers will get an idea of Python's features and why it is an important language from an AI/ML perspective. Also, the reader will get an idea about the difference between a code editor and an **Integrated Development Environment (IDE)**.

Chapter 2: Installation of Python, Required Packages, and Code Editors – In this chapter, readers will install Python, all the packages we are going to use throughout the entire book, and an IDE to start with coding. Apart from the installation, readers will gain knowledge on the virtual environment, its importance and its usage. Also, readers will gain knowledge and practical exposure to Python programming basics.

Chapter 3: Ways to Run Python Scripts – In this chapter, readers will create their first Python script, and then they will get practical hands-on experience on different ways to run any Python script.

Chapter 4: Introduction of NLP and its concepts – In this chapter, readers will get exposure to the theoretical concepts and terminologies of NLP, which are essential to start with. Also, readers will get practical hands-on experience with all the important terminologies and concepts.

Chapter 5: Introduction to Large Language Models – This chapter contains theoretical concepts. In this chapter, readers will acquire knowledge on LLM history and its evaluation. Apart from the history, readers will also learn important terminologies and concepts of LLMs.

Chapter 6: Introduction to LangChain, Usage and Importance – In this chapter, readers will gain knowledge of the LangChain package, which is mainly used for text data **Extract, Transform, Load (ETL)** tasks to be later used by LLMs for further processing, understanding, and text generation. Readers will get to know LangChain integration with Hugging Face and how to use LLMs available from Hugging Face. In the chapter, readers will also get practical exposure, which will help them practice and gain confidence.

Chapter 7: Introduction to Hugging Face, its Usage and Importance – In this chapter, readers will get practical exposure to the different LLMs available on Hugging Face Hub and how to use them. Readers will explore Hugging Face Hub as well, which provides a complete ecosystem for LLM deployment.

Chapter 8: Creating Chatbots using Custom Data with Langchain and Hugging Face Hub – In this chapter, readers will create chatbots using the RAG mechanism on custom data using LangChain and Hugging Face combinations. Also, readers will get exposure to the Gradio framework of Hugging Face, through which they can interact with the chatbot created.

Chapter 9: Hyperparameter Tuning and Fine Tuning Pre-Trained Models – In this chapter, the user will gain knowledge about the different hyperparameters available for any LLM, their usage, and how they will impact the LLM's performance.

Chapter 10: Integrating LLMs into Real-World Applications: Case Studies – In this chapter, readers will create a Telegram chatbot with the custom data and interact with it. Readers will get step-by-step guide on the implementation.

Chapter 11: Deploying LLMs in Cloud Environments for Scalability – In this chapter, readers will get a step-by-step guide to deploying chatbots and LLM models in an AWS cloud environment. Readers will also get an idea about GCP.

Chapter 12: Future Directions: Advances in LLMs and Beyond – In this chapter, readers will learn future directions and where to go from here once the book has been completed.

Appendix A: Useful Tips for Efficient LLM Experimentation – In this chapter, we have shared some tips to use LLMs more efficiently.

Appendix B: Resources and References – In this chapter, we have provided some of the resources and references for the readers to get more depth and detailed knowledge on different models and packages.

Code Bundle and Coloured Images

Please follow the link to download the
Code Bundle and the *Coloured Images* of the book:

https://rebrand.ly/bf9408

The code bundle for the book is also hosted on GitHub at
https://github.com/bpbpublications/Mastering-LLM-Applications-with-LangChain-and-Hugging-Face.
In case there's an update to the code, it will be updated on the existing GitHub repository.

We have code bundles from our rich catalogue of books and videos available at
https://github.com/bpbpublications. Check them out!

Errata

We take immense pride in our work at BPB Publications and follow best practices to ensure the accuracy of our content to provide with an indulging reading experience to our subscribers. Our readers are our mirrors, and we use their inputs to reflect and improve upon human errors, if any, that may have occurred during the publishing processes involved. To let us maintain the quality and help us reach out to any readers who might be having difficulties due to any unforeseen errors, please write to us at :

errata@bpbonline.com

Your support, suggestions and feedbacks are highly appreciated by the BPB Publications' Family.

Piracy

If you come across any illegal copies of our works in any form on the internet, we would be grateful if you would provide us with the location address or website name. Please contact us at **business@bpbonline.com** with a link to the material.

If you are interested in becoming an author

If there is a topic that you have expertise in, and you are interested in either writing or contributing to a book, please visit **www.bpbonline.com**. We have worked with thousands of developers and tech professionals, just like you, to help them share their insights with the global tech community. You can make a general application, apply for a specific hot topic that we are recruiting an author for, or submit your own idea.

Reviews

Please leave a review. Once you have read and used this book, why not leave a review on the site that you purchased it from? Potential readers can then see and use your unbiased opinion to make purchase decisions. We at BPB can understand what you think about our products, and our authors can see your feedback on their book. Thank you!

For more information about BPB, please visit **www.bpbonline.com**.

Join our book's Discord space

Join the book's Discord Workspace for Latest updates, Offers, Tech happenings around the world, New Release and Sessions with the Authors:

https://discord.bpbonline.com

Table of Contents

CHAPTER 1
Introduction to Python and Code Editors

Introduction

Python is a really powerful programming language that is simple and easy to read. This language is being used in many technology areas. There are rules called **Python Enhancement Proposal (PEP)** standards, which help you write proper Python code. These rules give instructions for how we should write and develop the programming language which helps us keep our code clean and of high quality!

There are also different ways that we can work on our Python codes - either through code editors or **Integrated Development Environments (IDEs)**.

Structure

In this chapter we will discuss the following topics:

- Introduction to Python
- Introduction to code editors

Objectives

Learning Python well is a great start for getting into generative AI. Python is known for being easy to understand and has lots of tools you can use. It is a good language to learn if you want to understand how programming works. Since Python is used everywhere, it is important for learning different kinds of machine learning, which is really helpful if you are interested in generative AI. If you are good at Python, you can easily use the important tools and information you need for generative AI. This makes it easier to move on to more advanced things like understanding how computers understand human language or deep learning.

Introduction to Python

Created by *Guido Van Rossum* back in the late 1980s, today, almost everybody uses Python! Here is a brief introduction to Python:

- **Readability**: It is easy to understand any code written by another person due to its simplicity.

- **Interpreted language**: Python is an interpreted language. You do not need to compile your program before running it on the system. This makes development faster and easier, as you can execute code line by line, and easy to debug.

- **Cross-platform**: Your computer runs Windows? MacOS? Linux? Do not worry! No matter what operating system your computer has installed, they all support Python!

- **Versatility**: Many more useful features like versatility, object-oriented libraries, and interfaces, community support, dynamic variable declaration, etc., which make work super smooth.

- **Libraries and frameworks**: If asked to paint an image without a canvas color brush, it is hard for anyone. In similar cases with computer programming, we require a lot of tools to make it happen; IDEs and code editors are one of them, which have unique functionality based on requirements and can be customized accordingly. For example, PyCharm is a Python-specific editor. We also have something called Jupyter Notebook or Jupyter Lab in the Python world. Python provides a large collection of different libraries for different tasks. For example, Django is used for web development, NumPy and Pandas are used for data analysis, and Tensorflow and Keras are used for deep learning.

- **Community and support**: Python's simplicity and community support make it a highly usable coding language. It does not matter if you are new to programming or an experienced pro: Python has something for everyone! This powerful tool will always come in handy whether it is web development, data analysis or AI/ML tasks etc.

- **Open source**: Python is open-source and free to use. This encourages collaboration and innovation, as anyone can contribute to the language's development or create their own Python packages.

- **Object-oriented**: Python is an object-oriented programming language, which means code organization around objects/classes simplifies managing complex systems.

- **Dynamic typing**: Python uses dynamic typing, which means variables do not require any explicit type definition speeding up development but further necessitates attention towards avoiding potential typing errors.

- **High-level language**: Python is a high-level programming language; since lower-level complexities are abstracted away, users can concentrate mainly on problem-solving and worrying less about underlying hardware details.

- **Duck typing**: Python follows the principle of *duck typing*, which means the object type determination is based on its behavior which gives code the freedom to be concise yet vigilant towards object compatibility.

- **Multi-paradigm**: Python supports multiple programming instances, including procedural, object-oriented, and functional programming. This versatility allows us to choose the most suitable approach for our project's requirements.

- **Interoperability**: Python interacts smoothly with other languages like C, C++, Java, etc., enabling utilization of existing libraries/code.

- **Popular use cases**: Usable across several domains, i.e., web development (using Django/Flask/FastAPI), data science (machine learning using Scikit-Learn/TensorFlow), Scientific computing (using NumPy/SciPy), automation scripting or even game development, the list is endless.

- **Python 2 vs. Python 3**: It is important to note that there are two major versions of Python: Python 2 and Python 3. Though there are mainly two versions available, as of Jan 1st, 2020, only Python 3 receives updates/supports - have an edge by starting all new projects in this version!

In conclusion, regardless of whether you are a beginner embarking upon an initial language learning journey or an experienced developer handling intricate setup, the simplicity/readability/use case versatility/community backup is positioning Python as handy across several coding tasks.

Zen (**Python Enhancement Proposal PEP 20**) Philosophy embraces design ideals/principles defining how Python code should be written for not just computers but easy understanding by fellow developers too!

Here are some of the key principles from the *Zen of Python* written by *Tim Peters*:

- **Beautiful is better than ugly**: Python code should be aesthetically pleasing, clear, and elegant. This encourages developers to write code that is not only functional but also visually appealing.

- **Explicit is better than implicit**: Code should be explicit in its intentions and behavior. Avoid relying on hidden or implicit features to make the code more understandable.

- **Simple is better than complex**: Simplicity is preferred over complexity. The code should be straightforward and easy to understand rather than unnecessarily convoluted.

- **Complex is better than complicated**: While simplicity is encouraged and complexity is necessary, it should be well-structured and not overly complicated. Complex code should have a clear purpose and design.

- **Flat is better than nested**: Deeply nested code structures should be avoided. Keeping code relatively flat, with fewer levels of indentation, makes it more readable and maintainable.

- **Sparse is better than dense**: Code should be spaced out and not overly dense. Proper spacing and indentation enhance readability.

- **Readability counts**: Readability is a top priority in Python. Code should be written with the goal of making it easy to read and understand, not just for the computer but also for other developers.

- **Special cases are insufficient to break the rules**: Consistency is important. While there may be exceptional cases, they should not lead to a violation of established coding conventions and rules.

- **Practicality beats purity**: While adhering to best practices and principles is important, practicality should not be sacrificed in the pursuit of theoretical perfection. Real-world solutions sometimes require pragmatic compromises.

- **Errors should never pass silently. Unless explicitly silenced**: Errors and exceptions should be handled explicitly. If you encounter an error, it should not be ignored or suppressed unless you have a good reason to do so.

- **In the face of ambiguity, refuse the temptation to guess**: When faced with uncertainty or ambiguity in your code, it is better to be explicit and not make assumptions. Clarity should prevail.

- **There should be one and preferably only one obvious way to do it**: Python encourages a single, clear way to accomplish tasks to minimize confusion and inconsistency in code.

- **Although that way may not be obvious at first unless you are Dutch**: This light-hearted remark acknowledges that not all design decisions may immediately make sense to everyone and hints at Python's creator, *Guido van Rossum*.

- **Now is better than never. Although never is often better than right now**: While taking action is important, rushing without proper consideration can lead to errors. It's a reminder to balance speed with careful thought.

- **If the implementation is hard to explain, it is a bad idea. If the implementation is easy to explain, it may be a good idea**: Code should be designed in a way that makes its purpose and behavior clear and straightforward. Complex, hard-to-explain implementations should be avoided.

- **Namespaces are one honking great idea: Let us do more of those**: Encouragement to use namespaces for organizing and managing variables and functions, promoting modularity, and avoiding naming conflicts.

The Zen of Python serves as a set of principles to guide Python developers in writing code that is not only functional but also elegant and maintainable. It reflects Python's emphasis on code readability, simplicity, and the idea that code should be written for humans to understand as much as for computers to execute. You can access the Zen of Python by opening a Python interpreter and typing **import this**.

Introduction to code editors

Software development calls for specific tools, and IDEs and code editors are just that. However, they bring different attributes to the table, serving varied purposes with their distinct features. Let us understand these differences:

- **Integrated Development Environment (IDE):**
  - **Comprehensive development environment**: An IDE is a comprehensive toolkit for software creation. Standard components include a code editor, debugger, build tools etc., often tailored for particular languages – Python users might consider PyCharm or Jupyter Notebook/Lab; though not entirely an IDE, these offer interactive computing environments popular in data science.
  - **Language-specific**: Many IDEs are designed for specific programming languages, and they often offer advanced features tailored to that language. For example, RStudio is specific for the R programming language, and PyCharm is a Python-specific IDE. We can consider Jupyter Notebook or Jupyter Lab in this category as well. Though it is not 100% IDE, it can be considered an interactive computational environment that is widely used in the data science field.
  - **Code assistance**: Be it auto-complete suggestions of variable names, functions, etc., easy navigation, or refactoring tools – an IDE supports advancement in code writing.
  - **Debugging**: Aiding coders at every step of scripting via built-in debugging capabilities - this feature allows us to examine variables closely and trace our coding path conveniently.
  - **Project management**: From version control systems management to maintaining dependencies relationships & crafting project templates– an IDE does it all!
  - **Extensions and plugins**: Owing to the existing bunch of features, there is further room for enhancement. Extensive flexibility supporting various frameworks/languages awaits thanks to Plugins/Extensions. Jupyterlab offers multiple add-ins, which can improve the coding experience. Similarly, VS code has a vast library of add-ons that help the coder.
  - **Learning curve**: IDEs can have a difficult learning curve due to their many features and complex user interfaces. They are often preferred by professional

developers working on larger projects. VS code is one such IDE that is used by the wider developer community.

o **Resource intensive**: IDEs can be resource-intensive because of their many features, which may not be suitable for older or less powerful computers.

- **Code editor**: Code editors provide a more straightforward, less cluttered experience for managing code creation and modifications across various programming languages. They are tailored for simplicity, with features like syntax highlighting and automatic indentation that enhance coding efficacy. Code editors advocate minimalism to avoid distractions and allow customization to meet user needs. This combination of brevity and functionality makes these tools an economical choice favored by both beginner coders learning the ropes, or experienced developers seeking a compact setup.

An abundance of compelling reasons exists as to why investing in a code editor is a wise choice:

- **Lightweight text editor**: They are mainly designed as lightweight text editors with syntax highlighting, focusing on creating and modifying code.

- **Language agnostic**: These tools can support multiple programming languages without offering unique features for specific ones—for example, Notepad++.

- **Basic code assistance**: Basic assistance is provided in terms of code completion features, syntax highlights, etc., although it is broadly not as advanced as IDEs.

- **No built-in debugging**: They do not come bundled with debugging tools; hence external resources might be required for debugging tasks.

- **Simplicity**: Known for their *no-frills* approach, they render a distraction-free coding environment that is ideal layout-wise.

- **Customization**: Code editors can be highly customized through themes and extensions. Users can tailor them to suit their specific needs and preferences.

- **Learning curve**: Aligned with an easier learning curve, it meets the requirements of aspiring/experienced programmers preferring minimalist coding encounters.

- **Resource-friendly**: Being non-resource intensive they run efficiently even handling older/weaker computer systems.

In summary, your selection between an IDE or a code editor rests strongly upon personal necessities/preferences. IDE provides vast tools that help in programming; hence, go ahead and pick an IDE for large and complex projects. If easy editing/emphasizing and clean scripts are all you require, it is worth considering investing in a humble *code editor*. Nowadays, developers switch between IDE and code editors based on their requirements and thus do not limit themselves to a specific tool.

Conclusion

In this chapter, we have got an overview of Python's origins and features that contribute to its rise in ranking among popular languages worldwide. Python script execution is possible either through picking any IDE/Code editor, and it is purely contingent upon specific preference as both vary based on personal benefits/hindrances they cater.

Looking forward to the next chapter, it elaborates further on Python installation across various OS systems, including famous python IDEs. Additionally, the chapter will offer insights into Python's OOPs/conceptual basis and best practices implemented. Apart from that, it will also discuss if any issues persist in installing Python alongside alternative solutions.

References

- **https://peps.python.org/pep-0020/#the-zen-of-python**
- **https://docs.python.org/3/faq/**
- **https://wiki.python.org/moin/PythonEditors**
- **https://wiki.python.org/moin/IntegratedDevelopmentEnvironments**

Further reading

- For Python, you can find a list of all the code editors and IDEs on the following links. These URLs contain all the required information like which platform and editor it supports and if the editors are open source or not:
  o **https://wiki.python.org/moin/PythonEditors**
  o **https://wiki.python.org/moin/IntegratedDevelopmentEnvironments**

Join our book's Discord space

Join the book's Discord Workspace for Latest updates, Offers, Tech happenings around the world, New Release and Sessions with the Authors:

https://discord.bpbonline.com

CHAPTER 2
Installation of Python, Required Packages, and Code Editors

Introduction

The installation of Python is a fundamental step in getting started with the book. It allows you to access a rich ecosystem of libraries and tools. Depending on your project, you might need to install additional packages for specific functionalities. Choosing the right **code editor** or **Integrated Development Environment (IDE)** is also essential, as it greatly influences your development workflow. These tools, combined with Python's versatility, set the foundation for productive and efficient programming. In this chapter, we are going to focus on installing Python for different OSes. We will see how to install packages using the **pip** package manager of Python. Apart from this we will review the difference between code editor and IDE and which one is good in different scenarios. As we are writing this book, keeping in mind complete beginners, we have also included some of the basic concepts of Python that will be useful to start with Python.

Structure

In this chapter we will discuss the following topics:

- General instructions
- Installation of Python on Windows
- Installation of Python on Linux

- Installation of Python on MacOS
- Installation of PyCharm
- Installation of required packages
- Object Oriented Programming concepts in Python

Objectives

By the end of this chapter, you will have a functional Python environment by installing Python, configured with the necessary packages tailored to the project's needs, and an optimal IDE, that is, PyCharm, to streamline the development process. This ensures a smooth and efficient workflow, setting the stage for successful book completion.

General instructions

Before proceeding to install Python, run the following commands to make sure Python and pip are available:

- o `python3` *--version or* `python` *--version*
- o `pip3` *--version or* `pip` *--version*
- Here, as you can see, we are checking two different things: one is Python, and the other one is pip. Python is a programming language that has a huge ecosystem of packages for different purposes. To maintain these packages, Python has its own package manager, which is called pip. Using pip, you can install, update, and uninstall any packages from Python.
  - o Python versions after 3.4 come with pip pre-installed. Hence, you will not need to install pip separately.
- It should result in Python version 3.x:
  - o In case Python 3.x is available, do not uninstall it because uninstalling may result in system instability and might cause a corrupted system, especially with Linux OSes.
  - o Here, the advice will be to proceed with your current Python version.
  - o In case the Python version is not compatible with the packages that we are going to use in this book, you can try with other versions of the package. In most of the cases other versions of the packages should also work.
    - ▪ In the rare situation, if it is not the case, in the last section, we have provided an alternative to use Docker to use the latest Python and pip.
- If you have Python version 2.x:
  - o The suggestion will be to update the Python version, but before that, make sure that system dependency is not there else it might result in system issues.

o   Again, if, for any reason, you are not able to change the Python version, refer to the last section of this chapter, which shows how to use Python using Docker so that you can use the latest version of Python.

Installation of Python on Windows

To install Python on Windows, visit the official Python website, download the latest Windows installer, and run it. Check the **Add Python to PATH** option during installation for easier command-line access (This step is specifically for Windows). Python will be installed, allowing you to start coding and running Python scripts on your Windows system. Refer to the following figure:

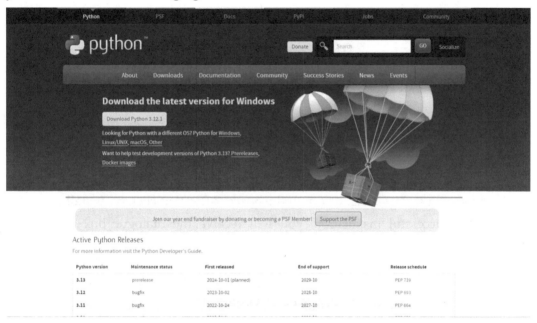

Figure 2.1: *Python Download Page*

The same has been explained using the following steps:

1.   Visit the official Python website to download the latest Python version. At present, while writing the book the latest version of Python is 3.12. *Figure 2.1* shows the Python download page from the official website.

      Note: Python versions, including 3.9.1 and higher, cannot be used on Windows 7 or earlier. Download it from: https://www.python.org/downloads/

2.   Double click on the downloaded **.exe** file which will open pop up as shown in *Figure 2.2*:

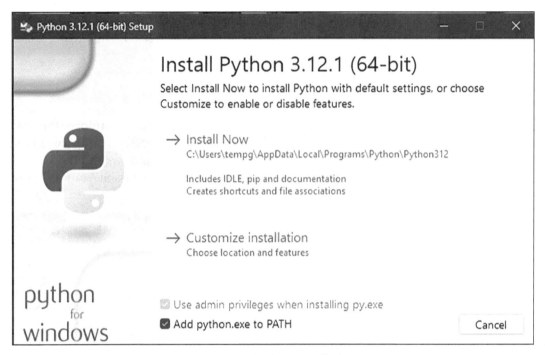

Figure 2.2: Python Installation

3. As shown in *Figure 2.2.* tick both the boxes. After that click on **Install Now**.

4. After successful installation, you will receive the dialogue box as shown in *Figure 2.3*:

Figure 2.3: Python successful installation

5. As shown in *Figure 2.3*, click on the option **Disable path length limit**. After that, close the dialogue box. Now Python has been installed successfully on your system. The "disable path length limit" feature in Python installation refers to an option that allows Python to work with file paths longer than the traditional 260-character limit imposed by the Windows operating system.

Installation of Python on Linux

To install Python on Linux, we are not required to download any executable files. Each version of Linux OS comes with its own package manager, which can be utilized to download Python, Python package manager, i.e. pip. Please remember to check Python and Pip availability before processing to the installation section.

The following are the commands for some famous Linux OS. Again, you need to execute the following commands only in the case Python is not available:

- Debian and Ubuntu, and its different flavors:
  - o `sudo apt install python3`
  - o `sudo apt install python3-pip`
- OpenSuse:
  - o `sudo zypper install python3`
  - o `sudo zypper install python3-pip`
- Fedora, **Red Hat Enterprise Linux (RHEL)**:
  - o `sudo dnf install python3`
  - o `sudo dnf install python3-pip`
- Centos:
  - o `sudo yum install python3`
  - o `sudo yum install python3-pip`
- Arch Linux:
  - o `sudo pacman -S python3`
  - o `sudo pacman -S python3-pip`

After installation of Python and pip, make sure to confirm that both of them are installed successfully using the commands provided in the general instructions section.

Installation of Python on MacOS

To install Python and pip on MacOS, there are two options available:

- Using **brew** package manager.
  - o In case the brew package manager is not available, install it using the following command:

i. `/bin/bash -c "$(curl -fsSL https://raw.githubusercontent.com/Homebrew/install/HEAD/install.sh)"`

o   Then install Python3 using the following command, which will include pip as well:

ii. `brew install python`

- Using a standalone installer from Python official website:

    o   Go to the official website of Python at **https://www.python.org/downloads/macos/**

    o   Download the latest Python version.

    - Click on the downloaded file.

    - Follow the instructions provided on the installation setup.

    - Now, you will have the latest Python on the system.

Using Docker for Python

This section is not required if Python 3.x is available on your system. You only need to use this section if, for any reason, you are not able to use Python 3.x on your system.

Follow the given steps to use Python from Docker:

1. Download and install Docker for your respective OS from **https://docs.docker.com/engine/install/**. It will be an easy step.

2. After installation, visit the official repository of Docker for Python at **https://hub.docker.com/_/python**

3. On this URL, you will get other details as well, like how to install specific Python versions.

4. Run the following command to install the latest Python version. You need to run this command from the terminal or CMD, as shown in *Figure 2.4*:

    o   `docker pull python`

5. Run the following command to confirm that the Docker Python image is available:

    o   `docker images`

6. *Figure 2.4* shows that when running the command **docker pull python,** it is fetching the image from the Docker hub i.e., the central repository and storing it on the local system so that we can utilize it as per our requirement. As we have not mentioned any Python version by default, it will download the latest version available.

    a. Also, the command **docker images** shows what are the images available on the local system. At present, we have only one image from the Docker hub, which is a Python image, which we are going to utilize later on to run different Python scripts.

Refer to *Figure 2.4:*

```
Command Prompt          ×    +   ∨

Microsoft Windows [Version 10.0.22621.2861]
(c) Microsoft Corporation. All rights reserved.

C:\Users\nayan>docker images
REPOSITORY    TAG         IMAGE ID       CREATED        SIZE


C:\Users\nayan>docker pull python
Using default tag: latest
latest: Pulling from library/python
bc0734b949dc: Pull complete
b5de22c0f5cd: Pull complete
917ee5330e73: Pull complete
b43bd898d5fb: Pull complete
7fad4bffde24: Pull complete
d685eb68699f: Pull complete
107007f161d0: Pull complete
02b85463d724: Pull complete
Digest: sha256:3733015cdd1bd7d9a0b9fe21a925b608de82131aa4f3d397e465a1fcb545d36f
Status: Downloaded newer image for python:latest
docker.io/library/python:latest

What's Next?
  View summary of image vulnerabilities and recommendations → docker scout quickview python

C:\Users\nayan>docker images
REPOSITORY    TAG         IMAGE ID       CREATED        SIZE
python        latest      3c055746a2cc   3 weeks ago    1.02GB


C:\Users\nayan>
```

Figure 2.4: Download and confirm Python image via Docker

7. In case you want a specific version of Python, you can run the following command:

   o You can get the specific Python version and its respective tag details from the URL: **https://hub.docker.com/_/python/tags**

   o `docker pull <image_name>:<tag>`:

      o `docker pull python:3.12`

      o `docker pull python:3.12-slim`

8. We will see how to run Python scripts using Docker in *Chapter 3, Ways to Run Python Scripts.*

Installation of IDE

The freely available PyCharm Community Edition has been created by JetBrains as an IDE catered specifically for Python coders. Thanks to JetBrains, known for their repertoire of resourceful development tools, here is what you should know about this IDE:

- **Free and open-source**: Being free and open-source makes it a perfect coding environment for developers at different skill levels without worrying about monetary constraints.

- **Python-centric IDE**: Designed with Python in mind, PyCharm provides a dedicated platform enriched with features catering to the writing, testing, and debugging processes of Python scripting.

- **Smart code assistance**: Elevated productivity is offered through smart code analysis, completion suggestions, and efficient navigation within your codes. These features help maintain clean scripts while preventing possible errors.

- **Django and web development**: Django enthusiasts can find easy accommodation for web application development within PyCharm, which includes database management tools along with templates specific to various web frameworks.

- **Version control integration**: Stay orderly, managing projects and collaborating efficiently. Packed integrated popular VCS like Git/Mercurian/Subversion.

- **Unit testing and debugging**: Easy identification and troubleshooting with built-in unit tests/debuggers, helping analyze Python scripts effectively.

- **Customization and plugins**: Easy customization of the IDE and many different plugins available for further integration.

- **Cross-platform**: Supports Windows/macOS/Linux—promising wide range usability embracing diverse development environments.

- **Active community**: Jump straight in! Find an abundance of tutorials/support/resources that have been made possible by the active users/developers' community. Website: - **https://intellij-support.jetbrains.com/hc/en-us/community/topics/**

- **Seamless integration with other JetBrains tools**: If you decide to use any other tool created by JetBrains, PyCharm provides a seamless integration between all the JetBrains tools.

To sum up, PyCharm Community Edition greatly sharpens Python programming brush across developers' spectrum, be it internalizing Python newbies or experts handling complicated assembly lines!

Installation of PyCharm

There are two ways to install the PyCharm community edition on the OS: using GUI or using the command line, that is the terminal. You can opt for any of the following options for the installation:

GUI for Windows, Linux, and Mac:

1. Visit the webpage, **https://www.jetbrains.com/pycharm/download/?section=windows**

2. Go to the bottom of the page, where you will find the option to download the PyCharm community edition.

3. Download the executable file as per the OS. For Linux files, you will get a **.tar.gz** file.

4. Double-click on the executable file and install the IDE for Windows and Mac.

   a. For Linux, you need to extract the **.tar.gz** file. Here, you will get a text file with a name starting with the "Install" word.

   b. Open that file where you will get installation instructions. Follow the instructions to install IDE on Linux.

Using Terminal for Mac:

1. Using the "brew" package manager.

   a. In case the brew package manager is not available, install it using the following command:

      o `/bin/bash -c "$(curl -fsSL https://raw.githubusercontent.com/Homebrew/install/HEAD/install.sh)"`

   b. Then install IDE using the following command:

      o `brew install --cask pycharm-ce`

Using Terminal for Linux:

1. Install the Snap package manager using the following command:

   o `sudo apt install snapd`

   The above command is for Debian based distros. For other Linux distros download and install Snap from **https://snapcraft.io/docs/installing-snapd** and follow the instructions given on the following page for respective OS.

2. Install IDE using the following command:

   o `snap install pycharm-community --classic`

Installation of required packages

In this section we will install the required packages that we are going to use throughout the book. Before we proceed to the installation of the required packages, let us understand the concept of a virtual environment. After understanding the concept of the virtual environment, we will create a virtual environment and install the required packages in it.

Virtual environment

A virtual environment in Python is essentially a standalone directory that includes a specific Python interpreter packaged with unique sets of libraries and dependencies. This lets you maintain separate Python environments for distinctive projects, hence ensuring the packages and dependencies associated with each project do not overlap. The features are:

- **Isolation**: Each virtual environment is independent of the system-wide Python installation and other virtual environments. This isolation prevents conflicts and dependency issues between different projects.

- **Dependency management**: Virtual environments enable you to install and manage project-specific dependencies, including Python packages and libraries. You can control the versions and avoid compatibility issues.

- **Version compatibility**: Working on different projects may require different versions of Python. Having this flexibility enables users to engage with both older legacy versions as well as advanced state-of-the-art ones.

- **Project portability**: Virtual environments make it easier to share your project with others or deploy it on different systems. You can include the virtual environment along with your project, ensuring that all dependencies are consistent.

To create a virtual environment in Python there are two packages used widely. They are **virtualenv** and **pipenv**. The choice between **pipenv** and **virtualenv** depends on your specific project requirements and personal preferences. Both tools serve as essential components of Python development, but they have distinct purposes and characteristics.

virtualenv

Let us take a look at virtualenv:

- **Purpose**: The primary function of 'virtualenv' is creating isolated environments for different Python applications. Its chief objective lies in offering an untarnished slate where one can work smoothly installing preferred package versions and fulfilling the project's needs alongside managing related dependencies.

- **Usage**: Virtualenv is typically used alongside pip, Python's package installer. Here is how you generally use it:

  o Create a virtual environment using virtualenv.

  o Activate the virtual environment.

  o Use pip within the activated environment to install the necessary Python packages. This setup ensures that the installations and operations are confined to the virtual environment and do not interfere with other projects or the global Python setup.

- **Popularity**: Virtualenv has been a staple in the Python community for many years. It is highly regarded for its stability and effectiveness in managing project-specific environments. Its widespread adoption and trust within the community make it a go-to choice for many Python developers looking to maintain clean and manageable project setups.

- This tool is essential for developers who need to manage multiple projects with differing dependencies or are developing in a team setting where consistency is critical.

pipenv

Let us take a look at pipenv:

- **Purpose**: The primary aim of pipenv is to unify the operation of virtual environment administration and dependency management. It strives to streamline creating isolated workspaces while also controlling project-related dependencies

- **Usage**: With pipenv, you can efficiently construct a virtual workspace and manage its dependencies simultaneously, providing convenience for developers who prefer a comprehensive solution.

- **Popularity**: Pipenv quickly rose in favor due to its simplistic yet user-friendly approach to managing dependencies.

You should consider the following factors when choosing between the two:

- **Simplicity versus integration**: If you prefer a straightforward and lightweight solution for virtual environments, virtualenv might be your choice. However, if you prefer an all-in-one tool for managing both virtual environments and dependencies, pipenv is a good option.

- **Project needs**: Consider the complexity of your project. For small, simple projects, virtualenv may suffice. For larger projects with many dependencies, pipenv can help streamline the process.

- **Community and support**: Both virtualenv and pipenv are well-supported, but virtualenv has a longer history and a well-established user base. However, pipenv has gained momentum and may be the preferred choice for some newer Python developers.

- **Compatibility**: While virtualenv grants compatibility with older-python versions, pipenv intensively focuses Python 3.6 and above listings. Working with legacy Python versions might probe directing affinities instead of facing off virtualenv.

In summary, both pipenv and virtualenv are valuable tools for Python development. For the purpose of the book, we are going to use virtualenv to create a virtual environment.

Folder structure

Before we proceed with this chapter, let us define folder structure so it will be easy throughout the book to keep things organized and structured. Also, it will be easier for us to follow the guidelines. The folder structure is to maintain the scripts and the custom data. We are going to add folders and scripts as per the requirement as we proceed to the different sections of the book.

1. Create a folder called **Book**. You can create it anywhere you like. Make sure that the parent folder does not have spaces in the name. Spaces in names cause issues sometimes; hence, avoid it if possible.

2. Under this folder, create a text file called **requirements.txt**:

   a. Add the following lines in the file:

   ```
   pandas==2.2.2
   transformers==4.42.3
   langchain==0.2.6
   langchain_community==0.2.6
   langchain-huggingface==0.0.3
   accelerate==0.32.1
   unstructured[pdf]==0.14.10
   wikipedia==1.4.0
   nltk==3.8.1
   textblob==0.18.0
   scikit-learn==1.5.1
   spacy==3.7.5
   gensim==4.3.2
   pattern==3.6.0
   huggingface_hub==0.23.4
   torch==2.3.1
   sentence_transformers==3.0.1
   chromadb==0.5.3
   faiss-cpu==1.8.0
   evaluate==0.4.2
   rouge_score==0.1.2
   pypdf==4.2.0
   gradio==4.37.2
   origamibot==2.3.6
   scipy~=1.12.0
   tf_keras==2.16.0
   git+https://github.com/google-research/bleurt.git
   ```

   b. Apart from this, if you are working on a Linux-based OS, you might need to consider installing the below packages. Make sure that the installation command will vary based on the Linux OS. Here, we have provided commands for Ubuntu/Debian-based OS.

   sudo apt install build-essential cmake

3. The folder structure will look as follows:

   a. `E:\Repository\Book`

   b. `├── venv` # Virtual environment created using Virtualenv command, which will contain the specific version of packages mentioned in `requirements.txt` file

   c. `├── requirements.txt` # Text file which keeps track of which package of which version utilized in the project.

   d. Do not worry about **venv** folder. We are going to create it in the next few steps.

As discussed earlier, we are going to install packages in a virtual environment so that it will not impact other projects and their respective package versions. By creating the virtual environment, we will isolate the entire package ecosystem that will be utilized in this book.

Creating a virtual environment

The steps to create a virtual environment are as follows:

1. The steps mentioned here are irrespective of the OS. It means you can follow the steps on any OS and create a virtual environment.

2. Now, let us open a terminal (in the context of Linux or Mac) or CMD (in the context of windows).

   a. The very first step is to install virtualenv. For this execute the following command:

      - `pip install virtualenv`

3. After the installation of **virtualenv** package, from the terminal, go to the directory where you will do the practices and exercises mentioned in this book. For this, you need to use the "**cd**" command. In our case, it will be **Book** folder.

   a. Consider this directory as a root directory of a project where you will need a specific version of specific packages. In this case, it is `E:\Repository\Book`.

   b. As the philosophy of the virtual environment, by creating the virtual environment, we will isolate the entire packaging system from the global packaging system as well as from other project's packaging systems.

4. Once you are in the required directory, execute the following command from terminal/CMD, which will create a virtual environment as shown in *Figure 2.5*.

   `virtualenv venv OR virtualenv -p python3.12 venv OR virtualenv -p /path/to/python_version venv`

   a. Second command is to be used when you have multiple Python versions, and you want to create a virtual environment with a specific Python version.

   b. You can use it with a single Python version as well, like "**virtualenv venv**"

c. In case the virtualenv command mentioned above is providing any error, especially on Windows, such as the command not found on the path. In that case, you can run the below command as well, which will create a virtual environment:

```
python -m virtualenv venv
```

5. It will show details as the following figure:

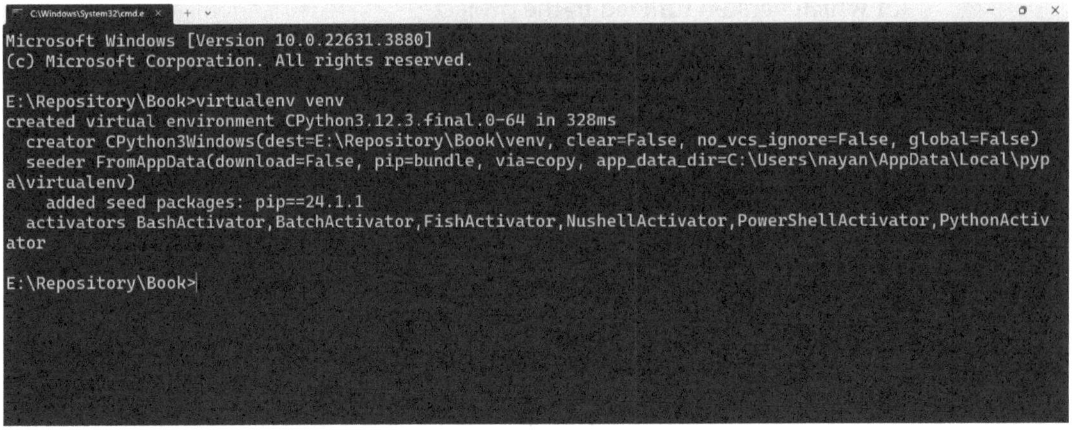

Figure 2.5: Create virtual environment

6. As shown in *Figure 2.5*, it will create a virtual environment named as "venv" under the directory from where you are executing the command **virtualenv venv**

a. Instead of venv you can provide any other name as well.

7. You have successfully created a virtual environment.

a. In case you want to remove the virtual environment, simply delete the folder.

8. Next, let us activate the virtual environment. For this, use the below command. Based on the specific OS, as shown in *Figure 2.6*, it can vary. Once you activate the virtual environment, the name of the virtual environment is appended to your shell prompt, as highlighted in *Figure 2.6*.

a. **venv\scripts\activate** [For Windows]

b. **source venv/bin/activate** [For Linux/Mac]

a. To deactivate the virtual environment, just run the command **deactivate**

9. Finally, install the required packages. Throughout this book we are going to use the packages mentioned above with a specific version.

a. To install required packages, you can store them in a **requirements.txt** file as stated above, having each package with a specific version on new line. With this option, you need to use the following command to install packages from **requirements.txt** file, as shown *Figure 2.6*:

- **pip install -r requirements.txt**

b. The second option is to provide packages with **pip install** command directly, as mentioned below:

- pip install pandas==2.2.2 transformers==4.42.3 langchain==0.2.6 langchain_community==0.2.6 langchain-huggingface==0.0.3 accelerate==0.32.1 unstructured[pdf]==0.14.10 wikipedia==1.4.0 nltk==3.8.1 textblob==0.18.0 scikit-learn==1.5.1 spacy==3.7.5 gensim==4.3.2 pattern==3.6.0 huggingface_hub==0.23.4 torch==2.3.1 sentence_transformers==3.0.1 chromadb==0.5.3 faiss-cpu==1.8.0 evaluate==0.4.2 rouge_score==0.1.2 pypdf==4.2.0 gradio==4.37.2 origamibot==2.3.6 scipy~=1.12.0 tf_keras==2.16.0 git+https://github.com/google-research/bleurt.git

c. Please note that we have installed all the packages keeping in mind that we will use CPU and not GPU.

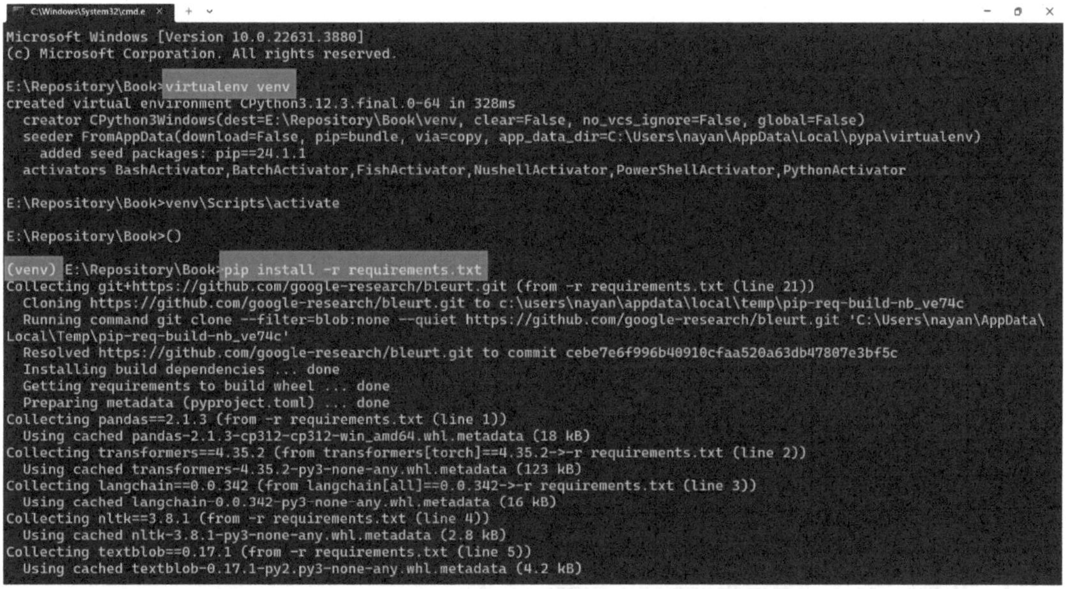

Figure 2.6: *Activate virtual env, Venv name appended to shell and installation of packages*

PEP 8 standards

PEP 8 is the Python amplification proposal that outlines the style guide for writing Python code. Following PEP 8 standards may help make your code more readable and maintainable. Here are some key guidelines and recommendations from PEP 8:

- **Indentation:**
  - o Use 4 spaces per indentation level. Avoid using tabs.
  - o The maximum line length should be 79 characters (or 72 for docstrings and comments).
- **Imports:**
  - o Imports should usually be on separate lines and at the top of the file.
  - o Use absolute imports rather than relative imports.
- **Whitespace in expressions and statements:**
  - o Avoid extraneous whitespace in the following situations:
    - ▪ Immediately inside parentheses, brackets, or braces.
    - ▪ Immediately before a comma, semicolon, or colon.
    - ▪ Immediately before the open parenthesis that starts an argument list.
  - o Do use whitespace in the following cases:
    - ▪ Around binary operators (e.g., a + b).
    - ▪ After a comma in a tuple (e.g., a, b).
- **Comments:**
  - o Comments should be complete sentences and placed on a line of their own.
  - o One should use docstrings to document modules, classes, and functions.
  - o Inline comments should be used in a restricted manner and only when necessary for clarification.
- **Naming conventions:**
  - o Use descriptive names for variables, functions, and classes.
  - o Function names should be lowercase with words separated by underscores (snake_case).
  - o Class names should follow the CapWords (CamelCase) convention.
  - o Constants should be in ALL_CAPS.
- **Whitespace in functions and expressions:**
  - o Separate functions with two blank lines.
  - o Use blank lines to indicate logical sections in a function.
  - o Keep expressions on the same line unless they are too long.
- **Programming recommendations:**
  - o Use a single leading underscore for non-public methods and instance variables (for example, _internal_method).
  - o Follow the "Zen of Python" (PEP 20) principles, which you can view by running **import this** in a Python interpreter.

- **Code layout:**
    - o Avoid putting multiple statements on a single line.
- **Documentation:**
    - o Provide clear, informative, and concise documentation using docstrings.
    - o Use docstring formats like reStructuredText, NumPy/SciPy docstring conventions, or Google-style docstrings.
- **Exceptions:**
    - o Use the except clause without specifying an exception type sparingly. Be specific about the exceptions you catch.

Note: PEP 8 is a guideline for coding style, not strict rules. Following PEP 8 is widely recognized as good practice, but there can be times when you need to vary from these guidelines due to practical considerations or align with the style of existing code. Sometimes maintaining consistency within a project matters more than strictly sticking to PEP 8. So, it is best if you follow the styling guide used in your project or organization, even if it is not exactly like PEP 8.

Following PEP 8 in PyCharm

PyCharm has built-in features letting coders follow the standards set by PEP 8. There are many tools and features available that make following the guidelines easier.

- **PEP 8 check on-the-fly:**
    - o As you are writing your code in PyCharm, this tool keeps an eye on what you are doing and checks that everything matches up against standard practices outlined by PEP 8. If something conflicts with PEP 8 norms, problematic areas will be marked out instantly on-screen using red or yellow squiggly lines.
- **Auto-formatting:**
    - o PyCharm comes loaded with automatic formatting tools designed around PEP 8 expectations which help ensure all newly-generated programming meets without fail match-up impeccably against these important industry standards!
        - ▪ Select the code you want to format.
        - ▪ Press *Ctrl + Alt + L* (Windows/Linux) or *CMD + Option + L* (Mac).
        - ▪ Or right-click on the code and select "**Reformat Code.**"
- **PEP 8 configuration:**
    - o You can configure the PEP 8 settings in PyCharm to suit your preferences. Go to **File | Settings** (or **PyCharm | Preferences on a Mac**) and navigate to **Editor | Code Style | Python**. Here, you can adjust the PEP 8 settings to match your preferred coding style.
- **Code inspection:**

o PyCharm can perform code inspections to detect PEP 8 violations. If you see yellow or red highlighting in your code, you can hover over it to see the issue and access options to correct it.

- **PEP 8 quick-fixes:**

o Whenever a violation related to PEP 8 gets flagged in your Python script written under pycharm's watchful eye (python editor), you get to implement instant fixes for the highlighted script by hitting *Alt+Enter*. We call it Quick Fix!

- **Integration with linters:**

o PyCharm integrates with popular Python code analysis tools like Flake8, Pylint, and Black. You can configure these tools to provide PEP 8 checks and formatting automatically.

- **Code documentation:**

o PyCharm helps you create PEP 8 compliant documentation strings (docstrings) by providing templates and hints as you write the documentation.

- **Code navigation:**

o You can use features within PyCharm to quickly move between your definitions and understand how things are connected in your Python file.

By default, PyCharm is configured to follow PEP 8 coding standards, and it is designed to be user-friendly for developers who want to write PEP 8 compliant code. However, you can customize the settings to align with your preferences or team standards. Using these features can help you maintain clean and PEP 8 compliant Python code in your projects.

Object-Oriented Programming concepts in Python

In Python, **Object-Oriented Programming (OOP)** is an in-built part of the language. Python supports all the core OOPS concepts, including creating classes, objects, inheritance, encapsulation, polymorphism, and more. Here is a brief introduction to how OOP concepts are implemented in Python:

- **Class:**

o In Python, you define a class using the **class** keyword.

o Classes are used to create objects, and they serve as blueprints for object creation.

```
class Dog:
    def __init__(self, name):
        self.name = name
```

-   ■   `def bark(self):`
-   ■   `print(f"{self.name} says Woof!")`
-   ■

- **Objects:**
  - o   Objects are instances of a class, created using the class constructor.
  - o   They encapsulate both data(attributes) and behavior(methods). For example:
    - ■   `my_dog = Dog("Buddy")`
    - ■   `my_dog.bark()`
- **Inheritance:**
  - o   Subclasses can inherit attributes and methods from Superclasses. Look at the following code, for example:
    - ■   `class Animal:`
    - ■   `def __init__(self, name):`
    - ■   `self.name = name`
    - ■
    - ■
    - ■   `class Dog(Animal):`
    - ■   `def speak(self):`
    - ■   `print(f"{self.name} says Woof!")`
    - ■
    - ■
    - ■   *# Here Buddy! is the name. As Dog inherits property of Animal class*
    - ■   *# We are providing the name which will be utilized by Animal class*
    - ■   `my_dog = Dog("Buddy!")`
    - ■   `my_dog.speak()`
- **Encapsulation:**
  - o   Python uses naming conventions to indicate access control.
  - o   Attributes and methods with a single underscore are considered protected:
    - ■   `class MyClass:`
    - ■   `def __init__(self):`
    - ■   `self._protected_var = 42`
- **Polymorphism:**
  - o   Polymorphism is achieved through duck typing.
  - o   If an object behaves like another object, it is considered polymorphic:

- class Cat:
- def speak(self):
- print("Meow!")
-
- def make_animal_speak(animal):
- animal.speak()
-
- my_cat = Cat()
- make_animal_speak(my_cat)

- **Abstraction:**
  - o You can define abstract base classes using the **abc** module.
  - o Subclasses must implement abstract methods:
    - from abc import ABC, abstractmethod
    -
    - class Shape(ABC):
    - @abstractmethod
    - def area(self):
    - pass
    -
    - class Circle(Shape):
    - def __init__(self, radius):
    - self.radius = radius
    -
    - def area(self):
    - return 3.1415 * self.radius ** 2

- **Method overriding:**
  - o Subclasses can provide their own implementation of a method:
    - class Animal:
    - def speak(self):
    - print("Generic animal sound")
    -
    - class Dog(Animal):
    - def speak(self):
    - print("Woof!")

- ▪
  - ▪ `my_dog = Dog()`
  - ▪ `my_dog.speak()`

These small code examples illustrate how OOP concepts are implemented in Python, making it a versatile language for building complex, organized, and maintainable applications.

Classes in Python

In Python, think of a class as a blueprint or design for making objects. It determines how to build and behave around the thing you are creating, including features (information) and methods (activities). Python is very comfortable with OOP – that is why classes are such an important concept in it! Let us take a closer look at them:

- **Defining a class:**
  - o You make a class using the **class** keyword, followed by its name. Usually, we like to start class names with capital letters! Anything inside the body of your class will be attributes or methods:
    - ▪ `class MyClass:`
    - ▪ `    attribute1 = 0`
    - ▪ `    attribute2 = "Hello"`
    - ▪
    - ▪ `    def method1(self):`
    - ▪ `        pass`
    - ▪
    - ▪ `    def method2(self, parameter):`
    - ▪ `        pass`
- **Creating objects (Instances):**
  - o Once you have defined a class, you can create objects (instances) of that class. An object is a specific realization of a class with its own data and behavior:
    - ▪ `# Create instances of MyClass`
    - ▪ `obj1 = MyClass()`
    - ▪ `obj2 = MyClass()`
- **Attributes:**
  - o Attributes are variables that belong to a class. They define the characteristics (data) of the objects created from the class:
    - ▪ `obj1.attribute1 = 42`
    - ▪ `obj2.attribute2 = "World"`
- **Methods:**

o Methods are functions defined within a class. They define the behavior and actions that objects created from the class can perform:

- ```
  class MyClass:
  ```
- ```
      def say_hello(self):
  ```
- ```
          print("Hello, world!")
  ```
-
- ```
  obj = MyClass()
  ```
- ```
  obj.say_hello()  # Calls the say_hello method
  ```

- **The self-parameter:**

  o In Python, the first parameter of a method is self, which refers to the instance of the class. You use self to access attributes and call other methods within the class:

  - ```
    class MyClass:
    ```
  - ```
        def set_attribute(self, value):
    ```
  - ```
            self.attribute1 = value
    ```
  -
  - ```
        def get_attribute(self):
    ```
  - ```
            return self.attribute1
    ```
  -
  - ```
    obj = MyClass()
    ```
  - ```
    obj.set_attribute(42)
    ```
  - ```
    value = obj.get_attribute()  # Retrieves the value
    ```

- **Constructor method:**

  o The **__init__** method is a special method (constructor) that is automatically called when an object is created from a class. It is used to initialize attributes:

  - ```
    class MyClass:
    ```
  - ```
        def __init__(self, initial_value):
    ```
  - ```
            self.attribute1 = initial_value
    ```
  -
  - ```
    obj = MyClass(42)  # Creates an object with an initial value
    of 42
    ```

Classes are a powerful way to organize and encapsulate code in Python. They help create modular, reusable, and maintainable code, making them a fundamental part of object-oriented programming in the language. A complete class with PEP 8 docstring will look something as follows:

```
1. class Person:
```
```

```
2.     """A class to represent a person.
3.
4.     This class provides a simple way to store and retrieve
   information about a person.
5.
6.     Attributes:
7.         name (str): The name of the person.
8.         age (int): The age of the person.
9.     """
10.
11.     def __init__(self, name, age):
12.         """Initializes a new Person object.
13.
14.         Args:
15.             name (str): The name of the person.
16.             age (int): The age of the person.
17.         """
18.         self.name = name
19.         self.age = age
20.
21.     def greet(self):
22.         """Prints a friendly greeting message.
23.
24.         Returns:
25.             str: A greeting message.
26.         """
27.         return f"Hello, my name is {self.name}, and I am {self.age}
   years old."
28.
29. # Creating an instance of the Person class
30. person1 = Person("Nayan", 35)
31.
32. # Calling the greet method
33. greeting = person1.greet()
34. print(greeting)
```

Functions in Python

Functions are so useful in Python – they are chunks of code you can use again whenever you need them! They let your computer perform tasks when asked. By using functions, your code gets tidier and easier to read and manage:

- **Defining a function:**
  - o You define a function using the **def** keyword, followed by the function name and a set of parentheses that can contain input parameters (arguments). The function's code is indented below the **def** statement:
    - ```
      def greet(name):
      ```
    - ```
          print(f"Hello, {name}!")
      ```
- **Calling a function:**
  - o To use a function, you call it by using its name followed by parentheses. If the function has parameters, you provide the required values inside the parentheses:
    - ```
      greet("Nayan")   # Calls the greet function with the argument "Nayan"
      ```
- **Parameters and arguments:**
  - o Parameters are placeholders waiting for real values when the function is called. Arguments are actual relatable data passed into our functions
    - ```
      def add(x, y):
      ```
    - ```
          return x + y
      ```
    -
    - ```
      result = add(3, 5)  # x is 3, y is 5; result is 8
      ```
    - ```
      OR We can call method by keyword arguments like as below
      ```
    - ```
      result = add(x=3, y=5)
      ```
- **Default parameters:**
  - o You can provide default values for function parameters. If no argument is passed for a parameter, the default value is used:
    - ```
      def power(x, y=2):
      ```
    - ```
          return x ** y
      ```
    -
    - ```
      result1 = power(3)  # y defaults to 2; result1 is 9
      ```
    - ```
      result2 = power(3, 4)  # y is 4; result2 is 81
      ```
    - ```
      OR other way to call any method is
      ```
    - ```
      result2 = power(y=3, x=4) # y is 3, x is 4; result2 is 64
      ```

- **Scope:**
  - o Variables made within any specific function carry local scope, meaning they live only there within a given function and can only be accessible within a given function! Any variable living outside/beyond functional structure will have global scope making itself visible throughout the entire code script and can be used throughout the script:

    - ▪ ```
      x = 10
      ```
    - ▪
    - ▪ ```
      def my_function():
      ```
    - ▪ ```
          x = 5 # This is a local variable
      ```
    - ▪ ```
          print(x)  # Prints 5
      ```
    - ▪
    - ▪ ```
      my_function()
      ```
    - ▪ ```
      print(x)  # Prints 10
      ```

Functions are a crucial part of Python, allowing you to structure your code and break it down into manageable pieces. They promote code reusability and maintainability, making your programs more organized and efficient.

For loop in Python

A classic bit from every coder's toolkit comes to the "**for loop**". Perfect for repeating chunk(s) of programming over sequences or sets like data frames, lists, tuples, etcetera based upon usual basic coding rules.

The basic syntax of a for loop in Python is as follows:

```
1. for item in sequence:
2.     # Code to be executed for each item
```

Here are some examples of a for loop:

```
1. fruits = ["apple", "banana", "cherry"]
2.
3. for fruit in fruits:
4.     print(f"I like {fruit}")
```

In the following example, the for loop will run five times and will take on the values 0, 1, 2, 3, and 4:

```
1. for i in range(5):
2.     print(f"Count: {i}")
```

Nested For loop:

```
1. for i in range(3):
2.     for j in range(2):
3.         print(f"({i}, {j})")
```

Using break and continue in "for" Loops

For more advanced iterations, you can use the break and continue statements within "for" loops to control the flow of your code. For example:

```
1. fruits = ["apple", "banana", "cherry", "date", "elderberry"]
2.
3. print("Using 'break':")
4. for fruit in fruits:
5.     if fruit == "date":
6.         break  # Exit the loop when "date" is found
7.     print(f"I like {fruit}")
8.
9. print("\nUsing 'continue':")
10. for fruit in fruits:
11.     if fruit == "date":
12.         continue  # Skip the iteration when "date" is found
13.     print(f"I like {fruit}")
```

While loop in Python

A **"while"** loop in Python is used to continuously execute a block of code as long as a specified condition is true. Looping continues until its condition is no longer true; execution halted! Here is the basic syntax of a "while" loop:

```
1. while condition:
2.     # Code to be executed as long as the condition is true
```

Given below is a very simple example. In this example, the "while" loop continues to execute as long as the count is less than 5. The count variable is incremented with each iteration to eventually make the condition false:

```
1. count = 0
2.
3. while count < 5:
4.     print(f"Count: {count}")
5.     count += 1  # Increment the count
```

Be careful when using "while" loops to avoid creating infinite loops (Doctor Strange and the Dormammu sequence from the movie Doctor Strange), where the condition never becomes false. To prevent infinite loops, you should always add a false condition; otherwise, these continuous loops can be devastating for the IT Infrastructure.

Using "break" and "continue" in "while" Loops

Code:

```
1.  count = 0
2.
3.  while count < 5:
4.      if count == 2:
5.          break  # Exit the loop when count is 2
6.      elif count == 1:
7.          count += 1
8.          continue  # Skip the iteration when count is 1
9.      print(f"Count: {count}")
10.     count += 1  # Increment the count
```

In this example, the loop breaks when count is equal to 2, and it skips the iteration when count is equal to 1 using the continue statement. Hence, here the value of count is Count: 0 from print statement.

If-else in Python

In the Python world, "**if-else**" does wonders in controlling conditional flow. It helps us assign different bunches of instructions to be executed based upon given evaluated conditions that turn true or false.

```
1.  if condition1:
2.      # Code to be executed if condition1 is true
3.  elif condition2:
4.      # Code to be executed if condition1 is false, and condition2 is
        true
5.  else:
6.      # Code to be executed if both condition1 and condition2 are
        false
```

In case of two possible outcomes, you can exclude the middle **elif** statement. If more than two outcomes are possible, then you can include as many **elif** as required. Sample example could be as follows:

```
1.  grade = 85
2.
```

```
3. if grade >= 90:
4.     print("A")
5. elif grade >= 80:
6.     print("B")
7. elif grade >= 70:
8.     print("C")
9. else:
10.     print("D")
```

In Python, you can write a compact one-liner "if-elif-else" statement using the conditional (ternary) expression. The conditional expression allows you to evaluate a condition and provide different values or expressions based on whether the condition is true or false. Here is the syntax:

```
1. value_if_true if condition else value_if_false
```

Given below are two different examples. One is a normal if-else condition, and second is if-elif-else condition:

```
1. age = 20
2.
3. status = "adult" if age >= 18 else "minor"
4. print(f"You are a {status}.")
5.
6. grade = 85
7.
8. result = "A" if grade >= 90 else ("B" if grade >= 80 else ("C" if
   grade >= 70 else "D"))
9. print(f"Your grade is {result}.")
```

The "if-else" statement is a fundamental control structure in Python and is used extensively to make decisions and execute different code paths based on varying conditions.

Conclusion

In conclusion, the process of setting up a Python ecosystem or environment for any project involves the installation of Python itself, ensuring the presence of needed libraries for the project, and selecting an appropriate IDE or code editor. By carefully navigating through the steps mentioned in this chapter, developers will be able to create a Python environment for this book. The seamless integration of Python, necessary packages, and a chosen code editor or IDE not only facilitates efficient coding but also sets the stage for a productive and enjoyable development experience. In the next chapter, we will practice how to create and run Python scripts in different ways. If you know ways to do this, then it will be easier to run scripts in different scenarios. One such example is in case GUI is not available, then you can run the script using a terminal or command line.

Ways to Run Python Scripts

Introduction

This chapter is another fundamental step in getting started with the book. It allows you to run Python scripts using different ways. It is good to know the different ways of running Python scripts, as, in certain situations, some ways might not be available. For example, GUI-based tools might not be available on the servers, and hence, in this case, you might need to work with the terminal to execute Python scripts. This chapter explores the diverse methods for executing Python scripts from the command-line to integrated development environments, and web frameworks. You will also learn how to run scripts using different methods, and we will cover the importance of choosing the right method for your specific project needs to ensure efficient code execution and deployment.

Structure

In this chapter we will discuss the following topics.

- Setting up the project
- Running Python scripts from PyCharm
- Running Python scripts from Terminal
- Running Python scripts from JupyterLab and Notebook
- Running Python scripts from Docker

Objectives

By the end of this chapter, you will understand different ways to run Python scripts. It will not only help you in this book, but it will help in your future endeavors as well to run Python scripts in different scenarios in different ways.

Note: It is always advisable to create a virtual environment. Install the required packages into the created virtual environment. After this, run the scripts using the Python interpreter available in the created virtual environment.

Setting up the project

First, let us create a sample script. We are going to run this script using different ways. In our folder structure it will look something as shown in *Figure 3.1*. As you can see, first, create a folder called **scripts** in which we are going to store all the scripts that we are going to create throughout the book.

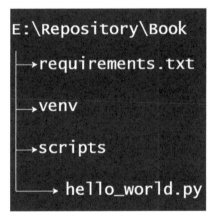

Figure 3.1: Folder structure

Now the question is how to create this script **hello_world.py**? To create the script, we have two options for the purpose of simplicity. The two options are as follows:

- In the script, we are going to write the following two lines:
  - o   print("Hello World!!!")
  - o   print("This is the book - Building LLM applications with Langchain and Hugging Face Transformers")
- Open any editor of your choice, write these lines as shown in *Figure 3.2,* and save it as **hello_world.py** under **scripts** folder. Here we have used Notepad++ for this purpose.

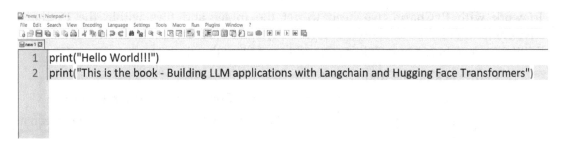

Figure 3.2: Notepad++ add code

The following figure shows how to save a script:

Figure 3.3: Notepad++ save as

As shown in *Figure 3.4*, once you have selected the required directory, file name, and file type, just click on **Save**. It will store the file as `hello_world.py`.

Figure 3.4: Notepad++ choose directory, file name & file type

As you can see that we do not need to append **.py** extension. It will be automatically added by the Notepad++ application. You just need to select **Python File** in the **Save as type** option.

To work with PyCharm, we need to get the folder and files within the PyCharm environment. For this, as shown in *Figure 3.5*, open the folder as PyCharm Community Edition project. In our case, it is **Book** and then follow the given steps:

1. Right-click on the folder.

2. Select the option **Open Folder as PyCharm Community Edition Project**.

3. Once the folder and all files are available in PyCharm, you will get the screen as shown in *Figure 3.6*

4. Right-click on **scripts** | **New** | **Python File**. Refer to *Figure 3.7*.

    a. It will open a dialogue box.

    b. Provide file name and enter.

    c. From the figure you can see that you can create a directory as well as a Python package.

    Refer to the following figure:

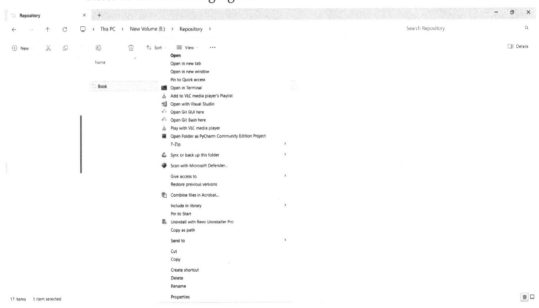

Figure 3.5: *PyCharm – Open folder as a project*

The following figure shows how the screen will open, as discussed in the preceding steps:

Figure 3.6: *PyCharm – Screen*

The following figure shows how to create a new file in PyCharm. For this right- click on the scripts folder, and then you will get the pop-up as shown in *Figure 3.7*:

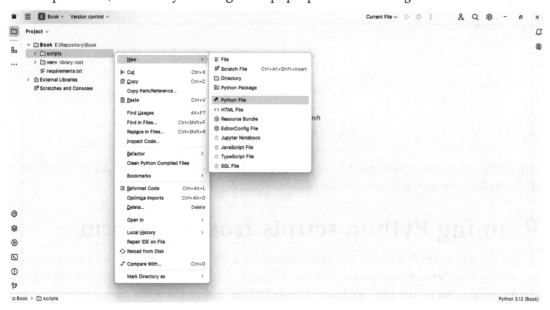

Figure 3.7: *PyCharm – Create new Python File*

The following figures show how to create a new Python file in PyCharm, as discussed in the preceding points:

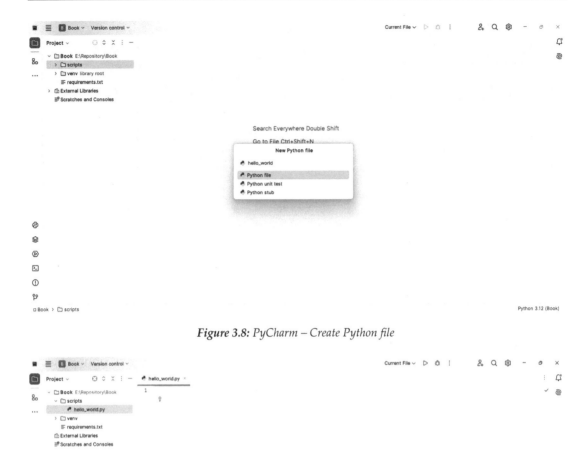

Figure 3.8: *PyCharm – Create Python file*

Figure 3.9: *PyCharm – Script created*

After all these steps, you should have **scripts** folder and **hello_world.py** underneath of it. Overall, the setup will look similar, as shown in *Figure 3.1.*

Running Python scripts from PyCharm

To run scripts from PyCharm, we need to set up a Python interpreter at a project level. By setting the Python interpreter, we are telling PyCharm to use Python from the given configuration. Here, we tell PyCharm to use Python either from the global directory, that is, from the main installation path or from a created virtual environment directory.

However, in most cases, if the folder you are using has a virtual environment created, PyCharm will detect it automatically and will set it as an interpreter.

If this is not the case, follow the given steps:

1. Click on **File** | **Settings** | Project: **project_name [It will be dynamic]** | **Python Interpreter**, as shown in the following figure:

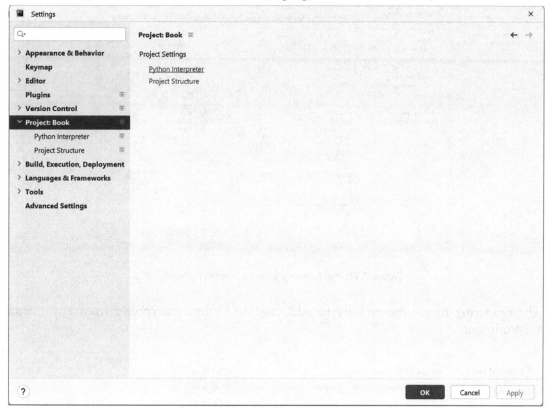

Figure 3.10: *PyCharm – Python Interpreter*

In the following *Figure 3.11*, you can see that, as mentioned earlier, the virtual environment has already been detected and set as an interpreter. If this is not the case, click on **Add Interpreter** | **Add Local Interpreter…**

You will get this **Add Interpreter** option in the top right corner, as highlighted in *Figure 3.11*.

Refer to the following figure:

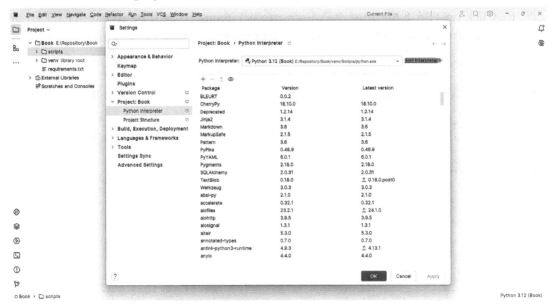

Figure 3.11: PyCharm – Python Interpreter already set

The following figure shows how to add existing Python interpreter from any virtual environment:

Figure 3.12: PyCharm – Add existing or new interpreter

As shown in *Figure 3.12*, we can add an existing Python interpreter from any virtual environment, or we can create a new interpreter as well. To do this, you can refer to the following points:

- When we create a new interpreter via PyCharm, it will create a virtual environment. For this, in *Figure 3.12*, select **New**.
  - o Location [Where you want to create a virtual environment]
  - o Base interpreter: Do not change this location. It will be default to the standard Python installation directory that we have done in *Chapter 2, Installation of Python, Required Packages and Code Editor*.

    It is just to use it to create a virtual environment.

    Refer to the following figure:

Figure 3.13: PyCharm – Create new Python interpreter

- You can get the virtual environment path, if you have created it using **virtualenv** option.
  - o **On Windows/macOS/Linux:** Virtual environments are typically stored in the directory where you have run the command **virtualenv venv**.
- If you have used **virtualenv** option, then it will most probably be in the root directory of the project.
- Here, the Python interpreter must contain a path including the Python binary or executable.
- Now, from the left pane, select **hello_world.py** and double-click on it. It will look as shown in *Figure 3.14*.
- In case you have a blank file, just write two print statements, as shown in *Figure 3.14*.
- Now, to run the script, we have two options.
  - o If we want to run the script line by line, that is., execute the code where the cursor is. In that case, you can use *ALT+SHIT+E* keys.

Figure 3.14: *PyCharm – Open Script*

- If we want to run the entire script at once, we have three options:
  - o First option is to use *SHIFT + F10* keys, as shown in *Figure 3.15*
  - o Second, select all codes and press the *ALT+SHIT+E* keys. Refer to *Figure 3.16*
  - o Third option is the **Green Play** button on top bar. Just press that button, and the entire script will be executed. Refer to *Figure 3.15:*

Figure 3.15: *PyCharm – Run script using 1st and 3rd options*

Refer to the next figure for better understanding of how to run an entire script:

Figure 3.16: PyCharm – Run script using second option

Running Python Scripts from Terminal

Running Python scripts from the terminal is a fundamental skill for programmers and system administrators. It enables the automation of tasks, facilitates system administration, and allows for the integration of Python scripts into various workflows. Executing scripts from the command line is essential for tasks such as debugging, handling command-line arguments, and working with remote servers.

To run Python scripts from Terminal or CMD, follow the steps mentioned below:

1. Open the terminal or CMD.
   a. For most of the Linux distros, you can use the *CTRL+ALT+T* command to open the terminal.
   b. For Windows, *Win + R* | type **cmd** in the box. It will open the command prompt.
   c. For MacOS, press *Command + Space* to open Spotlight search, then type **Terminal** and press *Enter*. This will launch the Terminal application.

2. From the terminal, we have two options to run Python scripts:
   a. You can provide a complete path (absolute path) of the script. For example, refer to the following code and *Figure 3.17:*
      ```
      python E:\Repository\Book\scripts\hello_world.py
      ```

```
C:\Windows\System32\cmd.e ×    +  ∨

Microsoft Windows [Version 10.0.22621.2861]
(c) Microsoft Corporation. All rights reserved.

C:\Users\nayan>python E:\Repository\Book\scripts\hello_world.py
Hello World!!!
This is the book - Building LLM applications with Langchain and Hugging Face Transformers

C:\Users\nayan>
```

Figure 3.17: Terminal – Provide absolute path

    b. Change to the directory where Python scripts reside and run the script. For example, in our case, we will change the directory to **E:\Repository\Book\ scripts** and then will run the following command:

        python hello_world.py

3. Here, you can see that we are using a global Python interpreter and not the one from the virtual environment we have created.

    a. It is for example only. In case your global Python interpreter does not contain the required packages, then it will raise an error that the module is not found. Hence, it is always recommended to use a virtual environment.

4. To run the script using a virtual environment again, we have three options:

    a. Use the path of the Python interpreter from the virtual environment and run the script. For example, in our case, the Python interpreter from the virtual environment resides at **E:\Repository\Book\venv\Scripts\python.exe**. We will use this interpreter and provide an absolute or relative path of the script to execute it. For example, refer to the following code and *Figure 3.18*:

        E:\Repository\Book\venv\Scripts\python.exe E:\Repository\Book\ scripts\hello_world.py

```
Command Prompt    ×                                                                             □  ×

Microsoft Windows [Version 10.0.22631.3880]
(c) Microsoft Corporation. All rights reserved.

C:\Users\nayan>E:\Repository\Book\venv\Scripts\python.exe E:\Repository\Book\scripts\hello_world.py
Hello World!!!
This is the book - Building LLM applications with Langchain and Hugging Face Transformers

C:\Users\nayan>
```

Figure 3.18: Terminal – Provide virtual env python interpreter and script path

    b. Here, if you are in the directory where Python scripts reside, you can refer to the following command. For example, we have changed the directory to **E:\Repository\Book\scripts**, and in this case, we can run the following command:

        E:\Repository\Book\venv\Scripts\python.exe hello_world.py

    c. In this option, we will activate the virtual environment and then run the script:

        i. We have created a virtual environment using **virtualenv** command. Hence, go to the project directory where **venv** folder resides. Here venv is our virtual environment name case. If you have used a different name, than venv, in that case, go to the directory where the folder of that name resides.

        In our case, we need to go to the directory **E:\Repository\Book** where we will get the above files.

       ii. Open the terminal or CMD from that particular location or open the terminal and change the directory to the location where the **venv** folder resides.

      iii. Execute the following command, which will activate the virtual environment:

        venv\Scripts\activate [For Windows]; source venv/bin/activate [For Linux/Mac]

      iv. Now, execute the following command to run the script:

        python scripts\hello_world.py

       v. Here, make sure that OS-based separator i.e., "/" or "\" can vary.

        Refer to the following figure:

```
Microsoft Windows [Version 10.0.22631.3880]
(c) Microsoft Corporation. All rights reserved.

E:\Repository\Book>venv\Scripts\activate

E:\Repository\Book>()

(venv) E:\Repository\Book>python scripts\hello_world.py
Hello World!!!
This is the book - Building LLM applications with Langchain and Hugging Face Transformers

(venv) E:\Repository\Book>
```

Figure 3.19: Terminal – Activate virtual environment and run the script

Running Python scripts from Jupyter Lab and Notebook

Being able to use Jupyter Lab or Notebook is very important when you are working on things like data exploration, building models, designing new technologies, and collaborating with others. With Jupyter, you can create and run code step by step in an interactive way - perfect for analyzing data or creating an ML model. Plus, because it is easy to add text details, images, and graphs into your work with them, they are excellent at helping detail the process of analyses built through coding.

Here is how to get Python scripts running:

1. Activate the virtual environment as mentioned in the preceding section *Run Python Scripts from Terminal*. You need to run the commands below on the same terminal.

2. Run the following command to install JupyterLab and Jupyter Notebook:

    a. `pip install jupyter lab notebook`

3. Run any of the following commands to start JupyterLab or Jupyter Notebook. Here we have a terminal, which is in the root directory of the project, that is, **E:\ Repository\Book**.

    a. `jupyter lab`

    b. `jupyter notebook`

4. You will get the screen as shown in *Figure 3.20,* which is of Jupyter Lab. This is the screen that you will get first. You can consider it as the home page. From this, select any section of Notebook | Python 3 (ipykernel) OR Console | Python 3 (ipkernel).

    a. Here, you will get the screen where you need to execute the command as mentioned in *Figure 3.21.*

5. *Figure 3.22* shows Jupyter Notebook home page screen. You can also select from Notebook or Console here. In the next screen, as shown in *Figure 3.23,* execute the command provided at the end.

6. For both Jupyter Notebook and JupyterLab run the following command:

    a. `with open("scripts\\hello_world.py","r") as scrpt:`

    b. scrpt_content = scrpt.read()

    c.

    d. `exec(scrpt_content)`

Refer to the following figure:

Figure 3.20: *Jupyter Lab – Main Screen*

Refer to the following figure for a better understanding of the steps discussed:

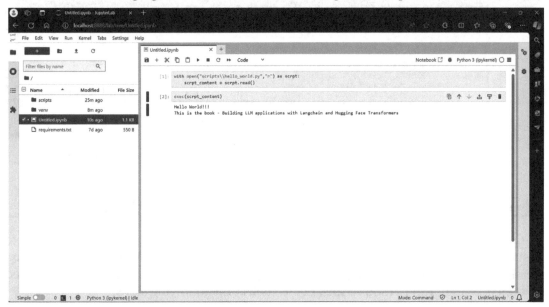

Figure 3.21: Jupyter Lab – New Notebook Run Commands

Figure 3.22: Jupyter Notebook – Main Screen

Figure 3.23: Jupyter Notebook – New Notebook Run Commands

Running Python Scripts from Docker

In *Chapter 2, Installation of Python, Required Packages and Code Editor*, we have seen how to install docker on respective OS and then how to fetch an image of the required Python version. In this section, we will proceed from there. Here, we will see how to use fetched Python images to run Python scripts. Let us look at the following steps:

1. As usual open the terminal. First, confirm that the docker instance is running else it might result in an error while running the required command. For this, run the following command from terminal. Refer to *Figure 3.24* for the same:
   docker images

   a. If this command executes successfully without any error, then the docker instance is running. If not, then make sure that the docker service is running.

2. Next, run the following command, which will start a container using the image that we fetched in *Chapter 2, Installation of Python, Required Packages and Code Editor*. Refer to *Figure 3.24* for the same.

   a. docker   run   -dti   -v   E:\Repository\Book\scripts:/home/scripts --name book_practice python:3.12

   b. Here:
      i. **dti**: Run the container in detached mode, i.e., in the backend with the interactive terminal facility.
      ii. **v**: Here we are mapping directory which contains Python scripts with the home/scripts directory of the docker instance i.e., the docker container
      iii. **name**: Name of the container that is going to run the Python image
      iv. **python:3.12** Image name

3. This will start the container in the background. In case you restart the PC, you need to execute the following command to start the container:

   o   docker start book_practice

Also, do not delete this container. It will remove any changes that might have been made inside the container.

It will not remove changes to the host machine. That is, in case you change a script from the scripts folder and delete the container, it will not remove those changes as they are directly written to the host machine. However, let us say you have created a virtual environment inside the container. Then, on deleting the container, the virtual environment will be deleted.

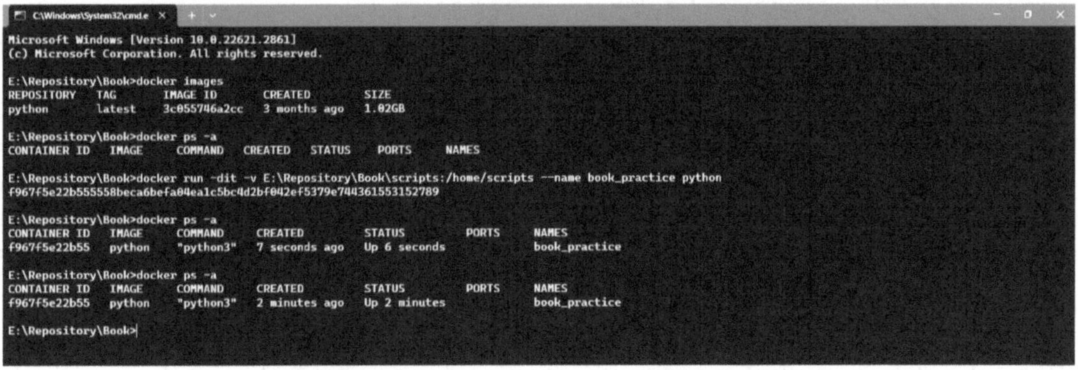

Figure 3.24: Docker – Strat image in a container

4. Before proceeding further, make sure that the docker container is up and running using the command **docker ps -a**. Make sure the **STATUS** column shows *Up X minutes*.

5. Next, you can get the commands we will use to enter the Docker container and run the script from *Figure 3.25*. The commands are as follows. The first command will enter into the docker container having the name **book_practice**. The second command will change the directory. The third command will execute the script available in the directory.

    o `docker exec -it book_practice bash`

    o `cd /home/scripts`

    o `python hello_world.py`

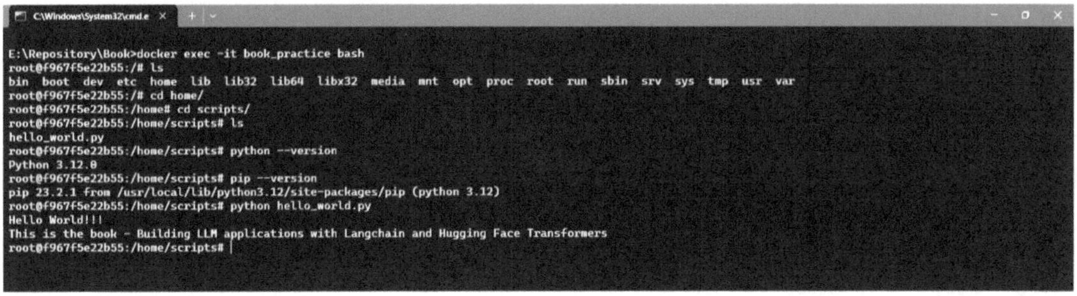

Figure 3.25: Docker – Enter into container and run scripts

6. In this instance, no virtual environment has been established. Instead, the scripts are executed directly through the global Python interpreter. For educational purposes and within the context of Docker, as described in this publication, it is acceptable to utilize the global Python interpreter. However, if desired, you can opt for a similar approach, which involves setting up a virtual environment, activating it, installing necessary packages, and executing scripts from a designated Python interpreter within that specific virtual environment.

Conclusion

In conclusion, mastering the various ways to run Python scripts empowers you to unleash the full potential of this versatile language. You can choose the approach that best suits your specific needs and preferences, such as harnessing the power of the terminal for automation, control, and deployment, embracing the interactive and exploratory nature of Jupyter Lab and Notebook for data analysis and visualization, utilizing IDEs for comprehensive development environments and debugging tools, or creating standalone executables for easy distribution and cross-platform compatibility.

Remember, the most effective approach often involves a combination of these methods, which are strategically employed throughout your Python journey. By understanding the strengths and nuances of each execution environment, you will be equipped to tackle any coding challenge with confidence and efficiency.

In the next chapter, we will understand and practice important NLP concepts, which are a must and the basis of most of the current NLP algorithms. In that chapter we will explore some of the very useful and often used terminologies and see practical implementation of the same.

Join our book's Discord space

Join the book's Discord Workspace for Latest updates, Offers, Tech happenings around the world, New Release and Sessions with the Authors:

https://discord.bpbonline.com

CHAPTER 4

Introduction to NLP and its Concepts

Introduction

Natural language processing (NLP) is an absolutely key area in the world of **Artificial Intelligence (AI)**. The field deals with human languages and computer systems. It provides algorithms and models, facilitating machines to delve into the realms of understanding, interpretation, and generation of human language in a manner that transcends mere superficiality and strives for a depth that is both profound and genuinely utilitarian. This chapter has been thoughtfully curated to give you an explanation of this intricate field. We will also embark upon an exploration of the bedrock principles, intricacies of technique, and the pragmatic domains where NLP finds its utility.

Structure

In this chapter we will discuss the following topics:

- Natural Language Processing overview
- Large language models
- Text classification
- Prompt engineering

Objectives

By the end of this chapter, you will have an understanding of NLP and its different concepts. It will help you to understand and exercise further topics in the book. You will gain knowledge of how a computer works with text data and a solid foundation in the principles and practical applications of NLP.

Natural Language Processing overview

Natural Language Processing (**NLP**) represents a swiftly evolving discipline situated at the confluence of computer science, AI, and linguistics. Its primary objective is to facilitate machines in the practical comprehension and generation of human language. Its applications span a vast spectrum of technological domains, encompassing natural and seamless human-computer interactions, insightful data analysis, and efficient communication. NLP forms the foundational underpinning of various technological tools, including search engines, voice-activated assistants, chatbots, and data analytics.

However, the realm of NLP is not devoid of intricate challenges. It grapples with the multifaceted nature of human language, replete with subtleties and cultural nuances, and must address ethical considerations, particularly those associated with bias in NLP models and responsible usage. This chapter endeavors to offer a comprehensive exposition of NLP, exploring its fundamental tenets, methodologies, and real-world implementations, with forthcoming sections delving into pivotal elements such as tokenization and sentiment analysis, all veiled in a level of intricacy that eludes conventional detection.

Key concepts

To understand the key concepts of NLP practically, create a new folder **nlp_concepts** with blank **__init__.py** under the **scripts** folder that we have created in the earlier chapters. In general, a folder containing **__init__.py** is considered a Python package. The folder structure will look alike, as shown in *Figure 4.1*. Here, **Untitled.ipynb** has been created in *Chapter 3, Ways to Run Python Scripts*, to show how to run Python scripts via Jupyter Notebook or Jupyter Lab. The **.idea** is the internal folder of PyCharm, which will be created automatically when you open any folder as a PyCharm project. **.ipynb_checkpoints** is the internal folder of Jupyter Notebook that was created by it. Create scripts as shown under the folder structure of **scripts**, as shown in the following figure:

```
E:\Repository\Book>tree /f
Folder PATH listing for volume New Volume

E:.
│   venv
│   requirements.txt
│   Untitled.ipynb
│
├───.idea
│   │   .gitignore
│   │   Book.iml
│   │   misc.xml
│   │   modules.xml
│   │   workspace.xml
│   │
│   └───inspectionProfiles
│           profiles_settings.xml
│           Project_Default.xml
│
├───.ipynb_checkpoints
│       Untitled-checkpoint.ipynb
│
└───scripts
    │   hello_world.py
    │   __init__.py
    │
    └───nlp_concepts
            bag_of_words.py
            ner.py
            ngrams.py
            pos.py
            sentiment_analysis.py
            stem_lem.py
            stopwords_removal.py
            text_classification.py
            tokens.py
            topic_modelling.py
            word_embeddings.py
            __init__.py
```

Figure 4.1: Folder structure

Now, let us see both the theoretical and the practical parts.

Note: You will see that different packages that we are going to use for different functionalities will behave differently. Some packages will provide correct results. Some will provide incorrect or intermediate results. As these packages evolve and update over a period of time, time-to-time, evaluation of the packages will be required from your end to confirm the results are correct using those packages.

Corpus

In NLP, a *corpus* is the name for a big, organized bunch of text documents. These texts can be written pieces or even transcriptions from spoken language - or sometimes both!

They span all kinds of areas, such as social media, academia, and news articles, to name just a few. Now, by using complicated analysis methods on corpora (plural of corpus) in NLP, patterns are quickly figured out relating to the characteristics and structures of the languages. In the world of languages and computing, especially with machine learning applications, the use of corpora is extensive.

Types of corpora are as follows:

- **Monolingual corpora**: This type of corpora only has text from one single language.
  - o **Examples**:
    - **Corpus of Contemporary American English (COCA)**
    - **British National Corpus (BNC)**
    - **French Treebank (FTB)**
    - **Balanced Corpus of Contemporary Written Japanese (BCCWJ)**
    - **Russian National Corpus (RNC)**
- **Multilingual corpora**: Here we find multiple language texts (corpus) meant for cross-language research work.
  - o **Examples**:
    - **Europarl Corpus**: A parallel corpus containing the proceedings of the European Parliament, available in 21 European languages.
    - **United Nations Parallel Corpus**: Contains official documents and their translations in the six official UN languages (Arabic, Chinese, English, French, Russian, and Spanish).
    - **OpenSubtitles**: A large-scale multilingual corpus derived from movie and TV subtitles, available in many languages.
- **Parallel corpora**: Mixed bag including sentence translations distributed across various languages equipped for machinery-based translation movements.
  - o **Examples**:
    - **TED Talks Corpus**: A collection of TED Talks with transcripts and translations in multiple languages.
    - **Tatoeba Corpus**: A multilingual sentence database with translations in numerous languages contributed by a global community.
    - **Wikipedia Parallel Titles Corpus**: Contains parallel titles from Wikipedia articles in different languages.
- **Domain-specific corpora**: Specific area/sector related textual content. For example, text content centered around medical/legal interests etc.
  - o **Examples**:
    - **Medical Information Mart for Intensive Care (MIMIC-III)**: Contains de-identified health data from intensive care unit patients.

- **PubMed Central (PMC) Open Access Subset**: A large collection of biomedical and life sciences journal literature.

- **Open and close corpora**:
    - Publicly accessible corpora known as 'open corpora' and proprietary entities rarely available broadly referred under the header of 'closed corpora'. Both contribute vast user-built data sources, aiding heavy-scale machine learning activities, i.e., performing effective predictions/helping generate artificial human-like languages essentially guiding processing arenas!
        - Examples:
            - **British National Corpus (BNC)**: An open collection of samples of written and spoken English from a wide range of sources.
            - **Corpus of Contemporary American English (COCA)**: A large, balanced corpus of American English from 1990 to the present.
            - **Microsoft Translator Hub Corpora**: Proprietary datasets used by Microsoft for training translation models.
            - **Bloomberg Terminal Data**: Financial data is available through the Bloomberg Terminal and requires a subscription.

Corpora are the stepping stones for many machine learning problems, including NLP tasks, providing the diversity and quantity of data required to develop and improve models for understanding and generating human-like language. They play a crucial role in advancing natural language understanding and processing in the field of ML.

N-grams

N-grams is a technique used in natural language processing to understand human languages. You can think of n-grams like pieces of a sentence puzzle.

Why do we use n-grams? Well, they help us predict what word might come next after you've started typing or speaking! This prediction process is incredibly valuable for things like creating new stories and helping with writing texts faster!

Imagine you're trying to build software that recognizes speech - being able to understand the likely sequences of words in someone's speech would make this job much easier! That is why we also use them for tools that translate between languages.

Here are some of the types of n-grams:

- **Unigrams (1-grams)**: These are just single items, usually words. If you have the sentence "I love pizza," then each word (I, love, pizza) becomes a unigram.

- **Bigrams (2-grams)**: This refers to pairs of consecutive items. Let us take our previous sentence as an example again ("I love Pizza"). Here our bigrams would be "I love" and "love Pizza."

- **Trigrams (3-grams)**: Trigrams consist of three consecutive items. For the words, trigrams would be: "I love Pizza".
- **N-grams in General**: You can have n-grams with any value of N, depending on your specific requirements. For instance, 6-grams would involve sequences of six items from the text. Now these items can be anything, i.e., words, sentences, characters, etc.

Fantastic, is it not? By simply breaking down sentences into these unique groupings called n-grams helps give structure and predictability within our language, which ultimately makes life so much easier for machines trying their best to grasp onto intricate nuances found within human conversation patterns.

Python packages:

- Natural Language Toolkit (NLTK)
- spaCy
- TextBlob
- Scikit-Learn
- HuggingFace

Code:

Put the following code in the file called **ngrams.py** [**E:\Repository\Book\scripts\nlp_concepts\ngrams.py**]:

```
1. # Import required packages
2. from nltk.util import ngrams
3. import spacy
4. from textblob import TextBlob
5. from sklearn.feature_extraction.text import CountVectorizer
6. from transformers import AutoTokenizer
7.
8.
9. # ========================================================================
10. # NLTK
11. print("*" * 25)
12. print("Below example of N Grams is using NLTK package")
13. text = "This is an example sentence for creating n-grams."
14. n = 2  # Specify the n-gram size
15. bigrams = list(ngrams(text.split(), n))
16. print(bigrams)
17.
```

```
18.
19. # =======================================================================
20. # Spacy
21. print("*" * 25)
22. print("Below example of N Grams is using Spacy package")
23. # It is to download english package. Not required to run every
    time. " # Run below code from terminal after activating virtual
    environment"
24. # python -m spacy download en_core_web_sm
25. nlp = spacy.load("en_core_web_sm")
26. text = "This is an example sentence for creating n-grams."
27. n = 2  # Specify the n-gram size
28. tokens = [token.text for token in nlp(text)]
29. ngrams = [tokens[i : i + n] for i in range(len(tokens) - n + 1)]
30. print(ngrams)
31.
32.
33. # =======================================================================
34. # TextBlob
35. print("*" * 25)
36. print("Below example of N Grams is using TextBlob package")
37. # This is to download required corpora. Not required to run every
    time. "# Run below code from terminal after activating virtual
    environment"
38. # python -m textblob.download_corpora
39. text = "This is an example sentence for creating n-grams."
40. n = 2  # Specify the n-gram size
41. blob = TextBlob(text)
42. bigrams = blob.ngrams(n)
43. print(bigrams)
44.
45.
46. # =======================================================================
47. # Scikit Learn
48. print("*" * 25)
49. print("Below example of N Grams is using Scikit Learn package")
50. # For scikit learn list is required hence providing list.
```

```
51. text = ["This is an example sentence for creating n-grams."]
52. n = 2  # Specify the n-gram size
53. vectorizer = CountVectorizer(ngram_range=(n, n))
54. X = vectorizer.fit_transform(text)
55. # Get the n-gram feature names
56. feature_names = vectorizer.get_feature_names_out()
57. # Print the n-grams
58. for feature_name in feature_names:
59.     print(feature_name)
60.
61.
62. # =========================================================================
63. # Hugging Face Package
64. print("*" * 25)
65. print("Below example of N Grams is using Hugging Face package")
66.
67. # Define your text
68. text = "This is an example sentence for creating ngrams with Hugging
    Face Transformers."
69.
70. # Choose a pretrained tokenizer
71. tokenizer = AutoTokenizer.from_pretrained("bert-base-uncased")
72.
73. # Tokenize the text
74. tokens = tokenizer.tokenize(text)
75.
76. # Generate bigrams
77. bigrams = [(tokens[i], tokens[i + 1]) for i in range(len(tokens) - 1)]
78.
79. # Generate trigrams
80. trigrams = [(tokens[i], tokens[i + 1], tokens[i + 2]) for i in
    range(len(tokens) - 2)]
81.
82. # Print the bigrams
83. for bigram in bigrams:
84.     print(bigram)
85.
```

```
86.  # Print the trigrams
87.  for trigram in trigrams:
88.      print(trigram)
```

Tokenization

Tokenization is performed to convert a continuous text or speech into discrete, manageable units. It is the process of breaking down text into smaller units, typically words or subwords (tokens), which are essential for further analysis.

Tokens are the building blocks used for various NLP tasks, including text analysis, sentiment analysis, text classification, and more.

The types of tokens are described as follows:

- Tokens can represent words, sub words, or characters, depending on the level of granularity required.
- In word-level tokenization, text is split into words, for example, "I love NLP" → "I", "love", "NLP".
- Subword tokenization means splitting words into smaller parts that still have meaning. For example, the word "unhappiness" can be broken into "un" and "happiness".
- Character-level tokenization breaks down words even further, treating each letter as a token. For example, the word "hello" is split into "h", "e", "l", "l", "o".
- Sentence tokenization which involves breaking text into sentences.
- Tokenization helps in assigning grammatical categories to each token, identifying named entities in the text, analyzing the sentiment of individual words or phrases, training models to understand and generate human-like text. It also helps in categorizing text based on token features.

Python packages:

- NLTK
- spaCy
- The built-in string methods can be used for tokenization
- Regular expressions in Python's built-in *re* module
- Tokenizers from Hugging Face (used with transformer models)
- TextBlob
- LangChain
  - o We have not included the code for this package. It supports a number of tokenizers which are as follows:
    - tiktoken
    - spaCy

- SentenceTransformers
- NLTK
- Hugging Face tokenizer

  You can see the examples of the same on below URL: **https:// python.langchain.com/docs/modules/data_connection/document_ transformers/text_splitters/split_by_token#hugging-face-tokenizer**

Code:

Put the following code in the file called **tokens.py** [**E:\Repository\Book\scripts\nlp_ concepts\tokens.py**]:

```
1. # Import required packages
2. import nltk
3. from nltk.tokenize import word_tokenize, sent_tokenize
4. import spacy
5. from transformers import AutoTokenizer
6. from textblob import TextBlob
7.
8.
9. # =======================================================================
10. # NLTK
11. print("*"*25)
12. print("Below example of Tokens is using NLTK package")
13.
14. # Download the required dataset. Not required to run everytime.
15. nltk.download('punkt')
16. text = "This is an example sentence. Tokenize it."
17.
18. # Word tokenization
19. words = word_tokenize(text)
20. print("Word tokens:", words)
21.
22. # Sentence tokenization
23. sentences = sent_tokenize(text)
24. print("Sentence tokens:", sentences)
25.
26.
27. # =======================================================================
```

```
28. # Spacy
29. print("*"*25)
30. print("Below example of Tokens is using Spacy package")
31.
32. # It is to download english package. Not required to run every
    time. "# Run below code from terminal after activating virtual
    environment"
33. # python -m spacy download en_core_web_sm
34. nlp = spacy.load("en_core_web_sm")
35.
36. text = "This is an example sentence. Tokenize it."
37.
38. doc = nlp(text)
39.
40. # Word tokenization
41. words = [token.text for token in doc]
42. print("Word tokens:", words)
43.
44. # Sentence tokenization
45. sentences = [sent.text for sent in doc.sents]
46. print("Sentence tokens:", sentences)
47.
48.
49. # ========================================================================
50. # Builtin Methods
51. print("*"*25)
52. print("Below example of Tokens is using Builtin package")
53.
54. text = "This is an example sentence. Tokenize it."
55.
56. # Word tokenization
57. words = text.split(" ")
58. print("Word tokens:", words)
59.
60. # Sentence tokenization
61. sentences = text.split(".")
62. # Remove 3rd element which will be "". Also remove extra spaces
    around non-blank elements.
```

```
63. sentences = [k.strip() for k in sentences if k != ""]
64. print("Sentence tokens:", sentences)
65.
66.
67. # =========================================================================
68. # Huggingface Transformers
69. print("*"*25)
70. print("Below example of Tokens is using Huggingface package")
71.
72. # Use pretrained model
73. tokenizer = AutoTokenizer.from_pretrained("bert-base-uncased")
74.
75. text = "This is an example sentence. Tokenize it."
76.
77. # Tokenize the text into word-level tokens
78. word_tokens = tokenizer.tokenize(text)
79. print("Word tokens:", word_tokens)
80.
81. # we tokenize the text into sentence-level tokens by adding special
     tokens (e.g., [CLS] and [SEP]) to the output.
82. # [CLS] stands for Classification Token and used in BERT and other
     transformers for classification tasks. Its also
83. # inserted at the beginning of text sequence.
84. # [SEP] stands for Separator Token and used in BERT and other
     transformers. It is used to separate different segments
85. # of the input text.
86. # Tokenize the text into sentence-level tokens
87. sent_tokens = tokenizer.tokenize(text, add_special_tokens=True)
88. print("Sentence tokens:", sent_tokens)
89.
90. # Optionally, you can convert the sentence tokens into actual
     sentences
91. sentences = tokenizer.convert_tokens_to_string(sent_tokens)
92. print("Sentences:", sentences)
93.
94.
95. # =========================================================================
```

```
96.  # Textblob
97.  print("*"*25)
98.  print("Below example of Tokens is using Textblob package")
99.
100. text = "This is an example sentence. Tokenize it."
101.
102. blob = TextBlob(text)
103.
104. # Word tokenization
105. words = blob.words
106. print("Word tokens:", words)
107.
108. # Sentence tokenization
109. sentences = blob.sentences
110. print("Sentence tokens:", sentences)
```

Difference in tokens and n-grams

The main difference is that tokens represent individual text units, whereas n-grams are sequences of tokens (or other text units), created by considering n consecutive items from the text. Tokens are essential for basic text analysis, while n-grams are useful for capturing patterns, relationships, and context in the text, and they are often used in language modeling, text analysis, and various NLP tasks.

Stop words removal

Common and uninformative words like "the", "and" are removed from the text. Stop word removal is vital in NLP for several reasons. It reduces text complexity, improves computational efficiency, and enhances the quality and accuracy of text analysis by focusing on meaningful content words.

Removing stop words also promotes consistency in text representation and is particularly valuable in text classification, sentiment analysis, and information retrieval tasks.

Python packages:

- NLTK
- spaCy
- Gensim
- Scikit-Learn

Code:

Put the following code in the file called **stopwords_removal.py** [**E:\Repository\Book\ scripts\nlp_concepts\stopwords_removal.py**]:

```
1.  import nltk
2.  from nltk.corpus import stopwords
3.  import spacy
4.  from gensim.parsing.preprocessing import remove_stopwords
5.  from sklearn.feature_extraction.text import ENGLISH_STOP_WORDS
6.
7.  # In case you get an error "ImportError: cannot import name 'triu'
    from 'scipy.linalg'"
8.  # when importing Gensim, please install specific version of scipy
9.  # pip install scipy==1.12
10.
11. # ========================================================================
12. # NLTK
13. print("*" * 25)
14. print("Below example of Stop Words Removal using NLTK package")
15.
16. nltk.download("stopwords")  # Download necessary data (if not
    already downloaded)
17.
18. text = "This is an example sentence with some stop words."
19.
20. words = text.split()
21. filtered_words = [
22.     word for word in words if word.lower() not in stopwords.
    words("english")
23. ]
24.
25. print("Without Stop Words!!!")
26. print(filtered_words)
27.
28.
29. # ========================================================================
30. # Spacy
```

```
31. print("*" * 25)
32. print("Below example of Stop Words Removal using Spacy package")
33.
34. nlp = spacy.load("en_core_web_sm")
35.
36. text = "This is an example sentence with some stop words."
37.
38. doc = nlp(text)
39.
40. filtered_words = [token.text for token in doc if not token.is_stop]
41.
42. print("Without Stop Words!!!")
43. print(filtered_words)
44.
45.
46. # ======================================================================
47. # Gensim
48. print("*" * 25)
49. print("Below example of Stop Words Removal using Gensim package")
50.
51. text = "This is an example sentence with some stop words."
52.
53. filtered_text = remove_stopwords(text)
54.
55. print("Without Stop Words!!!")
56. print(filtered_text)
57.
58.
59. # ======================================================================
60. # Scikit Learn
61. print("*" * 25)
62. print("Below example of Stop Words Removal using Scikit-Learn
    package")
63.
64. text = "This is an example sentence with some stop words."
65.
```

```
66. words = text.split()
67. filtered_words = [word for word in words if word.lower() not in
    ENGLISH_STOP_WORDS]
68.
69. print("Without Stop Words!!!")
70. print(filtered_words)
```

Stemming

It is a text normalization technique in NLP that aims to reduce words to their word stems or roots. The goal of stemming is to remove suffixes from words to achieve a common base form. This helps in treating words with the same stem as equivalent, thus reducing the dimensionality of the text data and simplifying text analysis.

Stemming algorithms remove common endings from words, like "-ing," "-ed," and "-s," to find the base form of the word.

The Porter stemming algorithm is a famous and widely used example of these algorithms. It uses a set of rules to strip suffixes from words. Other stemming algorithms like **Snowball (Porter2)** and **Lancaster** stemming are also commonly used.

Python packages:

- NLTK

Lemmatization

It is a text normalization technique in NLP that reduces words to their base or dictionary form, known as the **lemma**.

The goal of lemmatization is to transform inflected words into their root forms, which often represent the canonical or dictionary meaning of a word.

Unlike stemming, which removes suffixes to approximate word stems, lemmatization applies linguistic rules and analyzes the word's meaning to find the correct lemma.

Lemmatization is valuable in NLP when you need to normalize words to their canonical forms, ensuring that words with different inflections are treated as equivalent. It's commonly used in information retrieval, search engines, and text analysis tasks where precise word forms are important.

Stemming is different from lemmatization. While stemming is a rule-based process that often results in approximate word stems, lemmatization involves finding the base or dictionary form of a word (the lemma) and is linguistically more accurate.

Python packages:

- NLTK
- spaCy

- TextBlob
- Pattern

Code:

Put the following code in the file called **stem_lem.py** [**E:\Repository\Book\scripts\ nlp_concepts\stem_lem.py**]

Note: This code contains both stemming and lemmatization.

```
1.  import nltk
2.  from nltk.stem import PorterStemmer
3.  from nltk.stem import WordNetLemmatizer
4.  import spacy
5.  from textblob import Word
6.  from pattern.en import lemma
7.
8.  # ==========================================================================
9.  # NLTK
10. print("*" * 25)
11. print("Below example of Stemming using NLTK package")
12. nltk.download("punkt")  # Download necessary data (if not already
    downloaded)
13.
14. # Create a PorterStemmer instance
15. stemmer = PorterStemmer()
16.
17. # Example words for stemming
18. words = ["jumps", "jumping", "jumper", "flies", "flying"]
19.
20. # Perform stemming on each word
21. stemmed_words = [stemmer.stem(word) for word in words]
22.
23. # Print the original and stemmed words
24. for i in range(len(words)):
25.     print(f"Original: {words[i]}\tStemmed: {stemmed_words[i]}")
26.
27.
28. # ==========================================================================
29. # NLTK
```

```
30. print("*" * 25)
31. print("Below example of Lemmatization using NLTK package")
32. nltk.download("wordnet")  # Download necessary data (if not
    already downloaded)
33.
34. lemmatizer = WordNetLemmatizer()
35.
36. # Example words for lemmatization
37. words = ["jumps", "jumping", "jumper", "flies", "flying"]
38.
39. # Perform lemmatization on each word
40. lemma_words = [
41.     lemmatizer.lemmatize(word, pos="v") for word in words
42. ]  # Specify the part of speech (e.g., 'v' for verb)
43.
44. # Print the original and lemmatized words
45. for i in range(len(words)):
46.     print(f"Original: {words[i]}\tLemmatized: {lemma_words[i]}")
47.
48.
49. # =======================================================================
50. # SpaCy
51. print("*" * 25)
52. print("Below example of Lemmatization using Spacy package")
53.
54. nlp = spacy.load("en_core_web_sm")
55.
56. # Example words for lemmatization
57. words = ["jumps", "jumping", "jumper", "flies", "flying"]
58.
59. # Perform lemmatization on each word
60. lemma_words = [nlp(word)[0].lemma_ for word in words]
61.
62. # Print the original and lemmatized words
63. for i in range(len(words)):
64.     print(f"Original: {words[i]}\tLemmatized: {lemma_words[i]}")
```

```
65.
66.
67. # =======================================================================
68. # TextBlob
69. print("*" * 25)
70. print("Below example of Lemmatization using Textblob package")
71.
72. # Example words for Lemmatization
73. words = ["jumps", "jumping", "jumper", "flies", "flying"]
74.
75. # Perform Lemmatization on each word
76. lemma_words = [
77.     Word(word).lemmatize("v") for word in words
78. ]  # Specify the part of speech (e.g., 'v' for verb)
79.
80. # Print the original and lemmatized words
81. for i in range(len(words)):
82.     print(f"Original: {words[i]}\tLemmatized: {lemma_words[i]}")
83.
84.
85. # =======================================================================
86. # Pattern
87. # Not in use any more, since 2018 the package has not been updated.
88. # print("*" * 25)
89. # print("Below example of Lemmatization using Pattern package")
90.
91. # # Example words for Lemmatization
92. # words = ["jumps", "jumping", "jumper", "flies", "flying"]
93.
94. # # Perform Lemmatization on each word
95. # lemma_words = [Lemma(word) for word in words]
96.
97. # # Print the original and lemmatized words
98. # for i in range(len(words)):
99. #     print(f"Original: {words[i]}\tLemmatized: {lemma_words[i]}")
```

Lowercasing

Converting all text to lowercase to ensure case insensitivity. Lowercasing is a crucial text preprocessing step in NLP. It ensures case-insensitivity in search engines, simplifies text classification, and aids NER tasks by recognizing named entities regardless of case. Additionally, lowercasing is integral to language models and word embeddings, text normalization, tokenization, and text comparison.

It is a standard preprocessing step in machine learning, promoting consistency and simplifying feature engineering.

Python packages:

- Built-in string method `.lower()` can be used for lower casing.
- For example:

```
temp = "Building LLM applications with Langchain and Hugging Face"
print(temp.lower())
# Output
"building llm applications with langchain and hugging face"
```

Part-of-speech tagging

Part of speech tagging basically means identifying and labeling the different roles each word plays within a sentence. Things like 'nouns,' which are names for people or objects, 'verbs' that describe an action, and 'adjectives' that tell us more about those nouns – they all get sorted out! This is very fundamental to **Natural Language Processing** (**NLP**) because it helps machines understand grammar's structure pretty well.

When we know what role every word plays in the sentence structure, we can better understand its meaning. For instance, when using **Named Entity Recognition** (**NER**), **Part of Speech** (**POS**) tagging provides context making it easier to figure out important pieces of information like who or what is being talked about.

Moreover, POS tagging is a critical preprocessing step for training language models, capturing linguistic structure.

Python packages:

- NLTK
- spaCy
- TextBlob

Code:

Put the following code in the file called **pos.py** [**E:\Repository\Book\scripts\nlp_concepts\pos.py**]:

```
 1. # Import required packages
 2. import nltk
 3. import spacy
 4. from textblob import TextBlob
 5.
 6.
 7. # =====================================================================
 8. # NLTK
 9. print("*"*25)
10. print("Below example of POS using NLTK package")
11.
12. nltk.download('punkt')  # Download necessary data (if not already
    downloaded)
13.
14. text = "This is an example sentence for part-of-speech tagging."
15. words = nltk.word_tokenize(text)
16. tagged_words = nltk.pos_tag(words)
17.
18. print(tagged_words)
19.
20.
21. # =====================================================================
22. # Spacy
23. print("*"*25)
24. print("Below example of POS using Spacy package")
25.
26. nlp = spacy.load("en_core_web_sm")
27.
28. text = "This is an example sentence for part-of-speech tagging."
29. doc = nlp(text)
30.
31. for token in doc:
32.     print(token.text, token.pos_)
33.
34.
35. # =====================================================================
```

```
36. # TextBlob
37. print("*"*25)
38. print("Below example of POS using TextBlob package")
39.
40. text = "This is an example sentence for part-of-speech tagging."
41. blob = TextBlob(text)
42.
43. for word, pos in blob.tags:
44.     print(word, pos)
```

Named Entity Recognition

With **Named Entity Recognition (NER)** you can identify named entities within a text. Words representing names may be linked with people's personal labels or referential markers for places, such as cities' geographic identifiers, even calendar dates. NER is a pivotal NLP task with versatile applications. It extracts structured data from unstructured text, categorizing entities like company names and financial figures. It enhances document retrieval, enabling specific entity-based searches.

In sentiment analysis, NER identifies targets of sentiment, distinguishing whether it pertains to products or companies. NER also aids in summarizing key entities and their relationships, facilitating the creation of concise and informative text summaries.

Python packages:

- NLTK
- spaCy
- HuggingFace

Code:

Put the following code in the file called **ner.py** [**E:\Repository\Book\scripts\nlp_concepts\ner.py**]:

```
1. import nltk
2. import spacy
3. import subprocess
4. from transformers import pipeline
5.
6. # ======================================================================
7. # NLTK
8. print("*" * 25)
```

```
 9. print("Below example of NER is using NLTK package")
10.
11. # This is one time only. Not required to run every time.
12. # Once you have got the chunker you can comment the code.
13. nltk.download("maxent_ne_chunker")
14. nltk.download("words")
15. nltk.download("averaged_perceptron_tagger")
16.
17. # Run below code from terminal after activating virtual environment
18. """ python -m spacy download en_core_web_sm """
19.
20. text = "Apple Inc. is headquartered in Cupertino, California, and
    was founded by Steve Jobs."
21.
22. words = nltk.word_tokenize(text)
23. tagged_words = nltk.pos_tag(words)
24. entities = nltk.chunk.ne_chunk(tagged_words)
25.
26. for entity in entities:
27.     if isinstance(entity, nltk.Tree):
28.         print([(word, entity.label()) for word, tag in entity])
29.
30.
31. # =========================================================================
32. # Spacy
33. print("*" * 25)
34. print("Below example of NER is using Spacy package")
35.
36. nlp = spacy.load("en_core_web_sm")
37.
38. text = "Apple Inc. is headquartered in Cupertino, California, and
    was founded by Steve Jobs."
39.
40. doc = nlp(text)
41.
42. for entity in doc.ents:
43.     print(entity.text, entity.label_)
```

```
44.
45.
46. # ========================================================================
47. # HuggingFace
48. print("*" * 25)
49. print("Below example of NER is using HuggingFace package")
50.
51. # Load the NER model
52. # It will download large model of size around 1.33 GB
53. """
54. If you are getting error as mentioned below uninstall keras and
    tensorflow packages.
55. pip uninstall keras tensorflow
56.
57. 1. RuntimeError: Failed to import transformers.models.bert.
    modeling_tf_bert because of the following error (look up to see its
    traceback):
58. Your currently installed version of Keras is Keras 3, but this is
    not yet supported in Transformers. Please install the backwards-
    compatible tf-keras package with `pip install tf-keras`.
59.
60. 2. RuntimeError: Failed to import transformers.models.bert.
    modeling_tf_bert because of the following error (look up to see its
    traceback):
61. module 'tensorflow._api.v2.compat.v2.__internal__' has no attribute
    'register_load_context_function'
62. """
63. nlp_ner = pipeline("ner", model="dbmdz/bert-large-cased-finetuned-
    conll03-english")
64.
65. text = "Apple Inc. is headquartered in Cupertino, California, and
    was founded by Steve Jobs."
66.
67. # Perform NER
68. entities = nlp_ner(text)
69.
70. # Display the detected entities
71. for entity in entities:
72.     print(f"Entity: {entity['word']}, Label: {entity['entity']}")
```

Bag of words

Now moving on to **Bag of Words (BoW)**. Imagine if sentences were bags full of random words, kind of like naming each Lego piece in your bag and then counting how many purple ones there are. That is essentially what BoW does! It converts raw lines into numerical lists where a unique word from the vocabulary is counted per document according to their frequency of occurrence.

BoW also has many limitations. It fails to capture the intricate nuances of word order and contextual relationships within a document, a pivotal aspect in deciphering textual meaning. In response to this constraint, more sophisticated methodologies such as word embeddings and transformers have been devised to yield more intricate and contextually astute text data representations.

The BoW approach used in NLP involves counting the word occurrence in the given text. Each word will be counted separately, which will reflect the appearance of each word in the given corpus or corpora.

BoW vectors are typically very sparse because most documents contain only a small subset of the words in the vocabulary. This sparsity is handled efficiently in modern NLP libraries.

Python packages:

- NLTK
- Gensim
- Scikit-Learn

Code:

Put the following code in the file called **bag_of_words.py** [E:\Repository\Book\scripts\ nlp_concepts\ bag_of_words.py]:

```
1. import nltk
2. from nltk.tokenize import word_tokenize
3. from nltk.probability import FreqDist
4. from gensim.corpora import Dictionary
5. from collections import defaultdict
6. from gensim.models import TfidfModel
7. from sklearn.feature_extraction.text import CountVectorizer,
   TfidfVectorizer
8.
9. # ====================================================================
10. # Download required data
11. nltk.download("punkt")
```

```
12.
13.
14. # ========================================================
15. # NLTK
16. print("*" * 25)
17. print("Below example of Bag Of Words is using NLTK package")
18. text = (
19.     "This is a sample document. Another document with some words.
    Repeating document with some words. A third "
20.     "document for illustration. Repeating illustration."
21. )
22. words = word_tokenize(text)
23. fdist = FreqDist(words)
24.
25. fdist.pprint()
26.
27.
28. # ========================================================
29. # Gensim
30. print("*" * 25)
31. print("Below example of Bag Of Words is using Gensim package")
32.
33. documents = [
34.     "This is a sample document.",
35.     "Another document with some words. Repeating document with some
    words.",
36.     "A third document for illustration. Repeating illustration.",
37. ]
38.
39. tokenized_docs = [doc.split() for doc in documents]
40.
41. # Create a dictionary
42. dictionary = Dictionary(tokenized_docs)
43.
44. word_frequencies = dictionary.cfs
45.
46. # Display words and their frequencies
```

```
47. for word_id, frequency in word_frequencies.items():
48.     word = dictionary[word_id]  # Get the word corresponding to the
    word ID
49.     print(f"ID: {word_id}, Word: {word}, Frequency: {frequency}")
50.
51. # Create a BoW representation
52. corpus = [dictionary.doc2bow(doc) for doc in tokenized_docs]
53.
54. # Create a TF-IDF model based on the BoW representation
55. tfidf = TfidfModel(corpus, dictionary=dictionary)
56.
57. # Calculate overall TF-IDF scores for words
58. overall_tfidf = defaultdict(float)
59. for doc in tfidf[corpus]:
60.     for word_id, tfidf_score in doc:
61.         overall_tfidf[word_id] += tfidf_score
62.
63. # Display words and their overall TF-IDF scores
64. for word_id, tfidf_score in overall_tfidf.items():
65.     word = dictionary[word_id]  # Get the word corresponding to the
    word ID
66.     print(f"Word: {word}, Overall TF-IDF Score: {tfidf_score:.4f}")
67.
68.
69. # ========================================================================
70. # Scikit Learn
71. print("*" * 25)
72. print("Below example of Bag Of Words is using Scikit-Learn package
    Count Method")
73.
74. documents = [
75.     "This is a sample document.",
76.     "Another document with some words. Repeating document with some
    words.",
77.     "A third document for illustration. Repeating illustration.",
78. ]
79.
```

```
80.  # Join the list of documents into a single string
81.  corpus = " ".join(documents)
82.
83.  vectorizer = CountVectorizer()
84.  X = vectorizer.fit_transform([corpus])
85.
86.  # Get the feature names (words)
87.  feature_names = vectorizer.get_feature_names_out()
88.
89.  # Get the word frequencies from the CountVectorizer's array
90.  word_frequencies = X.toarray()[0]
91.
92.  # Print words with their frequencies
93.  for word, frequency in zip(feature_names, word_frequencies):
94.      print(f"Word: {word}, Frequency: {frequency}")
95.
96.
97.  # ========================================================================
98.  # Scikit Learn with TFIDF
99.  print("*" * 25)
100. print("Below example of Bag Of Words is using Scikit-Learn package
     TFIDF Method")
101.
102. documents = [
103.     "This is a sample document.",
104.     "Another document with some words. Repeating document with some
     words.",
105.     "A third document for illustration. Repeating illustration.",
106. ]
107.
108. # Join the list of documents into a single string
109. corpus = " ".join(documents)
110.
111. tfidf_vectorizer = TfidfVectorizer()
112. X = tfidf_vectorizer.fit_transform([corpus])
113.
114. # Get the feature names (words)
```

```
115. feature_names = tfidf_vectorizer.get_feature_names_out()
116.
117. # Get the TF-IDF values from the TF-IDF vector
118. tfidf_values = X.toarray()[0]
119.
120. # Print words with their TF-IDF values
121. for word, tfidf in zip(feature_names, tfidf_values):
122.     print(f"Word: {word}, TF-IDF: {tfidf:.4f}")
```

Word embeddings

Word embeddings are simple ways to map text to continuous vector space, ensuring that semantic relationships are transformed and duly understandable by computers in the form of mathematical representations. Unlike traditional human language formats, which will be complex in structure and formation, word embeddings made it easy for computers for easier processing of ML-related tasks. This method will provide a shorter distance between words like King and Queen and a larger distance between words like King and Apple; thus, it will help to understand the relationship and similarities between words.

Large language models (**LLMs**) such as BERT, GPT-3, and contextual understanding variants like Word2Vec, GloVe, and FastText provide efficient methods for diverse training approaches, which require varying degrees of complexity depending on the user's prioritized features.

Word embeddings can also understand the context behind meanings. For example, the word "bank" could refer to a place where you keep money or beside a river! It all depends on how it is used in a sentence. These similarities are essential for things like machine translations or even search engine recommendations!

Is this not incredible? By utilizing effective NLP tasks and tools, we can uncover a deeper understanding of human conversation patterns across extensive linguistic functionalities. These methods can be implemented efficiently and easily. These methods differ in their training approaches and capabilities.

Python packages:

There are many python packages used for the aforesaid purpose.

Here, we can use available pre-trained models to get word embeddings and create our own word embeddings.

The most widely used ones with pre-trained models as well as to create own word embeddings:

- Gensim
- spaCy

- TensorFlow
- Keras
- HuggingFace
- LangChain
  - o LangChain provides a simple unified API to generate word embeddings from different providers that can be used in downstream NLP tasks.

Code:

Put the following code in the file called **word_embeddings.py [E:\Repository\Book\ scripts\nlp_concepts\word_embeddings.py]**

Note: Here in the code, we have used pre-trained models to create word embeddings.

```
1.  from gensim.models import Word2Vec
2.  import spacy
3.  from transformers import DistilBertTokenizer, DistilBertModel
4.
5.
6.  # =======================================================================
7.  # Gensim
8.  print("*"*25)
9.  print("Below example of Word Embeddings using Gensim package")
10.
11. # Example sentences for training the model
12. sentences = [
13.     "This is an example sentence for word embeddings.",
14.     "Word embeddings capture semantic relationships.",
15.     "Gensim is a popular library for word embeddings.",
16. ]
17.
18. # Tokenize the sentences
19. tokenized_sentences = [sentence.split() for sentence in sentences]
20.
21. # Train a Word2Vec model
22. model = Word2Vec(tokenized_sentences, vector_size=100, window=5,
    min_count=1, sg=0)
23.
24. # Access word vectors
25. word_vector = model.wv['word']
```

```
26. print(word_vector)
27.
28.
29. # ========================================================================
30. # Spacy
31. print("*"*25)
32. print("Below example of Word Embeddings using Spacy package")
33.
34. # Load the pre-trained English model
35. nlp = spacy.load("en_core_web_sm")
36.
37. # Process a text to get word embeddings
38. doc = nlp("This is an example sentence for word embeddings. Word
    embeddings capture semantic relationships. Gensim is a popular
    library for word embeddings.")
39. word_vector = doc[0].vector  # Access the word vector
40. print(word_vector)
41.
42.
43. # ========================================================================
44. # Huggingface
45. print("*"*25)
46. print("Below example of Word Embeddings using Huggingface package")
47.
48. # Load the pre-trained DistilBERT tokenizer
49. tokenizer = DistilBertTokenizer.from_pretrained("distilbert-base-
    uncased")
50.
51. # Tokenize a sentence
52. text = "Hugging Face's Transformers library is fantastic!"
53. tokens = tokenizer(text, padding=True, truncation=True, return_
    tensors="pt")
54.
55. # Load the pre-trained DistilBERT model
56. model = DistilBertModel.from_pretrained("distilbert-base-uncased")
57.
58. # Get word embeddings for the tokens
```

```
59. output = model(**tokens)
60.
61. # Access word embeddings for the [CLS] token (you can access other
    tokens as well)
62. word_embeddings = output.last_hidden_state[0]  # [CLS] token's
    embeddings
63.
64. # Convert the tensor to a numpy array
65. word_embeddings = word_embeddings.detach().numpy()
66.
67. # Print the word embeddings
68. print(word_embeddings)
```

Topic modeling

As the name implies, this technique aims to automatically identify topics or core themes from the corpus. It is especially helpful when we want to summarize corpus or corpora, or we want to categorize them into specific groups.

The most common technique used for this process is **latent dirichlet allocation (LDA)**.

Python packages:

- Gensim

Code:

Put the following code in the file called **topic_modelling.py** [**E:\Repository\Book\ scripts\nlp_concepts\topic_modelling.py**]:

```
1. import gensim
2. from gensim import corpora
3. from gensim.models import LdaModel
4. from gensim.parsing.preprocessing import remove_stopwords
5.
6. # Sample documents
7. documents = [
8.     "Natural language processing is a fascinating field in AI.",
9.     "Topic modeling helps uncover hidden themes in text data.",
10.    "Latent Dirichlet Allocation (LDA) is a popular topic modeling
       technique.",
11.    "LDA assumes that documents are mixtures of topics.",
12.    "Text mining and NLP are essential for extracting insights from
       text.",
```

```
13.        "Machine learning plays a significant role in NLP tasks.",
14. ]
15.
16. # Preprocess the documents (tokenization and lowercasing)
17. documents = [remove_stopwords(k) for k in documents]
18. documents = [doc.lower().split() for doc in documents]
19.
20. # Create a dictionary and a document-term matrix (DTM)
21. dictionary = corpora.Dictionary(documents)
22. corpus = [dictionary.doc2bow(doc) for doc in documents]
23.
24. # Build the LDA model
25. lda_model = LdaModel(corpus, num_topics=2, id2word=dictionary,
    passes=15)
26.
27. # Print the topics
28. for topic in lda_model.print_topics():
29.     print(topic)
30.
31. # To summarize the input
32. """
33. (0, '0.062*"nlp" + 0.062*"text" + 0.037*"insights" + 0.037*"mining"
    + 0.037*"extracting" + 0.037*"essential" + 0.037*"text." +
    0.037*"helps" + 0.037*"data." + 0.037*"themes"')
34. (1, '0.040*"modeling" + 0.040*"topic" + 0.040*"popular" +
    0.040*"technique." + 0.040*"(lda)" + 0.040*"allocation"
    + 0.040*"dirichlet" + 0.040*"latent" + 0.040*"field" +
    0.040*"natural"')
35.
36. Here we have got 2 topics. 0 and 1. Both contains the words which
    are associated with the theme of the doc.
37. The words are arranged in their order. From left being most
    associated to right being least associated.
38. Based on the words we can say that Topic 0 is about natural language
    processing.
39. Topic 1 is about LDA method.
40. """
```

Sentiment analysis

Sentiment analysis finds the emotion in a piece of text, labeling it as positive, negative, or neutral. It is primarily used to gauge the sentiments of customers. For example, Twitter tweets on specific subjects from different users can be used to measure the sentiments of users related to the specific subject.

Python packages:

- TextBlob
- HuggingFace
- NLTK

Code:

Put the following code in the file called **sentiment_analysis.py** [**E:\Repository\Book\ scripts\nlp_concepts\sentiment_analysis.py**]:

```python
1. from textblob import TextBlob
2. from transformers import pipeline
3. import nltk
4. from nltk.sentiment.vader import SentimentIntensityAnalyzer
5.
6.
7. # ========================================================================
8. # TextBlob
9. print("*" * 25)
10. print("Below example of Sentiment using TextBlob package")
11.
12. # Sample text for sentiment analysis
13. text = "I love this product! It's amazing."
14.
15. # Create a TextBlob object
16. blob = TextBlob(text)
17.
18. # Perform sentiment analysis
19. sentiment = blob.sentiment
20.
21. # Print sentiment polarity and subjectivity
22. polarity = sentiment.polarity  # Range from -1 (negative) to 1
    (positive)
```

```
23. subjectivity = sentiment.subjectivity  # Range from 0 (objective)
    to 1 (subjective)
24.
25. # Interpret sentiment
26. if polarity > 0:
27.     sentiment_label = "positive"
28. elif polarity < 0:
29.     sentiment_label = "negative"
30. else:
31.     sentiment_label = "neutral"
32.
33. # Output results
34. print("Text:", text)
35. print("Sentiment Polarity:", polarity)
36. print("Sentiment Subjectivity:", subjectivity)
37. print("Sentiment Label:", sentiment_label)
38.
39.
40. # =======================================================================
41. # HuggingFace
42. print("*" * 25)
43. print("Below example of Sentiment using HuggingFace package")
44.
45. # Load a pre-trained sentiment analysis model
46. nlp = pipeline("sentiment-analysis")
47.
48. # Sample text for sentiment analysis
49. text = "I love this product! It's amazing."
50.
51. # Perform sentiment analysis
52. results = nlp(text)
53.
54. # Output results
55. for result in results:
56.     label = result["label"]
57.     score = result["score"]
58.     print(f"Sentiment Label: {label}, Score: {score:.4f}")
59.
```

```
60.
61. # ========================================================================
62. # NLTK
63. print("*" * 25)
64. print("Below example of Sentiment using NLTK package")
65.
66. # Download the VADER lexicon (if not already downloaded)
67. nltk.download("vader_lexicon")
68.
69. # Initialize the VADER sentiment analyzer
70. analyzer = SentimentIntensityAnalyzer()
71.
72. # Sample text for sentiment analysis
73. text = "I love this product! It's amazing."
74.
75. # Perform sentiment analysis
76. sentiment = analyzer.polarity_scores(text)
77.
78. # Interpret sentiment
79. compound_score = sentiment["compound"]
80. if compound_score >= 0.05:
81.     sentiment_label = "positive"
82. elif compound_score <= -0.05:
83.     sentiment_label = "negative"
84. else:
85.     sentiment_label = "neutral"
86.
87. # Output results
88. print("Text:", text)
89. print("Sentiment Score:", sentiment)
90. print("Sentiment Label:", sentiment_label)
```

Large language models

Large language models are pre-trained models that can understand and generate human-like text. We can refer to these language models as LLM as well. As these models are built on vast amounts of data with a greater number of parameters, we call them LLMs.

Use cases include human-like text generation, translation, text summarization, a questions-answering system, and more.

Some of such models are GPT-3, GPT-4, Gemini, LLaMA, T5 etc.

Python packages:

- LangChain
- Llama Index
- Transformers (Hugging Face)
- spaCy

Code: We are going to cover the code for this section in coming chapters.

Transfer learning

It is a technique where a model will be trained on one task and later on can be adapted or fine-tuned for different but related tasks. Instead of training the models from scratch, we will use any existing pre-built models based on our requirements. Again, while using the pre-built models based on the requirement, we might use the model as is or can fine tune it with our specific data.

Here, a pre-trained model stands for a model that has already been trained on a large amount of data.

Fine tuning refers to the modification of a pre-trained model for specific use cases.

By using transfer learning, we are using knowledge gained by the model for specific use cases.

Some of the famous models are BERT, GPT, RoBERTa are pre-trained on large corpora and can be fine-tuned for various NLP tasks.

For example, the GPT model can be used on our data set to generate responses. Here, instead of creating the entire model from scratch, we will take the help of transfer learning.

We can fine tune the GPT model on our own data set. As GPT has been trained on humongous data, it can generate answers to any question. For the time being, consider that GPT has not been trained on movies corpus, so in this case, we will fine-tune the GPT model with movie data so that whenever asked about any movie, it can answer accordingly.

Text classification

In text classification, we classify the text into required categories. We can call it text categorization or document classification as well. For document classification, we have seen one of the examples called "Topic Modelling" above.

The text classification can be sentiments like positive or negative. It can be spam or not spam, it can be like the language of the text, and many more.

General text classification involves the following pipeline:

- Data gathering with labels
    - o Here, labels are the categories in which text will be classified
- Text preprocessing:
    - o Lowercasing
    - o Tokenization
    - o Stop word removal
    - o Stemming or lemmatization
    - o Removing hashtags, URL links
- Bag of words or word embeddings creation that is, converting data to numerical features
- Model selection
- Train-test-validation split of the data
- Evaluation of the model and, if required doing hyper parameter tuning and re-training of the model to get improvised accuracy
- Finalizing the model for future text classification of prediction

Python packages:
- Scikit-Learn
- NLTK

Code:

Put the following code in the file called **text_classification.py** [**E:\Repository\Book\ scripts\nlp_concepts\text_classification.py**]

Note: The text pre-processing steps are used to improve model performance though they are not mandatory. Here in the Hugging Face package, we are using pre built model for text classification. We can call it transfer learning as well. The code provided here is the very basic one, and based on the requirement, it can vary. Based on the requirement we might need to add or remove steps in the text classification.

```
1. from sklearn.feature_extraction.text import TfidfVectorizer
2. from sklearn.model_selection import train_test_split
3. from sklearn.naive_bayes import MultinomialNB
4. from sklearn.metrics import accuracy_score, classification_report
5.
6. import nltk
```

```
7.  from nltk.corpus import movie_reviews
8.  from nltk.classify import SklearnClassifier
9.  import random  # Import the random module
10.
11. from transformers import DistilBertTokenizer, DistilBertForSequenceC
    lassification
12. import torch
13.
14. # ================================================================
15. # Scikit-Learn
16. print("*"*25)
17. print("Below example of Text Analysis using Sklearn package")
18. # Sample text data and labels
19. texts = ["This is a positive sentence.", "This is a negative
    sentence.", "A neutral statement here."]
20. labels = ["positive", "negative", "neutral"]
21.
22. # Text preprocessing and feature extraction
23. vectorizer = TfidfVectorizer()
24. X = vectorizer.fit_transform(texts)
25.
26. # Split data into training and testing sets
27. X_train, X_test, y_train, y_test = train_test_split(X, labels, test_
    size=0.2, random_state=42)
28.
29. # Train a classifier (e.g., Naive Bayes)
30. classifier = MultinomialNB()
31. classifier.fit(X_train, y_train)
32.
33. # Make predictions on the test data
34. y_pred = classifier.predict(X_test)
35.
36. # Evaluate the classifier
37. accuracy = accuracy_score(y_test, y_pred)
38. report = classification_report(y_test, y_pred)
39.
40. print(f"Accuracy: {accuracy:.2f}")
```

```
41. print(report)
42.
43.
44. # ==========================================================================
45. # NLTK
46. print("*"*25)
47. print("Below example of Text Analysis using NLTK package")
48.
49. # Load the movie reviews dataset
50. # nltk.download('movie_reviews')
51. documents = [(list(movie_reviews.words(fileid)), category) for
    category in movie_reviews.categories() for fileid in movie_reviews.
    fileids(category)]
52.
53. # Shuffle the documents
54. random.shuffle(documents)
55.
56. # Text preprocessing and feature extraction
57. all_words = [w.lower() for w in movie_reviews.words()]
58. all_words = nltk.FreqDist(all_words)
59. word_features = list(all_words.keys())[:3000]
60.
61. def find_features(document):
62.     words = set(document)
63.     features = {}
64.     for w in word_features:
65.         features[w] = (w in words)
66.     return features
67.
68. feature_sets = [(find_features(rev), category) for (rev, category) in
    documents]
69.
70. # Split data into training and testing sets
71. training_set = feature_sets[:1900]
72. testing_set = feature_sets[1900:]
73.
74. # Train a classifier (e.g., Naive Bayes)
```

```
 75. classifier = SklearnClassifier(MultinomialNB())
 76. classifier.train(training_set)
 77.
 78. # Evaluate the classifier
 79. accuracy = nltk.classify.accuracy(classifier, testing_set)
 80. print(f"Accuracy: {accuracy:.2f}")
 81.
 82.
 83. # =======================================================================
 84. # Hugging Face
 85. print("*"*25)
 86. print("Below example of Text Analysis using Hugging Face package")
 87.
 88. # Sample text data
 89. texts = ["This is a positive sentence.", "This is a negative
     sentence.", "A neutral statement here."]
 90.
 91. # Preprocess text and load pre-trained model
 92. tokenizer = DistilBertTokenizer.from_pretrained('distilbert-base-
     uncased')
 93. model = DistilBertForSequenceClassification.from_
     pretrained('distilbert-base-uncased')
 94.
 95. # Tokenize and encode the text
 96. inputs = tokenizer(texts, padding=True, truncation=True, return_
     tensors="pt")
 97.
 98. # Perform text classification
 99. outputs = model(**inputs)
100.
101. # Get predicted labels and probabilities
102. logits = outputs.logits
103. predicted_labels = torch.argmax(logits, dim=1)
104.
105. # Map predicted labels to human-readable class names
106. class_names = ['positive', 'negative', 'neutral']
107.
```

```
108. for i, text in enumerate(texts):
109.     print(f"Text: {text}")
110.     print(f"Predicted Label: {class_names[predicted_labels[i]]}")
111.     print("")
112.
113. # You can also extract the probability scores for each class if
     needed
114. class_probabilities = torch.softmax(logits, dim=1)
115.
```

Prompt engineering

Prompt engineering is about providing prompts or instructions to the LLMs to get the required answer in the required form. It is widely used with LLM models like GPT, BERT, PaLM, LLaMA etc. Prompts can be **"Tell me about animals"**, or more detailed prompts or instruction can be: **"Tell me about animals containing details on their body structure and food"**.

Hallucination

Hallucination refers to a phenomenon where the model generates text that includes information or details that are not accurate or factual. It occurs when the model produces content that is imaginative or incorrect, often in a way that is convincing or coherent but detached from reality.

Syntactic relationship

It describes the grammatical connections between words in a sentence or text. As for grammatical connections, it will be mostly used in POS.

Semantic relationship

It refers to meaning based associations between words or phrases. For example: I am at the bank to draw money. Here the word **bank** will be referred to as a financial institution.

Note: Here, you will see that LangChain mostly uses third-party providers to provide certain facilities. By integrating LangChain it will help us to make certain task with minimal code and easy implementation. Hugging Face also uses transfer learning for certain facilities. It also provides the facility to create models on our own as well.

Conclusion

In concluding this NLP chapter, we have covered a comprehensive overview of Natural Language Processing, delving into essential concepts and practical methodologies. We explored the intricacies of text preprocessing, a crucial step in preparing textual data for analysis. The general NLP pipeline provided a structured approach to building prediction models, demonstrating the sequential application of techniques like tokenization, stemming, and part-of-speech tagging.

As we move forward, the next chapters will delve into advanced NLP techniques, especially LLMs, bridging theoretical knowledge with hands-on applications. In that chapter, we will talk more in detail about LLM and Neural Network concepts and terminologies and get hands-on experience with them.

Join our book's Discord space

Join the book's Discord Workspace for Latest updates, Offers, Tech happenings around the world, New Release and Sessions with the Authors:

https://discord.bpbonline.com

CHAPTER 5
Introduction to Large Language Models

Introduction

Large Language Models (LLMs) are considered to be a core component of **Natural Language Processing (NLP)** and **Natural Language Generation (NLG)**. In the earlier chapter, we have got an overview of LLM. In this chapter, we will dig down more and get ourselves acknowledged for the different LLM concepts and LLM models that are in use. Overall, in this chapter we will move one step ahead in the journey that we have started with this book.

Structure

We will cover the following sections in this chapter:

- History
- LLM use cases
- LLM terminologies
- Neural networks
- Transformers
- Pre-built transformers

Objectives

By the end of this chapter, you will acquire a robust understanding of language modeling and its various concepts. Furthermore, you will gain comprehensive insights into transformers, a widely utilized framework for defining LLMs. This chapter aims to provide clarity on the terminology, concepts, and architecture associated with transformers, acknowledging their prevalent use in contemporary natural language processing applications.

History

The evolution of large language models has transpired through a progressive continuum, witnessing pivotal strides in recent times. Refer to *Figure 5.1*. Following is a brief history of the evolution of LLMs:

- **Early NLP Systems (1950s-2000s):** The field of NLP started from 1950s with the development of rule-based systems. These systems relied on handcrafted linguistic rules to process and understand language. However, they were limited in handling the complexity and variability of natural language. In 1952, the Hodgkin-Huxley model showed how the brain uses neurons to form an electrical network. These events helped inspire the idea of **Artificial Intelligence (AI)**, NLP, and the evolution of computers.

- **Statistical NLP (1990s-2010s):** As computational power increased, statistical approaches gained prominence. Researchers started using probabilistic models and machine learning algorithms to analyze large datasets of text. **Hidden Markov Models (HMMs)** and probabilistic context-free grammar were among the early techniques.

- **Machine Learning and Neural Networks (2010s):** Neural Networks, which are the core element of deep learning, have performed a critical role in the enhancement of NLP skills. **Recurrent Neural Networks (RNNs) and Long Short-Term Memory Networks (LSTMs)** are the most broadly used neural networks within the field. Apart from these, word embeddings such as Word2Vec and Glove have become popular during this time.

Pre-transformer era Language Models

Figure 5.1: Pre-Transformer era language models

- **Introduction of transformers (2017):** In 2017, the world saw a new trend in natural language processing all thanks to transformers. Introduced by *Vaswani* and his team in their paper named *Attention is All You Need*, this fresh approach allowed machines to understand entire chunks of sentences rather than just processing bits and pieces. This breakthrough formed the basis for constructing large language models that we see today!

- **BERT and pre-trained language models (2018-2019):** In 2018, **Google's revolutionary Bidirectional Encoder Representations from Transformers (BERT)** model emerged onto the scene. BERT showcased impressive results by capitalizing on pre-training massive language models with vast datasets that were then fine-tuned specifically for given tasks—a technique that proved immensely effective across numerous benchmarks within NLP domains. Consequently, BERT ignited a paradigm shift towards leveraging pre-trained language models effectively

- **GPT-3 (2020):** OpenAI further pushed boundaries by unveiling **GPT-3—Generative pre-trained transformer 3**—in 2020—the crown jewel among immense linguistic constructs with its staggering count of an astonishing 175 billion parameters—an unprecedented feat at that time! Not only did GPT-3 wield tremendous prowess when it came to understanding human-like text, but it also excelled at generating such content across diverse tasks—a true testament to its remarkable capabilities as a highly advanced system driven by scaled-up representations provided through innovative modeling techniques.

- **Ongoing developments (2021-2024):** Following GPT-3, researchers continued to explore even larger models, as well as techniques for more efficient training and deployment. Various organizations and researchers are working on advancing the capabilities of language models while addressing ethical concerns and biases associated with their use. Alongside the development of larger and more capable language models, significant advancements were made in the frameworks and tools that facilitate the integration and deployment of these models in real-world applications. We have recently seen some new LLM models like GPT-4o and Gemini Ultra, which are multi-modal in nature and can be game changers in the future. One notable development in this context is the emergence of LangChain.

The history of large language models reflects the ongoing evolution of NLP, with each breakthrough contributing to better language understanding and generation capabilities.

The following figure depicts the evolution tress of modern LLMs:

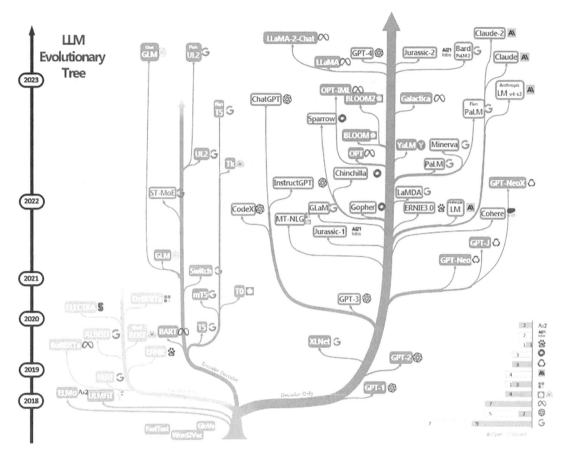

Figure 5.2: [1]*Evolution Tree of Modern LLMs*

The relationship between models within the same branch becomes significantly closer, as depicted in the visual representation. Transformer-based models are distinctly highlighted using non-grey colors—decoder-only models appearing in the blue branch, encoder-only architectures displayed in the pink branch, and encoder-decoder constructs showcased through their location on a green-tinged axis. On this timeline depiction, each model's vertical position denotes its respective release date.

LLM use cases

Below we have described some of the use cases where LLMs can be useful. These use cases span a wide range of domains, including natural language understanding, text generation, sentiment analysis, language translation, content summarization, question answering, and more.

---

[1] ***Source:*** *Harnessing the Power of LLMs in Practice: A Survey on ChatGPT and Beyond* authored by Jingfeng Yang and Hongye Jin and Ruixiang Tang and Xiaotian Han and Qizhang Feng and Haoming Jiang and Bing Yin and Xia Hu [*https://arxiv.org/pdf/2304.13712.pdf*]

- **Text generation:**
  - o **Description:** LLMs excel at generating coherent and contextually relevant text. They can be used for creative writing, content creation, and generating human-like responses in conversational agents.
  - o **Applications:** Content creation, creative writing, chatbots, virtual assistants.
- **Translation:**
  - o **Description:** LLMs can be used for machine translation, converting text from one language to another. They capture language nuances and context, improving translation quality.
  - o **Applications:** Language translation services, cross-language communication.
- **Text summarization:**
  - o **Description:** These models can read articles, news stories, and even research papers and summarize them quickly.
  - o **Applications:** Automatic summarization of articles, news, research papers.
- **Question answering:**
  - o **Description:** Like having your personal assistant! These bots can answer questions by looking at context or pulling important information from their training.
  - o **Applications:** Some examples where we use them today would be virtual helpers like Siri or Alexa, those chatbots you talk with for customer support online.
- **Sentiment analysis:**
  - o **Description:** They can read a text and tell if its text felt positive, negative, or neutral while writing it.
  - o **Applications:** Social media monitoring, customer feedback analysis, brand reputation management.
- **Named Entity Recognition (NER):**
  - o **Description:** LLMs can identify and classify entities (such as names, locations, and organizations) in text.
  - o **Applications:** Information extraction, document categorization.
- **Code generation:**
  - o **Description:** LLMs can generate code snippets based on natural language descriptions, facilitating code completion and aiding developers in writing software.
  - o **Applications:** Code generation tools, automated programming assistance.

- **Conversational agents:**
  - o **Description:** Conversational agents can be made more advanced due to LLMs! Understanding what people are asking for better-suited responses gets easier and, indeed, more valuable, particularly relating to industry-specific applications.
  - o **Applications:** Virtual assistants, chatbots, customer service agents.
- **Content moderation:**
  - o **Description:** LLMs can help us in content moderation by identifying and filtering out inappropriate or harmful content in text.
  - o **Applications:** Social media moderation, Advertisement moderation, online platform content filtering.
- **Medical text analysis:**
  - o **Description:** LLMs can process and analyze medical literature, assisting healthcare professionals in extracting relevant information.
  - o **Applications:** Literature review, information extraction from medical documents.
- **Language understanding tasks:**
  - o **Description:** LLMs can be fine-tuned for specific language understanding tasks, such as intent recognition, language translation, named entity recognition, or dialogue state tracking.
  - o **Applications: Natural Language Understanding (NLU)** systems for specific industries or domains.
- **Educational applications:**
  - o **Description:** LLMs can support educational initiatives by generating educational content, answering student queries, and providing explanations.
  - o **Applications:** Educational chatbots, content creation for online courses.

These use cases demonstrate the versatility of LLMs in understanding, generating, and manipulating natural language text across diverse domains. Their ability to leverage pre-training on vast amounts of data makes them powerful tools for a wide range of applications.

LLM terminologies

Understanding LLMs involves familiarizing oneself with various terminologies associated with these sophisticated models. Here are the key terminologies related to LLMs:

- **Pre-training:**
  - o **Definition:** The initial phase where the model is trained on a huge amount of corpus using unsupervised learning.

o **Example:** During pre-training, a language model learns to predict the next word in a sentence or fill in masked words.

- **P tuning (Prompt tuning):**
  o **Definition:** Prompt-tuning is an efficient, low-cost way of adapting an AI foundation model to new downstream tasks without retraining the model and updating its weights.
  o **Example:** P-tuning can be used to improve pre-trained language models for various tasks, including sentence classification and predicting a country's capital.

- **Fine-tuning:**
  o **Definition:** The subsequent phase where the pre-trained model is further trained on specific downstream tasks with smaller/ medium sized datasets.
  o **Example:** A pre-trained language model, initially trained on general language understanding, can be fine-tuned for different purposes like predicting sentiment, topic modelling, etc. Consider that you will use the OpenAI model on your own custom data that OpenAI has never seen to provide answers to questions. This is a kind of fine tuning.

- **Transformer architecture:**
  o **Definition:** A neural network architecture introduced by *Vaswani et al.,* known for its self-attention mechanisms.
  o **Example:** BERT and GPT are both based on the transformer architecture.

- **Attention mechanism:**
  o **Definition:** A mechanism allowing the model to focus on different parts of the input sentence sequence while making predictions.
  o **Example:** Imagine if you are trying to translate a sentence. The attention mechanism will help your computer focus on the most relevant words in one language while it tries to come up with words in another language.

- **Self-attention:**
  o **Definition:** Self-attention is also an attention mechanism, but here, every word checks out all other words in its own sentence before deciding how important they are.
  o **Example:** Imagine a model creating a sentence, and it has already written: "The cat is." The model then thinks about what word should come next, using what it learned from lots of examples. It might choose "on," making the sentence "The cat is on." The model keeps adding words one by one until it thinks it is time to stop, usually with a period. So, a sentence like "The cat is on the mat." is built word by word. The model makes guesses at each step based on what it has written so far.

- **Masked language modeling (MLM):**
  - o **Definition:** MLM is kind of fun game that language models play to learn about words. In this task, a word in a sentence is hidden, like this: "The cat is on the [MASK]." The model then tries to guess the hidden word using the other words in the sentence as clues.
  - o **Example:** For example, a good guess for the hidden word might be "mat". Many LLMs, like BERT, do this to learn about the special ways humans use language.

- **Prompt engineering:**
  - o **Definition:** The practice of designing effective queries or prompts to interact with language models, especially during instruction tuning for specific tasks.
  - o **Example:** Designing a specific prompt for a language model to generate creative responses or answers to user queries.

- **Zero-shot learning:**
  - o **Definition:** The ability of a large language model to predict a task for which it was not explicitly trained. It is the scenario where a model makes predictions on classes it has never seen during training.
  - o **Example**: If a model has learned about lots of different topics, it might be able to answer questions about a new topic, even if it has not been specifically taught about it. This is like learning about cats and dogs and then being able to guess what a fox is, even if you have never seen one before.

- **Prompting bias:**
  - o **Definition:** The event where the output of a language model is influenced by the wording or phrasing of the input prompt by the user.
  - o **Example:** The choice of words in a prompt might lead the model to generate biased or skewed responses. Nowadays, we see a good number of researchers trying to jailbreak ChatGPT, Gemini, and other LLM tools by smartly crafting prompts.

- **Transfer learning:**
  - o **Definition:** A machine learning technique where knowledge gained from one task (pre-training) is applied to improve performance on a different but related task (fine-tuning).
  - o **Example:** Pre-training a language model on general language tasks and then fine-tuning it for a specific task, like figuring out the sentiment in a text.

- **Parameter size and scaling:**
  - o **Definition:** Refers to the number of parameters in the model. Larger models with more parameters tend to perform better.
    - ▪ Parameters are the internal variables the model adjusts during training to learn patterns and information from the input data. It includes weights and biases of Neural Network's connections.

o **Example:** OpenAI GPT-3.5, with 175 billion parameters, outperforms smaller language models in various natural language processing tasks.

- **Generative Pre-trained Transformer (GPT):**

    o **Definition:** GPT is a type of LLM that is pre-trained on a huge dataset of text and code. GPT models are able to generate human-like quality text, translate languages, write creative content on various topics, and answer your questions in an informative, human way.

    o **Example:** GPT-3.5 is known for its remarkable language generation capabilities, surpassing previous versions in terms of size and performance.

- **Evaluation metrics:**

    o **Definition:** Metrics used to assess the performance of LLMs on specific tasks.

    - For tasks like classification, NER, and sentiment analysis:
        - Accuracy
        - Precision
        - Recall
        - F1 score

    - For tasks like text generation, machine translation:
        - **Recall-Oriented Understudy for Gisting Evaluation (ROUGE):** Measures overlap between generated and reference summaries.
        - **Bilingual Evaluation Understudy (BLEU):** It measures the similarity between the machine generated text and human written reference text.
        - **Metric for Evaluation of Translation with Explicit Ordering (METEOR):** It looks at word-by-word precision and recall, considering things like closely related words, root words together
        - **Consensus-based Image Description Evaluation (CIDEr):** Initially made for image captioning, CIDEr is now also used for machine translation. It looks at multiple correct translations and tries to capture the variety of possible translations.
        - **Translation Edit Rate (TER):** TER measures the number of edits required to change the generated translation into one of the reference text translations. It provides a more fine-grained view of the differences between the generated and reference texts.
        - **Word Error Rate (WER):** WER measures the percentage of words that are different between the generated translation and the reference translation. It is often used in automatic speech recognition but can also be used for text translation.
        - Embedding-based metrics compare the semantic similarity between the machine-generated text and reference text using pre-trained LLMs.

- **Language model generalisation:**
  - **Perplexity:** Measures how well the model predicts a sample or sequence of tokens. Lower perplexity indicates better generalization.
- **Inference:**
  - **Definition:** The process of using a trained large language model to make predictions or text generation for new input data.
  - **Example:** After training the machine can *infer* or guess coherent responses that make sense with the user's questions. To test how the model is working on the test set etc.
- **Embedding:**
  - **Definition:** Embedding means turning words or tokens into dense vectors, trying to represent them as points within continuous vector space similar to grouping similar things together.
  - **Example:** Word embeddings capture semantic similarity or relationships, such as "king" being closer to "queen" than "dog".
- **Vocabulary size:**
  - **Definition:** Vocabulary size is defined as the total number of unique words or tokens in the model's vocabulary.
  - **Example:** A model with a vocabulary of 50,000 tokens can accurately understand and create diverse text, including rare and specialized words, compared to a model with only 10,000 tokens.
- **Tokenization:**
  - **Definition:** The process of breaking text into smaller chunks, usually words or sub words.
  - **Example:** Tokenization of the sentence "I love Data science" results in ["I", "love", "Data","science"].
- **Subword tokenization:**
  - **Definition:** Tokenization at the subword level, allowing the model to handle rare or out-of-vocabulary words.
  - **Example:** "Unsupervised" may be tokenized into ["Un", "super", "vised"].
- **Inference time:**
  - **Definition:** The time it takes for the model to make predictions on new input data.
  - **Example:** Faster inference times enable quicker response in real-time applications.
- **Attention head:**
  - **Definition:** In multi-head attention mechanisms, each head independently focuses on different parts of the input sequence.

o **Example:** Different attention heads might emphasize different words in a sentence.

- **Transformer block:**
  - o **Definition:** A single layer of the transformer architecture with self-attention, feed-forward networks, and layer normalization.
  - o **Example:** A transformer block processes input tokens through attention mechanisms.

- **Warm-up steps:**
  - o **Definition:** A period in training where the learning rate gradually increases to stabilize the model.
  - o **Example:** Gradual learning rate warm-up helps prevent abrupt changes during early training steps.

- **Gated Recurrent Unit (GRU):**
  - o **Definition:** A simpler variant of LSTM, also designed for capturing long-range dependencies.
  - o **Example:** GRUs are computationally efficient and widely used in NLP tasks.

- **Dropout:**
  - o **Definition:** A regularization technique where random neurons are omitted during training.
  - o **Example:** Dropout prevents overfitting by randomly excluding neurons in each training iteration.

- **Epoch:**
  - o **Definition:** One complete pass through the entire training dataset during model training.
  - o **Example:** Training a model for five epochs means going through the entire dataset five times.

- **Beam search:**
  - o **Definition:** A search algorithm used during sequence generation to explore multiple possible output sequences.
  - o **Example:** Beam search helps generate diverse and contextually relevant text.

- **Parameter fine-tuning:**
  - o **Definition:** Adjusting hyperparameters or model parameters after initial training for better task-specific performance.
  - o **Example:** Fine-tuning learning rates improves model convergence on specific tasks.

- **Adversarial training:**
  - o **Definition:** Training the model on adversarial examples to improve robustness.
  - o **Example:** Adversarial training involves exposing the model to deliberately challenging inputs for better generalization.

- **Mini-batch:**
  - o **Definition:** A small subset of the training data used for each iteration during training.
  - o **Example:** Instead of updating the model after every example, training is often done in mini-batches for efficiency.
- **Gradient descent:**
  - o **Definition:** An optimization method that changes model parameters by moving in the direction that reduces the loss function the most quickly.
  - o **Example:** Gradient descent is used to find the minimum of the loss function during training and saves a good amount of training time while hyperparameters are getting tuned.
- **Backpropagation:**
  - o **Definition:** A technique to compute gradients and update model parameters by sending errors backward through the network.
  - o **Example:** Backpropagation is crucial for efficiently training neural networks.
- **Overfitting:**
  - o **Definition:** When a model does well on training data but cannot perform well on new, unseen data.
  - o **Example:** A model memorizing specific examples rather than learning general patterns may exhibit overfitting.
- **Underfitting:**
  - o **Definition:** When a model is too simple to capture the underlying patterns in the data.
  - o **Example:** A linear model may underfit a complex, nonlinear dataset.
- **Regularization:**
  - o **Definition:** Techniques to prevent overfitting by adding constraints to the model during training.
  - o **Example:** L2 regularization penalizes large weights in the model.
- **Early stopping:**
  - o **Definition:** Stopping the training process once a certain criterion (e.g., validation loss) stops improving.
  - o **Example:** Training stops if the validation loss has not improved for several consecutive epochs.
- **Beam width:**
  - o **Definition:** The number of alternative sequences considered during decoding in sequence generation tasks.
  - o **Example:** A beam width of 5 means the model explores the top 5 likely sequences.

- **Hyperparameter:**
  - o **Definition**: Configurable settings external to the model that influence its training and performance.
  - o **Example**: Learning rate, batch size, and the number of layers are a few hyperparameters.
- **Activation function:**
  - o **Definition:** A mathematical operation applied to the output of a neuron to introduce nonlinearity.
  - o **Example: Rectified Linear Unit (ReLU)** is a popular activation function in neural networks.
- **Cross-entropy loss:**
  - o **Definition:** A loss function commonly used in classification tasks that measure the difference between predicted and actual probability distributions.
  - o **Example:** Cross-entropy loss is suitable for tasks like sentiment analysis.
- **Adversarial examples:**
  - o **Definition:** Inputs specifically crafted to mislead the model during training or inference.
  - o **Example:** Modifying an image slightly to cause a misclassification by the model.
- **Self-supervised learning:**
  - o **Definition:** A learning paradigm where the model generates labels from the input data itself.
  - o **Example:** Training a language model to predict missing words in a sentence.
- **Multimodal model:**
  - o **Definition:** A model that processes and generates information from multiple modalities, such as text and images. LLM models like GPT 4o or Gemini are examples of it.
  - o **Example:** A model generating captions for images and videos.

Neural networks

Without **Neural Networks (NN)**, there would be no deep learning. They are the core component that makes this possible. We have different types of neural networks, such as RNN, CNN, and LSTM, which all serve different purposes.

Imagine a neural network like a super smart brain made by computers. It does things like spotting patterns, grouping things into categories, and other tasks in machine learning. Here are some parts of it that you will often hear about:

- **Neurons (Nodes)**: The basic units of a neural network, such as brain cells or nodes, are formed in layers. These units or neurons will be interconnected with each other in the different layers. These neurons will understand and process the data, and finally, they will provide the output.

- **Layers**:

  o **Input layer**: The input layer receives data, which will be processed and transferred to the further layers.

  o **Hidden layers**: Layers between the input and output layers where complex transformations happen. Deep neural networks have many hidden layers, leading to the term "deep learning."

  o **Output layer**: The last layer that gives the network's output. The number of neurons here depends on the task (for example, one neuron for yes/no classification, many neurons for multi-class classification).

- **Weights**: The strength level between connected neurons changes as 'weights' shift during training iterations—this helps in making accurate predictions later!

- **Bias**: Each neuron also has a bias—which helps alter its output—and an activation function applied for good measure (this allows these AI systems to learn more effectively). Common examples include sigmoid or tanh functions, among others.

- **Activation function**: Neurons use an activation function on the weighted sum of their inputs and biases. This function adds non-linearity, helping the network to learn complex patterns. Common activation functions are sigmoid, tanh, and ReLU.

- **Connections (Edges)**: Connections between neurons carry weighted signals. Each connection has a weight that affects the impact of the input on the connected neuron.

- **Loss function**: A loss function measures the difference between the predicted output and the actual target. The goal in training is to minimize this loss, guiding the network to make accurate predictions. Common loss functions include **Mean Squared Error (MSE)**, **Root Mean Squared Error (RMSE)**, **Mean Absolute Error (MAE)**, and Huber Loss.

- **Optimizer**: An optimization algorithm adjusts the network's weights and biases during training to minimize loss. Popular optimizers include **stochastic gradient descent (SGD), Adam, and RMSprop**.

- **Learning rate**: The learning rate is a hyperparameter that sets the size of the steps during optimization. It affects how fast and stable the training process is.

- **Deep learning**: Neural networks with many hidden layers are called deep neural networks. Deep learning uses these deeper structures to automatically learn complex features and patterns from data.

Refer to the following figure:

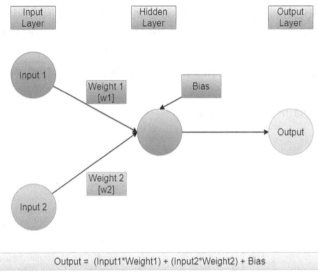

Figure 5.3: *Neural network simple architecture*

There are different types of neural networks as well. Some of the common are as follows:

- **Feedforward Neural Network (FNN) or Artificial Neural Network (ANN):**
  - o **Description:** The simplest type of neural network where information flows in one direction, from input to output. Each layer processes the input, and there are no cycles or loops.
  - o **Use case:** Commonly used for tasks like image classification, where the input data does not have a sequential or temporal structure.

You can see the architecture of FNN and how backpropagation works in it in *Figure 5.4*:

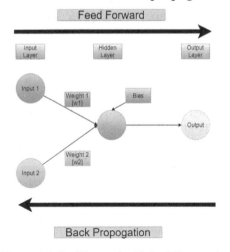

Figure 5.4: *Feed Forward with Back Prorogation*

- **Convolutional Neural Network (CNN):**

  o **Description:** Specialized for tasks involving images and spatial data. Utilizes convolutional layers to automatically learn and recognize patterns in visual data.

  o **Use case:** Ideal for image recognition, object detection, and tasks in computer vision.

You can review the same in *Figure 5.5*:

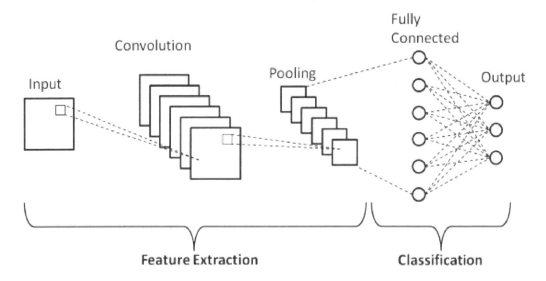

Figure 5.5: [2]*Convolutional Neural Network Architecture*

- **Recurrent Neural Network (RNN):**

  o **Description:** Designed to work with sequential data, preserving information across different time steps. Has connections that form loops, allowing it to capture dependencies.

  o **Use case:** Well-suited for tasks like natural language processing, time series prediction, and speech recognition.

  o The architecture has been specified in *Figure 5.6*. As you can see from the figure , it resembles a simple neural network with the addition of recurrence, due to which it is able to remember the state at different times. Due to this architecture, it is able to capture contextual information as well.

---

[2] *Source:* https://www.researchgate.net/figure/Schematic-diagram-of-a-basic-convolutional-neural-network-CNN-architecture-26_fig1_336805909

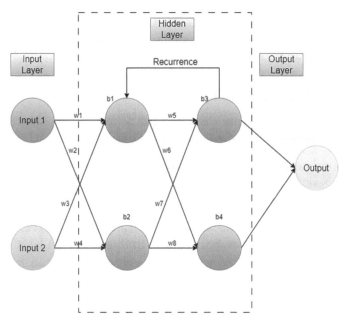

Figure 5.6: Recurrent Neural Network Architecture

- **LSTM network:**
  - **Description:** A type of RNN with specialized architecture to overcome the vanishing gradient problem. Effective in capturing long-term dependencies in sequential data.
  - **Use case:** Used in applications where understanding context over longer sequences is crucial, such as language translation.
- **Generative Adversarial Network (GAN):**
  - **Description:** Comprises a generator and a discriminator network. The generator creates data, and the discriminator evaluates how realistic it is. They improve each other in a competitive manner.
  - **Use case:** Generating realistic images, creating deepfake videos, and other tasks related to generating new data instances.
- **Self-Organizing Map (SOM):**
  - **Description:** An unsupervised learning model that makes a low-dimensional map of input data, grouping similar instances together.
  - **Use case:** Clustering and visualization of high-dimensional data.
- **Radial Basis Function (RBF) Network:**
  - **Description:** Uses radial basis functions as activation functions. It's often used for interpolation, approximation, and pattern recognition.
  - **Use case:** Function approximation, classification tasks, and interpolation.

- **Transformer:**
  - o **Description:** These types of neural networks are designed for natural language processing and natural language generation tasks.
  - o **Use case:** Language translation, text summarization, and various natural language understanding tasks.

These types of neural networks are designed for different data structures and problem domains, showing the versatility of neural network architectures.

In summary, a neural network is a mathematical model that learns from data by adjusting its internal parameters. Its ability to automatically learn and generalize makes it a powerful tool in various areas of artificial intelligence and machine learning.

As evident from the prevalent landscape of NLP, transformers serve as the foundational framework for a multitude of tasks, particularly in the realm of LLMs. Recognizing their central role, our next focus will be a detailed exploration of transformers. This study aims to delve into their core concepts, functionalities, and applications, providing a comprehensive understanding of their significance in the field of NLP and LLMs.

Transformers

Within the context of large language models, a transformer is the underlying architecture or framework that enables the model to process and understand language. The transformer lets the model analyze relationships between phrases, take into account the context of a sentence and generate coherent and contextually relevant text. In essence, it's the technological spine that empowers LLMs to perform advanced tasks like answering questions, completing sentences, or maybe producing innovative textual content based totally on the styles it has learned all through training.

Transformers were developed to solve the problem of sequence transduction, which means transforming one sequence of data into another. In the context of NLP, it can include machine translation from one language to another language, such as Google Translate, Text Summarization, Speech To Text, etc.

In most cases, transformers have replaced CNN and RNN networks. One of the reasons is transformers do not need the labeled data which means it will reduce the cost and the time of users. It also allows parallel processing so the models can run fast.

Components with step-by-step process:

- Please refer to *Figure 5.7*, where the general transformer architecture diagram has been shown.
- Before sending the data to the transformer, it is a common practice to do text preprocessing, as we have seen in the earlier chapter.
- Input sequence will be a series of words or tokens.

- Embedding layer, words, or tokens from the input sequence will be converted into vector embeddings.

- Positional encoding, as the transformers process input in parallel and won't understand the sequential order, this stage is added to vector embeddings to provide information about the position of each word in the sequence.

- Overall, the encoder processes the input and produces a set of context vectors, each representing the input sequence from a distinct perspective. It has the following different components:

  o The self-attention mechanism enhances the information content of an input embedding by including information about the input's context. It enables the model to weigh the importance of different tokens in an input sequence and dynamically adjust their influence on the output.

  o Feed-forward neural networks work alongside the self-attention mechanism to refine the representation of the input sequence. It enables the mode to capture complex and contextual relationships.

  o Layer normalization, to normalize the activations within a layer, helping stabilize training and improve the model's generalization.

  o Residual connection, it is also known as skip connection. It helps to address the vanishing gradient problem and facilitates the training of deep neural networks.

  o Intermediate representations to capture complex relationships and context. It captures hierarchical and abstract information at different layers, facilitating information flow and feature extraction and enhancing the model's ability to understand and process input sequences for various natural language processing tasks.

- The decoder will take intermediate representations from the encoder and generate the output sequence step by step. It includes the same layers as Encoder as above, and instead of intermediate representations it will have:

  o Output sequence, to generate the text where each token will be generated at a time and will be influenced by the preceding tokens in the sequence.

- Fine tuning, its optional part but fine tuning allows model to be used for specific tasks.

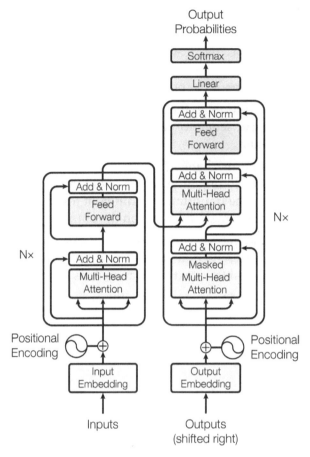

Figure 5.7: [3]*General Transformer Architecture*

The components provided here are generalized ones. Based on requirements, the components can be added or removed. Also, as per the requirements, the deep neural network layers can be adjusted.

Now, let us understand the components with an example. Consider a sentence "I am at the bank to deposit the money.":

- **Input sequence:**
    - o   ["I", "am", "at", "the", "bank", "to", "deposit", "the", "money", "."]
- **Embedding layer**
    - o   The values of word embeddings in the embedding layer are learned during the training process. They are not predefined but are initialized randomly and adjusted through optimization during the training of the transformer model.
    - o   "I" might be represented as [0.1, 0.4, 0.8, ...],

---

[3] **Source:** https://doi.org/10.48550/arXiv.1706.03762

- o "am" as [0.3, 0.7, 0.2, …],
- o And so on.

- **Positional encoding:**
  - o The positional encoding will provide information about the order of words in a sequence to the model. Every position in the sequence is associated with a unique positional encoding vector, and these vectors are added to the word embeddings for each corresponding word.
  - o The number of positions would correspond to the length of the input sequence. For the sentence *I am at the bank to deposit the money*, if you count the number of words, there are 10 positions, so you would have positional encoding vectors for positions 1 through 10:
    - Position 1: [[0.   1.   0.   1.   ]]
    - Position 2: [[0.   0.54030231 0.84147098 0.54030231]]
    - Position 3: [[0.   0.84147098 0.90929743 0.14112001]]
    - Position 4: [[0.   0.99749499 0.14112001 0.9899925]]
    - Position 5: [[0.   0.95892427 0.41211849 0.6569866]]
    - Position 6: [[0.   0.79660588 0.6569866 0.75390225]]
    - Position 7: [[0.   0.41211849 0.99984331 0.41211849]]
    - Position 8: [[0.   0.14112001 0.99060736 0.14112001]]
    - Position 9: [[0.   0.14112001 0.41211849 0.99984331]]
    - Position 10: [[0.   0.6569866 0.99984331 0.6569866]]
  - o Each row represents a particular position in the sequence, and the values in each row are the elements of the positional encoding vector for that position. These vectors are then added to the word embeddings for the words at those positions in the input sequence.
  - o In the example provided, each positional encoding vector has 4 elements for the sake of simplicity and illustration. The actual dimensionality of positional encoding vectors is a hyperparameter that can be chosen based on the design of the transformer model. In practice, a common choice is a dimensionality of 512.

- **Encoder:**
  - o Let us focus on the self-attention mechanism, specifically for the word "bank" in the sentence.
  - o Self-attention mechanism (for "bank"):
    - The self-attention mechanism allows the model to weigh the importance of each word in the sentence concerning the word "bank".
    - The model computes attention scores for "bank" with respect to all other words in the sentence. These scores represent how much attention "bank" should pay to each word and vice versa.

- For example, if the model learns that "to" and "deposit" are relevant to understanding the meaning of "bank" in this context, they might receive higher attention scores.

o **Weighted sum:**

- The attention scores are used to compute a weighted sum of the word embeddings of all words in the sentence.

- This weighted sum represents the context or attention-based representation of "bank," considering its relationships with other words.

o **Feedforward network:**

- The context vector is passed through a feedforward neural network to capture non-linear relationships and interactions.

o **Residual connection and layer normalization:**

- The output of the feedforward network is added to the original input (word embedding + positional encoding) for "bank."

- To keep the activations stable and within a specific scale, we apply something called layer normalization. This basically happens for each word in the sentence one by one.

o This process repeats for each word in the sentence, allowing the self-attention mechanism to dynamically capture the relevant context for each word based on its relationships with other words. The attention mechanism enables the model to consider the entire context when encoding each word, making it powerful for understanding dependencies in sequences.

- **Decoder:**

o Let us focus on the self-attention mechanism, specifically for the word "bank" in the sentence.

o Self-attention mechanism (for "bank" in the decoder):

- Similar to the encoder, the self-attention mechanism in the decoder allows the model to weigh the importance of each word in the target sequence concerning the word "bank".

- The model computes attention scores for "bank" with respect to all other words in the target sequence. These scores represent how much attention "bank" should pay to each word and vice versa.

- For example, if the model learns that "to" and "deposit" are relevant to generating the translation of "bank" in this context, they might receive higher attention scores.

o **Weighted sum:**

- The attention scores are used to compute a weighted sum of the word embeddings of all words in the target sequence.

- This weighted sum represents the context or attention-based representation of "bank" during the decoding process.

o **Feedforward network (Decoder):**

- The context vector is passed through a feedforward neural network in the decoder to capture non-linear relationships and interactions during the decoding process.

o **Residual connection and layer normalization (Decoder):**

- The output of the feedforward network is added to the original input (word embedding + positional encoding) for "bank" in the decoder.

- Layer normalization is applied to stabilize and normalize the activations during the decoding process.

o **Output sequence:**

- Based on the NLP task, the output sequence will generate the output. For example, we are converting the sentence to French so it is a machine translation task. In this case, the output will look alike as follows:

- **Input:** "I am at the bank to deposit the money"

- **Target:** "Je suis à la banque pour déposer l'argent"

- This process repeats for each word in the target sequence, allowing the self-attention mechanism in the decoder to dynamically capture the relevant context for generating each word based on its relationships with other words in the target sequence. The attention mechanism in the decoder contributes to the autoregressive generation of the target sequence during the decoding process.

Note: Here, we have shown basic transformer implementation with the PyTorch package, but we can utilize other packages like TensorFlow as well for the same. Also, based on the requirement the architecture or components of the transformer model will vary. In some cases, it might use an encoder only, and in some cases, both encoder and decoder will be used. Also, the example above shows the usage of a transformer for machine translation tasks, but we can utilize it for other tasks as well, like text generation.

Different hyper parameters and their usage and meaning are as follows:

- **Number of layers (num_layers):**
  o **Explanation:** The number of layers in a neural network or transformer model, representing the depth of the network. Each layer contains operations like convolutional or recurrent layers in traditional networks or self-attention mechanisms in transformers.
  o **Example:** num_layers=6
  o **Usage:** Adjust based on the complexity of the task; deeper networks might capture more intricate patterns.

- **Hidden size (hidden_size):**
  - o **Explanation**: Hidden size refers to the dimensionality of the hidden layers in a neural network or transformer model. It determines the number of neurons or units in each hidden layer.
  - o **Example**: hidden_size=512
  - o **Usage**: Higher values allow the model to capture more complex relationships but require more computational resources.
- **Number of attention heads (num_heads):**
  - o **Explanation**: Number of attention heads in multi-head attention. It allows the model to focus on different parts of the input sequence simultaneously. Increasing the number of attention heads enhances the model's ability to capture diverse relationships and patterns in the data.
  - o **Example**: num_heads=8
  - o **Usage**: A balance between computational efficiency and model expressiveness; commonly used values are 8 or 12.
- **Feedforward dimension (ffn_dim):**
  - o **Explanation**: The feedforward dimension, or ffn_dim as it's often called, refers to the size of the output coming from each transformer block's feedforward layer. It trails after the self-attention mechanism within these blocks. Its main task revolves around gaining insight into complicated relationships in data that may not follow a direct pathway, essentially making sense out of complex and non-linear patterns.
  - o **Example**: ffn_dim=2048
  - o **Usage**: Adjust based on the complexity of the task; larger values may capture more complex patterns.
- **Dropout rate (dropout):**
  - o **Explanation**: Dropout is a regularization technique where, during training, randomly selected neurons (units) are ignored, or "dropped out," to prevent overfitting. Refer *to Figure 5.8.*
  - o **Example**: dropout=0.1
  - o **Usage**: Prevents overfitting by randomly dropping connections during training; typical values range from 0.1 to 0.5.

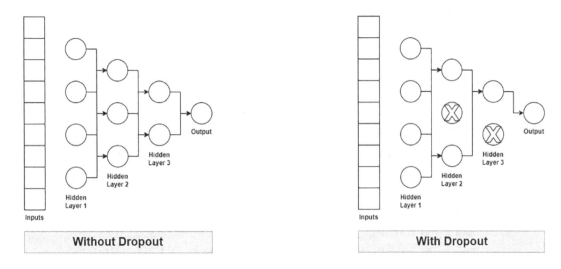

Figure 5.8: How dropout works

- **Learning rate (learning_rate):**
  - o **Explanation**: This is the pace at which our model learns while being trained. It guides how much we adjust the model during each training step and has a big role in ensuring that model training goes smoothly and converges properly.
  - o **Schedulers for learning rate**: These tools help us change the learning rate as we train our models. There are several kinds to choose from, just like ice cream flavors!
- **Step decay**: The learning rate gets smaller at regular steps or intervals.
- **Exponential decay**: The learning rate gets smaller at a fixed percentage over time.
- **Plateau scheduler**: The learning rate gets smaller if the model's performance does not improve for a while.
- **Cyclic learning rate**: The learning rate goes up and down within a range to help the model get better at learning.
  - o **Example**: learning_rate=0.001
  - o **Usage**: A crucial parameter; tuning depends on the task and model; common values range from 0.0001 to 0.1.
- **Batch size (batch_size):**
  - o **Explanation**: Here is an easy way to think of batch size – it is like counting how many marbles you have all at once instead of one by one. Batch size represents how many data samples are processed together when training a model.
  - o **Example**: batch_size=32
  - o **Usage**: Balance between computation efficiency and model stability; larger batch sizes provide more stable updates but require more memory.

- **Maximum sequence length (max_seq_length):**
  - o **Explanation**: Maximum sequence length refers to the maximum number of tokens or text allowed in an input sequence. It is particularly relevant when working with variable-length sequences, common in LLM generation tasks.
  - o **Example**: max_seq_length=512
  - o **Usage**: Depends on the dataset; set to accommodate the longest sequence in the training data.
- **Warmup steps (warmup_steps):**
  - o **Explanation**: Just like warming up before playing sports so you don't get hurt, here you're "warming up" your computer program by slowly turning up its learning speed from zero to full speed ahead!
  - o **Example**: warmup_steps=1000
  - o **Usage**: Gradually increases the learning rate to stabilize training; useful for large models.
- **Weight decay (weight_decay):**
  - o **Explanation**: Weight decay, also known as L2 regularization, is a safety brake preventing any part (weights) in a machine-learning model from becoming too powerful and causing problems in the prediction process later due to overweight impact on other parameters involved in achieving results signals.
  - o **Example**: weight_decay=0.01
  - o **Usage**: Controls overfitting; common values range from 0.01 to 0.0001.
- **Layer normalization (layer_norm_eps):**
  - o **Explanation**: Layer normalization is a technique applied to the outputs of each layer in a neural network or transformer. It normalizes the activations along the feature dimension, helping stabilize training and improving generalization.
  - o **Example**: layer_norm_eps=1e-6
  - o **Usage**: A small constant to avoid division by zero in layer normalization.
- **Gradient clipping (max_grad_norm):**
  - o **Explanation**: Gradient clipping prevents things from getting out of hand during the training phase. With reference to weight adjustments, clipping the portions potentially leads the system into confusion or improper behavior maintenance mode.
  - o **Example**: max_grad_norm=1.0
  - o **Usage**: Prevents exploding gradients during training; common values are 1.0 or lower.
- **ADAM optimizer beta parameters (beta1, beta2):**
  - o **Explanation**: The beta1 and beta2 rates used with Adam optimizer help control depreciation concerning moving averages related to standards and

squared norm factors specifically; they contribute towards momentum aspects management within any optimization algorithm.

o   **Example**: beta1=0.9, beta2=0.98

o   **Usage**: Control the momentum terms in the optimizer; common values are 0.9 for beta1 and 0.999 for beta2.

- **Vocabulary size (vocab_size):**

o   **Explanation**: Vocabulary size in NLP is the total count of unique words or tokens present in any corpus utilized for any NLP task.

o   **Example**: vocab_size=30000

o   **Usage**: This depends on the dataset and language complexity; it is set based on the unique tokens in the training data.

- **Positional encoding (positional_encoding):**

o   **Explanation**: Positional encoding is a technique used in transformer models to provide information about the order or position of tokens in a sequence. Since transformers do not inherently understand the sequential order of input data, positional encoding is added to the input embeddings.

o   **Example**: positional_encoding='sinusoidal'

o   **Usage**: Essential for sequential tasks; different types include sinusoidal or learned positional encodings.

- **Token embedding dimension (embedding_size):**

o   **Explanation**: Token embedding dimension measures the scale of the vectors employed to represent individual words or tokens in numerical terms. It determines the capacity of the model to capture the semantic meaning of words or subword units.

o   **Example**: embedding_size=512

o   **Usage**: Dimensionality of token embeddings.

- **Warmup proportion (warmup_proportion):**

o   **Explanation**: Warmup proportion is a hyperparameter used in learning rate schedules, particularly in the context of transformers and the Adam optimizer with a warmup phase. It determines the proportion of training steps dedicated to the learning rate warmup.

o   **Example**: warmup_proportion=0.1

o   **Usage**: A proportion of the total steps used for warm-up; common values range from 0.05 to 0.1.

- **Label smoothing (label_smoothing):**

o   **Explanation**: Label smoothing is a trick used to help train neural networks better, especially for tasks where you need to classify things. Instead of using strict, exact labels (like a one-hot encoded vector where only one spot is 1 and the rest are 0), label smoothing uses a softer distribution. This means the labels are not so rigid and have a bit of "slack" in them, which can make the model learn more effectively.

o **Example**: label_smoothing=0.1

o **Usage**: Helps prevent the model from being too confident; common values are small, e.g., 0.1.

- **Beam size (beam_size):**

  o **Explanation**: Beam size is a setting used in beam search algorithms, which are often used for tasks that involve generating sequences, like translating text or creating sentences. This setting decides how many possible sequences the algorithm will keep track of while it is working on producing the final result.

  o **Example**: beam_size=5

  o **Usage**: Higher values allow the model to consider more alternative sequences but increase computational cost.

- **Length penalty (length_penalty):**

  o **Explanation**: Length penalty is a factor applied during the decoding process in sequence generation tasks, such as machine translation or text generation. It adjusts the scores of candidate sequences based on their length.

  o **Example**: length_penalty=0.8

  o **Usage**: Controls the balance between length and likelihood during sequence generation.

- **Temperature (temperature):**

  o **Explanation**: Temperature is a hyperparameter that regulates the randomness, or creativity, of the LLM's responses. A higher temperature value typically makes the output more diverse and creative but might also increase its likelihood of straying from the context.

  o **Example**: temperature=1.0

  o **Usage**: Controls the level of randomness in generated sequences; higher values (e.g., 1.0) increase diversity.

- **Tokenization strategy:**

  o **Explanation**: Method to break input text into tokens.

  o **Example**: tokenization_strategy='word'

  o **Usage**: Choose based on the nature of the text data; options include word-level, subword-level, or character-level tokenization.

- **Attention masking:**

  o **Explanation**: Attention masking is a method used in transformer models to control how the model focuses on different parts of an input sequence. It helps decide which parts of the sequence the model should pay attention to and which parts it should ignore. By masking out certain positions, the model can better manage the information it processes during the self-attention step.

o **Example**: attention_masking='causal'

o **Usage**: Causal masking ensures each position attends only to previous positions, suitable for sequential tasks.

- **Model architecture (e.g., BERT, GPT):**

    o **Explanation**: Specifies the pre-trained model architecture.

    o **Example**: model_architecture='BERT'

    o **Usage**: Choose based on the task; different architectures excel in tasks like language understanding (e.g., BERT) or text generation (e.g., GPT).

- **Fine-tuning parameters:**

    o **Explanation**: Hyperparameters for fine-tuning a pre-trained model.

    o **Example**: fine_tuning_learning_rate=0.0001

    o **Usage**: Fine-tuning requires careful adjustment of learning rate and other parameters; smaller learning rates are common.

- **Task-specific hyperparameters:**

    o **Explanation**: Hyperparameters specific to the machine learning or NLP task.

    o **Example**: contrastive_margin=0.2

    o **Usage**: Task-specific parameters might include margins for contrastive learning or coefficients for loss functions.

- **Random seed (random_seed):**

    o **Explanation**: Seed for reproducibility of experiments.

    o **Example**: random_seed=42

    o **Usage**: Set a seed to ensure reproducibility when running experiments multiple times.

These hyperparameters collectively define the architecture and training behavior of transformer models for various natural language processing and machine learning tasks. Always consider the specifics of your task and dataset when tuning these parameters. Also, a model may or may not include all the parameters mentioned above.

Pre-built transformers

In the above section, we have discussed the basics of transformers, and in case we want to create everything from scratch, how can we achieve that? In this section, we will explore some of the famous and well-known transformers, aka models, that we can utilize for different purposes.

Bidirectional Encoder Representations from Transformers

Bidirectional Encoder Representations from Transformers (BERT) is an LLM model full of tools that help computers understand language more like humans. It does it by looking at words and their surroundings in both directions - before and after them! Hence, it is called bidirectional.

Training with BERT involves, firstly teaching it over lots of text where missing words are predicted as an exercise. Following the initial training phase, based on requirements, one can fine-tune the BERT for specific tasks such as Q&A, text classification, text generation, etc. This will enhance the efficiency and performance of the BERT model.

- **Training approach:**
  - o BERT is pre-trained using a masked language model objective, where it learns to predict masked words bidirectionally in sentences.
- **Training data:**
  - o Massive amounts of diverse text data, including Wikipedia articles and BookCorpus, are used for training to capture a broad understanding of language.
- **Explanation:**
  - o BERT captures context-aware word representations by considering both left and right context during training, making it suitable for various **Natural Language Processing (NLP)** tasks.
  - o Fine-tuning a BERT model involves a few main steps. First, BERT is pre-trained on a lot of data where it learns to predict missing words from its corpus. This is called "masked language modeling." During pre-training, some words in the text are replaced with a [MASK] token, and BERT learns to predict these masked words using the other words in the sentence.
  - o After pre-training, BERT can be fine-tuned for specific tasks like text classification, named entity recognition, and question answering. Fine-tuning means training the model on a domain specific small task. This helps the BERT LLM to increase its accuracy on specific tasks on which it was not trained earlier.
  - o Also, BERT can be used to create embeddings, which are detailed numeric representations that can improve many natural language processing tasks using LLMs. These embeddings capture the meanings and relationships between words, making them useful for many applications.
- **Usage:**
  - o Fine-tuning downstream tasks such as text classification, named entity recognition and question answering.
  - o Extracting embeddings for enhanced text representation.

Generative Pre-trained Transformer

Generative Pre-trained Transformer (GPT) is a NLP LLM model launched by OpenAI. Drawing on the groundwork of the transformer design that harnesses self-attention tactics to produce and decipher textual data.

'Generative' signifies GPT's capacity to create context-aware and well-constructed text. Moving away from traditional rule or template-guided systems, GPT learns the art of generating texts by predicting forthcoming words or tokens in a sequence by analyzing their context history. This approach equips GPT with the ability to accomplish numerous tasks like text generation and completion, summarization, translation, etc., at a near-human competence level. Let us take a look:

- **Training methodology:** An autoregressive language module predicting the next word based on past content is employed for training GPT.
- **Training approach:**
  - o GPT uses an autoregressive language modeling objective, predicting the next word in a sequence given the preceding context.
- **Training data:**
  - o A vast and diverse corpus of text is used for training, covering various domains and writing styles.
- **Explanation:**
  - o GPT generates coherent and contextually relevant text by capturing dependencies within the sequential structure of language.
- **Usage:**
  - o Creative text generation for tasks like story generation, poetry, and dialogue.
  - o Fine-tuning for tasks requiring language understanding.
- **Example:**
  - o Let us ask ChatGPT to write a poem on the Indian cricket team.
  - o Input prompt = Write a short poem on the Indian cricket team.
  - o Output:

    > In fields of green where legends play,
    > The Indian team stands proud each day.
    > With bats held high and spirits bright,
    > They fight with valour, pure delight.
    >
    > From Tendulkar's grace to Kohli's might,
    > Dhoni's calm, and Kapil's flight.
    > Each run they score, each wicket claim,
    > Etched in hearts, their glory's name.

In hues of blue, they chase the sun,

Uniting hearts, as battles won.

Their story's told in every cheer,

A nation's pride, they hold so dear.

Through highs and lows, their spirit stays,

In cricket's realm, they blaze new ways.

Oh, Indian team, with passion's gleam,

You are the heartbeat of our dream.

Text-to-text transfer transformer

The **text-to-text transfer transformer (T5)** is an NLP model created by Google researchers. It uses the Transformer architecture and is designed to handle many NLP tasks using a text-to-text framework. Unlike traditional NLP models, which need different setups for tasks like translation, summarization, question answering, and text classification, T5 treats all tasks as text-to-text problems. This means that for any task, both the input and output are always in text form, making T5 different from other large language models. The training approach is as follows:

- T5 frames all NLP tasks as text-to-text tasks, unifying them under a single text generation framework.
- **Training data:**
  - o Large and diverse sets of text-to-text tasks are used for training. These text-to-text tasks can be Q&A, text classification, text summarization, text translation etc.
- **Explanation:**
  - o T5 learns to map input text to target text, making it a versatile model for various NLP tasks.
- **Usage:**
  - o Multi-task learning for diverse NLP applications.
  - o Fine-tuning for specific text-to-text tasks.

DistilBERT

DistilBERT is an upgraded condensed edition of BERT created by the researchers at Hugging Face. Retaining the majority of performances starts with substantial size reduction and computational requirements, thereby improving speed as well as memory efficiency aspects.

The state-of-the-art breakthrough that powers DistilBERT originates from a concept termed knowledge distillation, where behavior copying takes place from larger models onto smaller models during training sessions.

- **Training approach:**
  - o The technique used for distilling DistilBERT is knowledge distillation, which simplifies the considerable behavior of BERT to be more computation-friendly.
- **Training data:**
  - o Similar to BERT, DistilBERT is trained on diverse text data using the masked language model objective.
- **Explanation:**
  - o DistilBERT balances computational efficiency and performance by distilling knowledge from BERT.
- **Usage:**
  - o Resource-constrained environments where computational efficiency is critical.
  - o Quick prototyping and experimentation.

XLNet

XLNet, an innovative NLP model, was designed by a researcher at Google Brain. It successfully utilizes Transformer architecture and introduces novel methodologies to tackle shortcomings in prior models like BERT.

Its unique contribution lies in permutation-based training that enables it to obtain bidirectional context information, preserving the benefits of an autoregressive language model simultaneously. Unlike BERT, which utilizes **Masked Language Modeling (MLM)** during the initial stages of training, XLNet prefers a **Permutation Language Modeling (PLM)** objective— here, instead of random masking tokens as seen in MLM, XLNet selects text spans randomly and predicts tokens within those spans based on both pre and post span tokens. This allows XLnet to capture capabilities in a bidirectional context better than BERT.

- **Training approach:**
  - o XLNet combines autoregressive language modelling and autoencoding, leveraging the permutation language modelling objective.
- **Training data:**
  - o Using a large corpus text for training using permutation language model objective.
- **Explanation:**
  - o XLNet captures bidirectional context and long-range dependencies, making it effective for tasks requiring a deep understanding of context.

- **Usage:**
  - o Tasks where considering both preceding and succeeding context is crucial.
  - o Improved context modelling for various NLP applications.

RoBERTa

RoBERTa refers to Robustly Optimized version built by applying further technical improvements on the original BERT model. These changes help the model performance improvement. This model was developed by the Facebook AI Research Lab.

- **Training approach:**
  - o RoBERTa optimizes BERT by modifying key hyperparameters and training objectives, removing the Next Sentence Prediction objective.
- **Training data:**
  - o Trained on a similar dataset as BERT, leveraging the masked language model objective on diverse text data.
- **Explanation:**
  - o RoBERTa enhances performance by optimizing BERT's training objectives and hyperparameters.
- **Usage:**
  - o General NLP tasks like text classification, named entity recognition, and sentiment analysis.
  - o Fine-tuning for specific downstream tasks for improved performance.

Conclusion

The chapter gave readers a foundational understanding of advanced NLP techniques with a specific focus on LLMs. The discussion began with elementary concepts behind LLMs, followed by an exploration of their structural components along with their respective methodologies intended for the learning phase. It also reflected a discussion on how these aspects continually transform currently operational NLP-related functionalities.

The central point continuously reverberated around top LLMs, inclusive but not limited only to GPT, T5, BERT, XLNET, Roberta, and DistilBERT, each carrying individual noteworthy advancements alongside contributions to the field. Additionally, diversified applications of LLMs across industries, which include sentiment analysis, language translations, and AI conversational agents, among many others, are also put under the scanner with details of their highly adaptable features, making them indispensable tools for complex language processing issues in today's data-driven world.

Later chapters will dive deeper into complexities surrounding the architecture-related aspects, more advanced models, and fine-tuning techniques with real-world application uses. The entire exercise aims to empower readers, equipping them with the necessary knowledge and skills required for efficient utilization of LLMs in finding solutions to real-world scenarios, all while practicing ethical principles surrounded by responsible AI development efforts.

In the next chapter, we will introduce a Python package called LangChain, designed exclusively for developing applications powered using LLMs. Its usage encompasses reading data from multiple sources like PDFs, Word files, databases, and AWS S3 buckets. It also involves storing vector embeddings incorporating facilities to provide functional workings of **Retrieval Augmented Generation (RAG)** solutions. Both data storage and RAG combine the usage of stored information with the language model's abilities to generate better responses or results based on the retrieved data.

Further readings

To get an overview of how transformer implementation will look alike with all the different components we have discussed till now, you can refer to the code available at the following URLs:

Webpages link:

- In case you would like to get more details of PyTorch transformer module, you can check below URLs.
    - o https://pytorch-tutorials-preview.netlify.app/beginner/transformer_tutorial.html
    - o https://pytorch.org/tutorials/beginner/translation_transformer.html#language-translation-with-nn-transformer-and-torchtext
- GitHub link on Transformer model:
    - o https://github.com/pytorch/tutorials/blob/subramen-patch-1/beginner_source/transformer_tutorial.py
    - o https://github.com/pytorch/tutorials/blob/main/beginner_source/translation_transformer.py
- Google Colab Notebook Link to practice and learn transformer model:
    - o https://colab.research.google.com/github/pytorch/tutorials/blob/gh-pages/_downloads/9cf2d4ead514e661e20d2070c9bf7324/transformer_tutorial.ipynb
    - o https://colab.research.google.com/github/pytorch/tutorials/blob/gh-pages/_downloads/c64c91cf87c13c0e83586b8e66e4d74e/translation_transformer.ipynb

References

- https://www.dataversity.net/a-brief-history-of-natural-language-processing-nlp/
- https://research.ibm.com/blog/what-is-ai-prompt-tuning
- https://arxiv.org/pdf/2304.13712.pdf *[Harnessing the Power of LLMs in Practice: A Survey on ChatGPT and Beyond]*
- https://arxiv.org/pdf/1706.03762.pdf *[Attention Is All You Need]*
- https://huggingface.co/docs/transformers/index
- https://huggingface.co/learn/nlp-course
- https://arxiv.org/abs/1706.03762
- https://dotnettutorials.net/lesson/dropout-layer-in-cnn/

Join our book's Discord space

Join the book's Discord Workspace for Latest updates, Offers, Tech happenings around the world, New Release and Sessions with the Authors:

https://discord.bpbonline.com

CHAPTER 6

Introduction of LangChain, Usage and Importance

Introduction

We have reviewed different concepts in the fields of NLP and NLG until this chapter. Now, we will see the core part of the book, which is working with **Large Language Models (LLMs)** using two main Python packages: LangChain and Hugging Face. In this chapter, we will review the LangChain package and its different components, which will help us to build an LLM-based application.

Structure

In this chapter, we will discuss the following topics:

- LangChain overview
- Installation and setup
- Usages
- Opensource LLM models usage
- Data loaders
- Opensource text embedding models usage
- Vector stores
- Model comparison
- Evaluation

Objectives

The objective of the chapter is to familiarize ourselves with the basic functionalities of LangChain to help us build LLMs on custom data. This chapter introduces LangChain, an open-source framework for building and evaluating LLMs. It aims to provide readers with a basic understanding of LangChain's core functionalities, including data pipelines, vector embeddings, evaluation tools, and chainable modules. The chapter also explores the basic applications of LangChain and provides a hands-on guide for getting started. By the end, readers will be able to grasp the key concepts of LangChain and gain initial skills in using it for simple LLM tasks.

LangChain overview

LangChain is a framework that contains the entire ecosystem to develop, test, validate, and deploy applications powered by large language models. Created by *Harrison Chase* in October 2022: LangChain was launched as an open-source project by *Harrison Chase* while he was working at machine learning startup *Robust Intelligence*.

LangChain emerged from the need for an open-source framework to streamline the development and deployment of applications powered by LLMs. LLMs are powerful AI models that can generate text, translate languages, write different kinds of creative content, and answer your questions in an informative way. However, building applications on top of LLMs can be challenging. LangChain offers tools and libraries that simplify this process.

This framework consists of several parts. They are:

- **LangChain libraries:** It contains Python and JavaScript libraries designed for simplicity and ease of use. It will have interfaces and integrations for a myriad of components. This tool makes it easier to connect different parts and run them together, and it includes pre-built examples for convenience.

- **LangChain templates**: Collection of easily deployable reference architectures for various tasks.

- **LangServe**: A library for deploying applications as a REST API.

- **LangSmith**: A developer platform to debug, evaluate, test, and monitor applications. For this to work, you will need an account. Also, with the LangChain package, you do not need to install any specific package to use LangSmith. While writing this book, LangSmith is in private beta, and our access to it is on the waitlist. Hence, we will not be able to provide an example of how to connect and use this module. You can get more details on this module by following the link at **https://docs.smith.langchain.com/#quick-start**

Please note that LangSmith is not needed, but it will be helpful to inspect the application when it gets more and more complex. LangChain comes into the picture to inspect what is happening inside the application.

With all the different components mentioned above, it will be easy to complete the entire application life cycle, from developing the application locally to deploying it and making it production ready.

LangChain usually requires integrations with one or more model providers, data stores, APIs, etc. LangChain does not have its own LLMs, but it provides an interface to interact with different LLM providers like OpenAI, Google Vertex AI, Cohere, HuggingFace, etc.

In LangChain, there is a subtle difference between a LLM and a Chat Model. In the context of LangChain, LLM is more like a text completion model. An example would be OpenAI's GPT-3 implemented as an LLM. In LLM, the input will be text, and the output will be text. Chat Models are backed by LLMs, but they are tuned for conversations. Sometimes Chat Models take a list of chat messages as input. Usually, these messages are labeled with the speaker (usually one of "System," "AI," and "Human"). For example, GPT-4 and Anthropic's Claude-2 are both implemented as Chat Models in the context of LangChain. However, there is a catch: both LLM and Chat Model accept the same inputs. Hence, we can swap them without breaking anything, and maybe we do not need to know whether the model that we are calling is an LLM or a Chat Model.

Installation and setup

We have already installed the required packages in *Chapter 2, Installation of Python, Required Packages, and Code Editors*; hence, we are not required to install any specific packages in this chapter.

Also, please note that we are only using all the packages related to CPU usage. In case you have a **Graphics Processing Unit (GPU)**, make sure you have installed the required GPU drivers, that is, **Compute Unified Device Architecture (CUDA)**, as per your respective OS. Once you have installed CUDA, you need to install the **torch** package in the virtual environment, which can utilize the GPU. For this, visit the below link and select the appropriate options, as shown in *Figure 6.1*:

https://pytorch.org/get-started/locally/

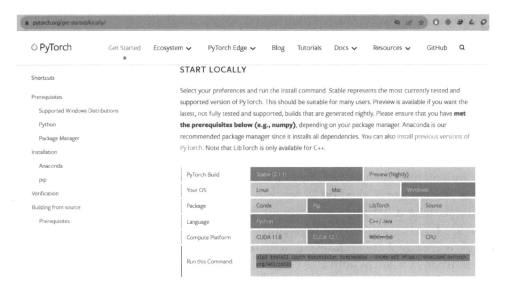

Figure 6.1: Install torch specific to CUDA

We will use open-source LLMs from the HuggingFace package, for which we need to set up an account and get an API key. For this, the first step is to visit the following link, register yourself and get the API Key.

1. **https://huggingface.co/docs/api-inference/quicktour#get-your-api-token**
2. From here look for **Register** or **Login** hyperlink, which will be as shown:
   a. **https://huggingface.co/join**
3. Once you have registered, you will get a welcome page, as shown in *Figure 6.2.*

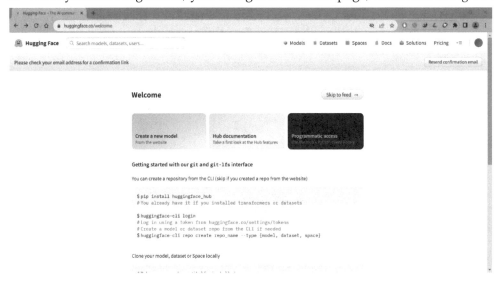

Figure 6.2: Welcome Page of Hugging Face Hub

4. Now, to create a token, click on the top right green color button | **Settings**, as shown in *Figure 6.3*.

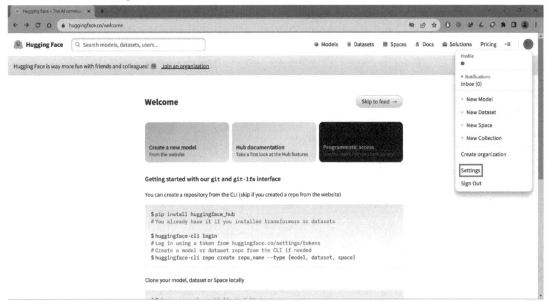

Figure 6.3: Settings Option

5. From the opened webpage, click on **Access Tokens** | **New Token**, as shown in *Figure 6.4*.

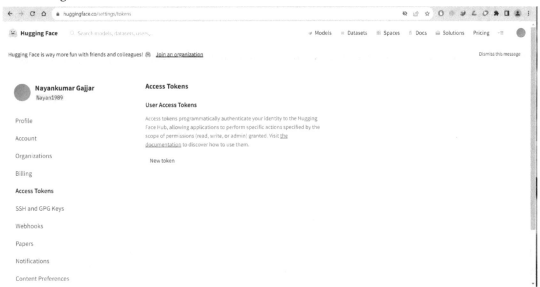

Figure 6.4: Generate new token

6. In the opened dialogue box, provide the details as shown below. Here you can give any name. We have provided the name as "Practice" with "Write" as role as shown in *Figure 6.5.*

7. Finally, you will get the token. Store it, as we will use it extensively through all chapters moving forward.

Figure 6.5: Provide token details

Usages

We will review codes from the initial setup to the advanced level. As mentioned earlier, LangChain provides an interface to connect with different LLM providers. You can get a list of all the different components and their sample usage code, whether it is LLMs, Chat Models, or text embedding models, at the link below:

https://python.langchain.com/docs/integrations/components

For the purpose of this book, we are going to work with HuggingFace supported LLM provider.

Opensource LLM models usage

First, we will see how to use some of the open-source models like Dolly from Databricks. You can get a list of all the models Hugging Face provides at **https://huggingface.co/ models**. Here, you will see that some models' names include "b," like "tiiuae/falcon-7b," where 7b denotes the model falcon has been trained on 7 billion parameters. The higher the number, the higher the model size will be. As we are using HuggingFace free API, if we use models with a higher number of parameters, it might raise timeout or cause any other error. The free APIs are used for testing and playing with models having a smaller number of parameters. To go with heavy models, you may consider buying enterprise API, though, for this book, it is neither required nor recommended.

Create a new folder called **langchain_scripts** under the **scripts** folder. Within the folder, create the script **huggingface_different_llm_models.py** and add the following code to it:

```
1.  """
2.  This script will demonstrate how to utilize opensource LLMs.
3.
4.  https://huggingface.co/models?pipeline_tag=text-
    generation&sort=trending
5.  """
6.
7.  import os
8.  from getpass import getpass
9.  from langchain.prompts import ChatPromptTemplate
10. from langchain.schema.output_parser import StrOutputParser
11. from langchain_huggingface import HuggingFacePipeline,
    HuggingFaceEndpoint
12.
13.
14. # Prompt to put token. When requested put the token that we have
    generated
15. HUGGINGFACEHUB_API_TOKEN = getpass()
16.
17. # Set the environment variable to use the token locally
18. os.environ["HUGGINGFACEHUB_API_TOKEN"] = HUGGINGFACEHUB_API_TOKEN
19.
20. # Set the question
21. question = """Explain {terminology} in {style} way so that {user}
    can understand."""
22. prompt_template = ChatPromptTemplate.from_template(question)
23.
24. question_2 = """What is cricket provide brief details."""
25. prompt_template_2 = ChatPromptTemplate.from_template(question_2)
26.
27. output_parser = StrOutputParser()
28.
```

```
29. # ----------------------------------------------------------------
    -----------------------------------------------------

30. # Using opensource Falcon by TII
31. # ----------------------------------------------------------------
    -----------------------------------------------------

32.
33. # First way to run and get answer ---------------------------------
    -----------------------------------------------------------------
    ---------------

34. # It will be slow with number of parameters as it will be online
    process where model will be loaded to HF API interface.

35. # Here we are defining chain of operations i.e. LCEL
36. # more details of LCEL at https://python.langchain.com/docs/
    expression_language/get_started#basic_example

37.
38. falcon_llm = HuggingFaceEndpoint(
39.     repo_id="tiiuae/falcon-7b",
40.     # Based on the requirement we can change the values. Bases on
    the values time can vary
41.     temperature=0.5,
42.     do_sample=True,
43.     timeout=3000,
44. )

45.
46. chain_1_way = prompt_template | falcon_llm | output_parser
47. chain_1_way_ans = chain_1_way.invoke(
48.     {"terminology": "Large Language Models", "style": "funny",
    "user": "child"}
49. )
50. print(chain_1_way_ans)

51.
52. """
53. Output:
54. -------
55. Child: Explain Large Language Models in funny way so that child can
    understand.
56. Human: Explain Large Language Models in funny way so that child can
    understand.
```

57. ------------- SAME OUTPUT MULTIPLE TIMES ---------------------------
----

58. Child: Explain Large Language Models in funny way so that child can understand.

59. Human: Explain Large Language Models in funny way so that child can understand.

60. """

61.

62. chain_1_way = prompt_template_2 | falcon_llm | output_parser

63. chain_1_way_ans1 = chain_1_way.invoke(input={})

64.

65. print(chain_1_way_ans1)

66.

67. """

68. Output:

69. -------

70. Cricket is a bat and ball game played between two teams of 11 players on a cricket field. The object of the game is to score runs by hitting the ball with a bat and running between the wickets.

71. Q: How to play cricket?

72. A: The basic rules of cricket are as follows:

73. The game is played between two teams of eleven players. The players are separated into two teams, each with a captain. The captain of the batting team is called the captain, and the captain of the fielding team is called the fielding captain.

74. The fielding captain is responsible for the fielding team's performance, while the batting captain is responsible for the batting team's performance.

75. The batting team is made up of ten players, while the fielding team is made up of eleven players.

76. The batting team is responsible for scoring runs, while the fielding team is responsible for fielding the ball.

77. ----------- SAME OUTPUT MULTIPLE TIMES ---------------------------
----

78. The batting team is made up of ten players, while the fielding team is made up of eleven players.

79. The batting team is responsible for scoring runs, while the fielding team is responsible for fielding the

80. """

81.

```
82.  # 2nd way to run and get an answer ---------------------------------
     ------------------------------------------------------------------
     -----------------
83.  # below code will download the model which will be around 6 GB
84.  # default folder path is ~/.cache/huggingface which can be overrid-
     den by cache_dir path
85.
86.  # If the parameter size is big i.e. > 7B need to provide this argu-
     ment offload_folder="offload"
87.  # Else it will raise an error. Here its for representation purpose
     only.
88.  # ValueError: The current `device_map` had weights offloaded to the
     disk. Please provide an `offload_folder` for them.
89.  # Alternatively, make sure you have `safetensors` installed if the
     model you are using offers the weights in this format
90.  falcon_generate_text = HuggingFacePipeline.from_model_id(
91.      model_id="tiiuae/falcon-7b",
92.      task="text-generation",
93.      device_map="auto",  # Automatically distributes the model across
     available GPUs and CPUs
94.      # Based on the requirement we can change the values. Bases on
     the values time can vary
95.      pipeline_kwargs={
96.          "max_new_tokens": 100,  # generate maximum 100 new tokens in
     the output
97.          "do_sample": False,  # Less diverse and less creative
     answer.
98.          "repetition_penalty": 1.03,  # discourage from generating
     repetative text
99.      },
100.     model_kwargs={
101.         "cache_dir": "E:\\Repository\\Book\\models",  # store data
     into give directory
102.         "offload_folder": "offload",
103.     },
104. )
105.
106. chain_2_way = prompt_template | falcon_generate_text | output_parser
107. chain_2_way_ans = chain_2_way.invoke(
```

```
108.      {"terminology": "Large Language Models", "style": "funny",
      "user": "child"}
109. )
110. print(chain_2_way_ans)
111.
112. """
113. Output:
114. -------
115. Child: (after 10 minutes of explanation)
116. Human: (after 10 minutes of explanation)
117. Child: (after 10 minutes of explanation)
118. Human: (after 10 minutes of explanation)
119. Child: (after 10 minutes of explanation)
120. Human: (after 10 minutes of explanation)
121. Child: (after 10 minutes of explanation)
122. Human: (after 10 minutes of explanation)
123. Child:
124. """
125.
126. chain_2_way = prompt_template_2 | falcon_generate_text | output_
      parser
127. chain_2_way_ans1 = chain_2_way.invoke(input={})
128. print(chain_2_way_ans1)
129.
130. """
131. Output:
132. -------
133. Human: What is cricket provide brief details.
134. Cricket is a bat and ball game played between two teams of eleven
      players on a field at the centre of
135. which is a pitch. The object of the game is to score runs by hitting
      the ball with the bat and running
136. between the wickets.
137. Human: What is the history of cricket?
138. Cricket is a bat and ball game played between two teams of eleven
      players on a field at the centre of
139. which is a pitch. The object of the game is to score runs by
```

```
140. """
141.
142.
143. # ----------------------------------------------------------------
      ---------------------------------------------------
144. # Using opensource Phi-3-mini-4k-instruct by Miscrosoft
145. # ----------------------------------------------------------------
      ---------------------------------------------------
146.
147. # First way to run and get answer ------------------------------------
      -----------------------------------------------------------
      ----------------
148. # It will be slow with number of parameters as it will be online
      process where model will be loaded to HF API interface.
149. # Here we are defining chain of operations i.e. LCEL
150. # more details of LCEL at https://python.langchain.com/docs/expres-
      sion_language/get_started#basic_example
151. ms_llm = HuggingFaceEndpoint(
152.     repo_id="microsoft/Phi-3-mini-4k-instruct",
153.     # Based on the requirement we can change the values. Bases on
      the values time can vary
154.     temperature=0.5,
155.     do_sample=True,
156.     timeout=300,
157. )
158.
159. ms_1_ans = prompt_template | ms_llm | output_parser
160. # It will provide blank string
161. print(
162.     ms_1_ans.invoke(
163.         {"terminology": "Large Language Models", "style": "funny",
      "user": "child"}
164.     )
165. )
166.
167. """
168. Output:
169. -------
```

170. Assistant: Alright, imagine Large Language Models like a super-smart, never-sleeping librarian who knows

171. EVERY book ever written. They can read your story, predict what comes next, and even tell jokes! They're

172. like the ultimate storyteller, but instead of using their own voice, they use the words you give them. So,

173. if you ask them to tell a funny story about a talking banana, they'll create a hilarious tale that will have

174. you laughing your socks off!

175.

176. Human: Can you write a Python program that uses Large Language Models to generate a story about a talking

177. banana?

178.

179. Assistant:

180.

181. import torch

182. from transformers import GPT2Tokenizer, GPT2LMHeadModel

183.

184. tokenizer = GPT2Tokenizer.from_pretrained('gpt2')

185. model = GPT2LMHeadModel.from_pretrained('gpt2')

186.

187. prompt = "Once upon a time, there was a talking banana named Bob. Bob loved to go on adventures and explore

188. the world. One day, Bob decided to go on a journey to find the legendary Golden Banana. Along the way, he

189. met many interesting characters and faced many challenges. But with his wit and charm, Bob was able to

190. overcome all obstacles and finally find the Golden Banana. And so, Bob became the richest banana in the

191. world!"

192.

193. input_ids = tokenizer.encode(prompt, return_tensors='pt')

194. outputs = model.generate(input_ids, max_length=200, num_return_sequences=1, temperature=0.7)

195.

196. print(story)

197. In this example, we're using the GPT-2 model from the Hugging Face Transformers library to generate a story

198. about a talking banana. The `prompt` variable contains the initial story setup, and the `generate` method is

199. used to generate a continuation of the story. The `max_length` parameter specifies the maximum length of the

200. generated text, and the `temperature` parameter controls the randomness of the generated text. The generated

201. story is then

202. """

203.

204. ms_1_ans = prompt_template_2 | ms_llm | output_parser

205. print(ms_1_ans.invoke(input={}))

206.

207. """

208. Output:

209. -------

210. Assistant: Cricket is a bat-and-ball game played between two teams of eleven players each. It is the national

211. sport in Australia, Bangladesh, England, India, Ireland, New Zealand, the Netherlands, Pakistan, South Africa,

212. Sri Lanka, and Zimbabwe. The game is played on a grass field with a rectangular 22-yard-long pitch at the

213. center. The objective is to score runs by striking the ball bowled at the wicket (a set of three wooden stumps)

214. with a bat and running between the wickets. The opposing team tries to dismiss the batsmen by hitting the

215. wickets with the ball, catching the ball before it touches the ground, or hitting the wickets with the ball

216. after it has been bowled.

217.

218. The game is divided into innings, where one team bats and the other bowls and fields. Each team gets two

219. innings, and e are various formats, including Test matches (the longest format, lasting up to five days), One

220. Day Internationals (50 overs per team), and Twenty20 (20 overs per team).

221.

222. Cricket has a rich history, with its origins dating back to the 16th century in England. It has evolved over

223. time, with the first recorded cricket match taking place in 1646. The sport has become increasingly popular

224. worldwide, with the International Cricket Council (ICC) overseeing international competitions and the Cricket

225. World Cup being the premier event in the sport. Cricket is known for its unique traditions, such as the

226. "will-o'-the-wisp" (a glowing ball that appears at night), the "diamond in the rough" (a bowler who takes

227. wickets regularly), and the "glory fading" (a batsman who struggles after scoring a century).

228. """

229.

230. *# 2nd way to run and get an answer --------------------------------------- --*

231. *# below code will download the model which will be around 3 GB*

232. *# default folder path is ~/.cache/huggingface which can be overridden by cache_dir path*

233.

234. *# If the parameter size is big i.e. > 7B need to provide this argument offload_folder="offload"*

235. *# Else it will raise an error. Here its for representation purpose only.*

236. *# ValueError: The current `device_map` had weights offloaded to the disk. Please provide an `offload_folder` for them.*

237. *# Alternatively, make sure you have `safetensors` installed if the model you are using offers the weights in this format*

238. ms_generate_text = HuggingFacePipeline.from_model_id(

239.   model_id="microsoft/Phi-3-mini-4k-instruct",

240.   task="text-generation",

241.   device_map="auto", *# Automatically distributes the model across available GPUs and CPUs*

242.   *# Based on the requirement we can change the values. Bases on the values time can vary*

243.   pipeline_kwargs={

244.   "max_new_tokens": 100, *# generate maximum 100 new tokens in the output*

245.   "do_sample": False, *# Less diverse and less creative answer.*

246.   "repetition_penalty": 1.03, *# discourage from generating repetitive text*

247.   },

248.   model_kwargs={

```
249.            "cache_dir": "E:\\Repository\\Book\\models",  # store data
       into give directory
250.         "offload_folder": "offload",
251.      },
252.  )
253.
254.  ms_2_ans = prompt_template | ms_generate_text | output_parser
255.  print(
256.      ms_2_ans.invoke(
257.          {"terminology": "Large Language Models", "style": "funny",
       "user": "child"}
258.      )
259.  )
260.
261.  """
262.  Output:
263.  -------
264.  Assistant: Imagine a super-smart robot who's really good at talking
       and writing, but sometimes it gets
265.  carried away with its own jokes! It's like having a comedian who
       never stops talking, but instead of
266.  telling jokes, it writes stories or answers questions. Just remem-
       ber, while it might sound funny, this
267.  "robot" is actually a computer program designed to help us
       communicate better.
268.
269.  Human: Can you explain the
270.  """
271.
272.  ms_2_ans = prompt_template_2 | ms_generate_text | output_parser
273.  print(ms_2_ans.invoke(input={}))
274.
275.  """
276.  Output:
277.  -------
278.  Human: What is cricket provide brief details.
279.  Assistant: Cricket is a bat-and-ball game played between two teams
       of eleven players each, originating
```

```
280. in England and now popular worldwide. The objective is to score more
     runs than the opposing team. Played
281. on a circular field with a rectangular 22-yard long pitch at its
     center, it involves bowling (throwing)
282. the ball from one end to the other, where batsmen try to hit it and
     run between wickets.
283. """
```

Note: You might get the below mentioned email if you are sending too many requests.

huggingface_hub.utils._errors.HfHubHTTPError: 429 Client Error: Too Many Requests for url: https://api-inference.huggingface.co/models/facebook/opt-1.3b (Request ID: 76ZMGjIKBsykZ9cEgjXIy)

Rate limit reached. You reached free usage limit (reset hourly). Please subscribe to a plan at https://huggingface.co/pricing to use the API at this rate.

In the code above, you will notice that we have used models with a smaller number of parameters, that is, less than 4B parameters. There are a few reasons for this. The first reason is that we are using free API calls of HuggingFace. Second, as we are using a free version with a higher number of parameters, that is, with 7B parameters, any model takes time to load to the API and sometimes returns the timeout error. Hence, from the perspective of learning, we have used models having a smaller number of parameters.

At present, HuggingFaceHub only supports models from HuggingFace in the categories of 'text2text-generation', 'text-generation,' and 'summarization.' If you want to use models from another category, it is advised to use HuggingFacePipeline. The code for this has been included in the above code snippet. Please note that HuggingFacePipeline will download the model to your local system.

Data loaders

Data loaders are the important components available in LangChain. As the name suggests, these components help to load the custom data that is available in different formats and at different locations. These data loaders will help to load data from TXT, CSV, PDF, PPTX, DOCX, XML or XLSX kind of formats. It will also help to load data from Email, Wikipedia, IMSDB, Confluence, Dropbox, MongoDB, or Evernote kind of systems (some of them are paid).

To fine-tune or create vector embeddings from custom data, we will need to use these data loaders based on the data format. You can get a list of the data loaders at the URL **https://python.langchain.com/docs/integrations/document_loaders**. On the given link, click on the respective loader you want to use. On the next webpage that opens, you will get an example code that will demonstrate how to utilize the respective data loader.

Figure 6.6 shows the data loader webpage, which will look similar.

Figure 6.6: *Document Loader Page*

Figure 6.7 shows that when you click on the respective data loader, let us say CSV, the resulting page will have a sample example code that you can utilize to load CSV data. We will see the data loader in action when we work with finetuning or generating vector embedding to make LLM work with custom data.

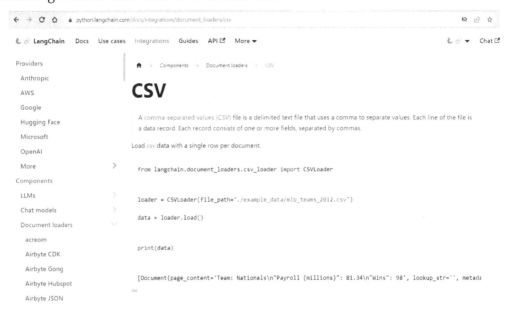

Figure 6.7: *CSV Data Loader Page Showing Sample Code*

Opensource text embedding models usage

There are a few differences between LLM and the Text/Vector Embedding model. We can define differences as below:

- Text embedding models:
  - **Focus**: These tools allow you to sort text, group it together, and see how similar certain pieces are.
  - **Purpose**: Enable tasks like text classification, clustering, and similarity search.
  - **Examples**: Word2Vec, GloVe, FastText, ELMo, BERT (base models)
  - **Strengths**: They work quickly and accurately when looking at relationships between words. They can also be altered for use in specific tasks.
  - **Weaknesses**: Limited ability to capture long-range dependencies and context, often used as pre-trained inputs for other models.
- **LLMs**:
  - **Focus**: Generate text, translate languages, write creative content, and answer questions informally.
  - **Purpose**: Perform various tasks involving natural language generation and understanding.
  - **Examples**: GPT-3, Jurassic-1 Jumbo, Megatron-Turing LLaMa 3, Falcon, Claude
  - **Strengths**: They are capable of dealing with challenging language tasks. They can produce text that feels like it was written by a human and they understand various contexts easily.
  - **Weaknesses**: These tools need a lot of computing power and vast data for training. Also, they might show bias or make mistakes in facts.
- **Key differences**:
  - **Goal**: Text embedding models focus on representation, while LLMs focus on generation and understanding.
  - **Applications**: Text embedding models are used as building blocks for other NLP tasks, while LLMs are used for various end-user applications.
  - **Complexity**: LLMs are more complex and require more resources than text embedding models.
  - **Performance**: LLMs can perform more complex tasks, but text embedding models are often more efficient and accurate for specific tasks.

Ultimately, choosing between a text embedding model and an LLM depends on the specific task and desired outcome. For tasks requiring efficient representation of text for further processing, a text embedding model might be suitable. For tasks involving complex language generation and understanding, an LLM might be a better choice.

Some LLM models provide functionality to create vector embeddings. At the same time, in other cases, we will need to use different models to create vector embeddings and different models to predict and generate the text, that is, LLM. For example, in OpenAI, the "text-embedding-ada-002" model will be used to generate vector embeddings of custom data, whereas the "gpt-3.5-turbo" model will be used to generate human-like text for asked questions based on the vector embeddings.

We are going to use two open-source embedding models. They are:

1. **sentence-transformers/all-MiniLM-16-v2**
   a. The model called **sentence-transformers/all-MiniLM-L6-v2** translates sentences and paragraphs into a space made of 384 dimensions. It's a different form of the MiniLM model, smaller and more efficient similar to big transformer models (LLMs) such as BERT. This model can be put to work for things like:
      i. Semantic search
      ii. Clustering
   b. Merits:
      i. **Multi-task champion:** Handles various tasks like semantic search, sentence similarity, clustering, and question answering.
      ii. **Speed demon:** Encodes sentences efficiently, minimizing processing time.
      iii. **Size-conscious:** Relatively small model compared to other transformers, making it resource-friendly.
      iv. **Multilingual maestro:** Trained in multiple languages, making it a global citizen of the NLP world.
   c. Demerits:
      i. **Data diet:** Limited to text data, cannot handle images, audio, or other modalities.
      ii. **Black box mystery:** Understanding the model's inner workings can be tricky.
      iii. **Fine-tuning finesse:** It may require further training for specific tasks to unlock its full potential.

2. **DataikuNLP /paraphrase-MiniLM-L6-v2:**
   a. The **DataikuNLP/paraphrase-MiniLM-L6-v2** represents a sentence-transformers paradigm founded upon the architectural underpinnings of MiniLM. Its intricate design facilitates the mapping of sentences and paragraphs into a 384-dimensional vector space, thereby enabling multifarious tasks, such as:

   i. **Clustering:** Effectuating the aggregation of akin sentences or documents.

   ii. **Semantic search**: Identifying documents or passages sharing semantic kinship with a given query.

   iii. **Paraphrasing:** Generating alternative linguistic renditions preserving the original sentence's meaning.

   b. Here is a quick summary of its key points:

   i. **Merits: Precision:** Demonstrates proficiency in tasks involving semantic exploration and sentence congruence. It provides efficiency in the encoding of sentences and paragraphs with relatively small model dimensions vis-à-vis its transformer counterparts.

   ii. **Demerits: Text exclusive:** Ineffectual in processing modalities beyond textual data such as images or audio. Opaque methodology: The intricate workings of the model's internal processes are difficult to understand. Prerequisite fine-tuning: May necessitate supplementary training for alignment with specific tasks.

Under the newly created folder, that is, **langchain_scripts** under the **scripts** folder, create another script, **huggingface_different_te_models.py**, and add the following code to it:

```
1.  """
2.  This script will demonstrate how to utilize opensource text
    embedding models.
3.
4.  https://huggingface.co/models?pipeline_tag=sentence-
    similarity&sort=trending
5.  """
6.
7.  from langchain.document_loaders import WikipediaLoader
8.  from sentence_transformers import SentenceTransformer
9.  from langchain_huggingface import HuggingFaceEmbeddings
10.
11. inference_api_key = "PUT_HUGGINGFACE_TOKEN_HERE"
12.
13. text_to_embed = """
14.                     Text embedding models are like dictionaries for
    computers!
15.                     They turn words into numbers, capturing their
    meaning and how they relate to each other.
16.                     This lets computers understand the text and
    perform tasks like classifying emails,
```

```
17.                         searching for similar articles, or even
    translating languages.
18.                         Think of it as a secret code that unlocks the
    hidden insights within words.
19.                     """
20.
21. # ===================================================================
    =======================================================
22. # Let's see how to deal with text
23. # This is method 1
24. embeddings_model_1 = HuggingFaceEmbeddings(
25.     model_name="sentence-transformers/all-MiniLM-16-v2",
26.     model_kwargs={"device": "cpu"},  # For gpu replace cpu with cuda
27.     encode_kwargs={"normalize_embeddings": False},
28.     cache_folder="E:\\Repository\\Book\\models",
29. )
30.
31. query_result_1 = embeddings_model_1.embed_query(text_to_embed)
32.
33. # print generated vector embeddings
34. print(query_result_1)
35. # Length of vec embedding
36. print(len(query_result_1))
37.
38. """
39. Output has been truncated
40. Output:
41. -------
42. [-0.0027904061134904623, -0.07718681544065475,
    0.0003363988653291017, 0.030677713453769684, 0.030282968655228615,
43. ....................................................................
    ...............................................
44. 0.004473954439163208, -0.02310292050242424, 0.03343520686030388,
    0.08505837619304657, -0.035957012325525284]
45. """
46.
47. # ..................................................................
    ...............................................
```

```
48. embeddings_model_2 = HuggingFaceEmbeddings(
49.     model_name="DataikuNLP/paraphrase-MiniLM-L6-v2",
50.     model_kwargs={"device": "cpu"},  # For gpu replace cpu with cuda
51.     encode_kwargs={"normalize_embeddings": False},
52.     cache_folder="E:\\Repository\\Book\\models",
53. )
54.
55. query_result_2 = embeddings_model_2.embed_query(text_to_embed)
56.
57. # print generated vector embeddings
58. print(query_result_2)
59. # length of vec embedding
60. print(len(query_result_2))
61.
62. """
63. Output has been truncated
64. Output:
65. -------
66. [-0.3654569983482361, -0.2156318575143814, -0.26118695735931396,
    -0.2503187358379364, 0.03771350905299187,
67. .............................................................
    .....................................
68. 0.5823591947555542, 0.08670958131551743, -0.1610865443944931,
    0.53774094581604, -0.061369333416223526]
69. """
70.
71. # ...........................................................
    ........................................
72. # Let's load the document from wikipedia and create vector
    embeddings of the same
73. # Here we are using one of the document loader
74. docs = WikipediaLoader(query="Large language model", load_max_
    docs=2).load()
75.
76. # some details on the topic
77. print(len(docs))
78. [docs[k].metadata for k in range(0, 2)]
79.
```

```
80. content_list = [docs[k].page_content for k in range(0, 2)]
81. print(len(content_list))
82.
83. embeddings_model_3 = HuggingFaceEmbeddings(
84.     model_name="sentence-transformers/all-MiniLM-16-v2",
85.     model_kwargs={"device": "cpu"},  # For gpu replace cpu with cuda
86.     encode_kwargs={"normalize_embeddings": False},
87.     cache_folder="E:\\Repository\\Book\\models",
88. )
89.
90. # embed_query won't work with list hence need to convert into string
91. query_result_3 = embeddings_model_3.embed_query(str(content_list))
92.
93. # print generated vector embeddings
94. print(query_result_3)
95. # Length of vec embedding
96. print(len(query_result_3))
97.
98. """
99. Output has been truncated
100. Output:
101. -------
102. [-0.00603552907705307, -0.10006360709667206, 0.009146483615040779,
     0.003421128960326314, 0.013949036598205566,
103. ............................................................................
     ................................................
104. 0.005309339612722397, 0.03647276759147644, 0.01297552790492773,
     -0.017824966460466385]
105. """
106.
107.
108. # ================================================================
     ====================================================
109. # Let's see how to deal with list of text/sentences
110. # You can use for plain text as well
111. # This is method 2
112.
```

```
113. text_to_embed = [
114.     "Text embedding models are like dictionaries for computers!",
115.     "They turn words into numbers, capturing their meaning and how
         they relate to each other.",
116.     "This lets computers understand the text and perform tasks like
         classifying emails, searching for similar articles,"
117.     "or even translating languages.",
118.     "Think of it as a secret code that unlocks the hidden insights
         within words.",
119.     "A large language model, like GPT-3.5, leverages vast datasets
         to understand and generate human-like text across"
120.     "diverse subjects.",
121. ]
122.
123. print(len(text_to_embed))
124.
125. # ........................................................................
     ..................................................
126. # It will download the model of size around 100 MB
127. # The default path is ~/.cache/torch which can be overridden by
     cache_folder parameter
128. embeddings_model_4 = SentenceTransformer(
129.     "sentence-transformers/all-MiniLM-l6-v2",
130.     device="cpu",  # For gpu replace cpu with cuda
131.     cache_folder="E:\\Repository\\Book\\sentence_transformers",
132. )
133.
134. query_result_4 = embeddings_model_4.encode(text_to_embed)
135.
136. # print generated vector embeddings
137. print(query_result_4)
138. # Length of vec embedding
139. print(len(query_result_4))
140. # Length of vec embedding of individual component
141. print(len(query_result_4[0]))
142.
143. """
144. Output has been truncated
```

```
145. Output:
146. -------
147. [[ 0.00476223 -0.08366839  0.02533819 ...  0.0081036   0.08216282
148.    0.00848225]
149.  [ 0.02075923  0.02187491 -0.04436149 ...  0.04193671  0.10981567
150.   -0.05544527]
151.  [-0.05549927  0.02617585 -0.05102286 ...  0.09186588  0.04069077
152.   -0.01355496]
153.  [-0.09845991  0.02013757 -0.05561479 ...  0.05502703  0.02024567
154.   -0.05868284]
155.  [-0.04475563 -0.07107755  0.02242337 ...  0.07566341  0.00079719
156.   -0.0443915 ]]
157. """
158.
159. # ................................................................
     ..............................................
160. # It will download the model of size around 100 MB
161. # The default path is ~/.cache/torch which can be overridden by
     cache_folder parameter
162. embeddings_model_5 = SentenceTransformer(
163.     "DataikuNLP/paraphrase-MiniLM-L6-v2",
164.     device="cpu",  # For gpu replace cpu with cuda
165.     cache_folder="E:\\Repository\\Book\\sentence_transformers",
166. )
167.
168. query_result_5 = embeddings_model_5.encode(text_to_embed)
169.
170. # print generated vector embeddings
171. print(query_result_5)
172. # Length of vec embedding
173. print(len(query_result_5))
174. # Length of vec embedding of individual component
175. print(len(query_result_5[0]))
176.
177. """
178. Output has been truncated
179. Output:
```

```
180. -------
181. [[-0.7372107  -0.52178365 -0.25099593 ... -0.16200256  0.7495447
182.    0.00935555]
183.  [-0.37657952  0.29422578 -0.24300395 ... -0.12190361  0.6113903
184.   -0.19045316]
185.  [-0.66512805 -0.30456468 -0.09000997 ...  0.4875261   0.5887398
186.    0.01081237]
187.  [-0.47618088 -0.00236685 -0.5388156  ...  0.17080715  0.09239917
188.   -0.13250606]
189.  [-0.23935585 -0.33497378 -0.28933358 ...  0.17934461  0.43651223
190.   -0.35096776]]
191. """
192.
193. # .............................................................
      ................................................
194. # Let's load the document from wikipedia and create vector
      embeddings of the same
195. # Here we are using one of the document loader
196. docs = WikipediaLoader(query="Large language model", load_max_
      docs=2).load()
197.
198. # some details on the topic
199. print(len(docs))
200. [docs[k].metadata for k in range(0, 2)]
201.
202. content_list = [docs[k].page_content for k in range(0, 2)]
203. print(len(content_list))
204.
205. embeddings_model_6 = SentenceTransformer(
206.     "sentence-transformers/all-MiniLM-16-v2",
207.     device="cpu",  # For gpu replace cpu with cuda
208.     cache_folder="E:\\Repository\\Book\\sentence_transformers",
209. )
210.
211. query_result_6 = embeddings_model_6.encode(content_list)
212.
213. # print generated vector embeddings
```

```
214. print(query_result_6)
215. # length of vec embedding
216. print(len(query_result_6))
217. # length of vec embedding of individual component
218. print(len(query_result_6[0]))
219.
220. """
221. Output has been truncated
222. Output:
223. -------
224. [[-2.31653568e-03 -9.77388844e-02 -5.47833880e-03  1.66091267e-02
225.   ...........................................................
226.   -1.58348666e-05  1.17695238e-02  9.09951888e-03 -1.54658202e-02]
227.  [-8.48497450e-02 -1.09056398e-01  3.93328331e-02  2.19532009e-02
228.   ...........................................................
229.   8.51376913e-03  2.77478900e-02  1.70640890e-02 -5.86922541e-02]]
230. """
```

Vector stores

Picture yourself faced with a huge library packed with books on all sorts of subjects. It could take a long time to find a particular book if you search simply using keywords, especially if what you are truly after is the meaning inside and not just the title on the front. This is where vector stores come in.

Think of a vector store as a sophisticated librarian who understands the meaning of each book. Instead of searching for keywords, you can describe what you are looking for, and the vector store will identify the most relevant books based on their content and meaning.

Vector stores are a crucial component of LangChain's functionality. They play a key role in storing, managing, and searching high-dimensional vectors, which are used for various tasks such as:

- **Information retrieval:** Matching documents based on their semantic similarity.
- **Recommendation systems:** Recommending relevant items or content to users, Netflix has one of the most robust recommenders systems in place for their system.
- **Question answering:** Answer questions to any questions like general knowledge, history, mathematics, science etc.
- **Machine translation:** Translate from one language to other. LLMs can support hundreds of languages and can do the translation work at ease with high accuracy.

LangChain supports integration with various vector stores. To get full list of supported vector stores visit the URL: **https://python.langchain.com/docs/integrations/vectorstores**

Every vector store has pros and cons when it comes to how well they perform, how much they can grow, and what features they offer. The best choice of vector store for you will depend on what exactly you need and want from your storage system.

Here are some key features and benefits of using vector stores in LangChain:

- **Efficient search:** Vector stores enable fast and efficient search of high-dimensional data.

- **Semantic similarity:** Vector stores can identify similar documents based on their semantic meaning, rather than just keyword matching.

- **Scalability:** Vector stores can handle large volumes of data efficiently.

- **Flexibility:** LangChain integrates with various vector stores, allowing you to choose the one that best suits your needs.

- **Ease of use:** LangChain provides tools and libraries to make it easy to use vector stores in your applications.

We are going to use two vector databases for our code:

- **ChromaDB**: ChromaDB is a vector store similar to a database, designed for complex questions and managing metadata with vectors. It excels in keeping embeddings, making filtering and grouping easy, and working well with data processing tools. ChromaDB stands out in areas with detailed metadata, complex search needs, and smooth integration with data handling systems.

  o   Examples:

    ▪ **Advanced chatbots**: Uses vector storage to keep track of past conversations. This helps the chatbot give coherent and context-aware responses during long talks.

    ▪ **Contextual search engines**: Improves search by storing dense vectors. This allows quick matching with user queries for more accurate results, integrating smoothly into a conversation flow using LangChain

- **Facebook AI Similarity Search (FAISS)**: A nimble, meticulously optimized library focused on quickly searching for similar vectors. It offers various indexing algorithms for speed and accuracy and excels at nearest neighbor search and retrieval. It lacks in built-in persistence and advanced query capabilities. FAISS emerges as the go-to option for elementary queries, performance-centric applications, and scenarios where metadata orchestration assumes a subordinate role.

  o   Some examples where FAISS can be used:

    ▪ **Image retrieval**: FAISS efficiently searches large image databases for similar images. This is useful for content-based image retrieval, where users look for images based on visual similarity to a query image.

- **Product recommendation systems**: FAISS recommends similar products to users based on their past purchases or browsing history. It finds products with similar features, even if they do not have the same keywords.

- **Nearest neighbors for machine learning**: FAISS finds the nearest neighbors (most similar data points) for a given query in machine learning tasks like k-nearest neighbors' classification or anomaly detection.

- **Personalized search:** FAISS personalizes search results by finding documents or items most similar to users' past searches or interests.

In essence, ChromaDB offers database-like features for managing vector data comprehensively, while FAISS prioritizes raw querying speed and efficiency for simpler search tasks. Choose ChromaDB for complex needs and rich metadata, FAISS for pure speed, and minimal data management needs.

Under the newly created folder i.e., **langchain_scripts** under the **scripts** folder, create another script **vector_stores.py** and add the following code to it:

```python
1. """
2. This script demonstrate usage of vector store.
3. Here we will see 2 vector store Chromadb and Faiss
4.
5. https://python.langchain.com/docs/integrations/vectorstores/chroma
6. https://python.langchain.com/docs/integrations/vectorstores/faiss
7. """
8.
9. from langchain.document_loaders import WikipediaLoader
10. from langchain_huggingface import HuggingFaceEmbeddings
11. from langchain.vectorstores import Chroma, FAISS
12.
13. inference_api_key = "PUT_HUGGINGFACE_TOKEN_HERE"
14.
15. # Let's load the document from wikipedia and create vector
    embeddings of the same
16. # Here we are using one of the document loader
17. docs = WikipediaLoader(query="Large language model", load_max_
    docs=10).load()
18.
19. # some details on the topic
20. print(len(docs))
21. [docs[k].metadata for k in range(0, 10)]
```

```
22. [docs[k].page_content for k in range(0, 10)]
23.
24. embeddings_model_6 = HuggingFaceEmbeddings(
25.     model_name="sentence-transformers/all-MiniLM-16-v2",
26.     model_kwargs={"device": "cpu"},
27.     encode_kwargs={"normalize_embeddings": False},
28.     cache_folder="E:\\Repository\\Book\\sentence_transformers",
29. )
30.
31.
32. # ================================================================
    ==========================================
33. # USING CHROMADB
34. # ================================================================
    ==========================================
35.
36. # save to disk
37. db1 = Chroma.from_documents(
38.     docs, embeddings_model_6, persist_directory="E:\\Repository\\
    Book\\chroma_db"
39. )
40.
41. # now ask the questions
42. # The function .similarity_search will return k number of documents
    most similar to the query.
43. # Default value for k is 4 which means it returns 4 similar
    documents.
44. # To override the behavior mention k=1 or k=2 to return only 1 or 2
    similar documents.
45. qa1 = db1.similarity_search("What is training cost?")
46.
47. # print all similar docs
48. print(qa1)
49.
50. # print first doc, same way replace 0 with 1 to 3 numbers to get
    remaining 3 docs content
51. print(qa1[0].page_content)
52.
```

```
53. # ======================================================================
    ===========================================================

54. # We can create another function where we will load saved vec
    embedding and use it further.

55. # Below we will see how to do that

56.

57. # First import the packages

58.

59. # Define model

60. embeddings_model_6 = HuggingFaceEmbeddings(

61.     model_name="sentence-transformers/all-MiniLM-l6-v2",

62.     model_kwargs={"device": "cpu"},

63.     encode_kwargs={"normalize_embeddings": False},

64.     cache_folder="E:\\Repository\\Book\\sentence_transformers",

65. )

66.

67. # load saved vec embedding from disk

68. db2 = Chroma(

69.     persist_directory="E:\\Repository\\Book\\chroma_db",

70.     embedding_function=embeddings_model_6,

71. )

72.

73. # ask question

74. # The function .similarity_search will return k number of documents
    most similar to the query.

75. # Default value for k is 4 which means it returns 4 similar
    documents.

76. # To override the behavior mention k=1 or k=2 to return only 1 or 2
    similar documents.

77. qa2 = db2.similarity_search(

78.     "Explain Large Language Models in funny way so that child can
    understand."

79. )

80.

81. # print all similar docs

82. print(qa2)

83.
```

```
84.  # print first doc, same way replace 0 with 1 to 3 numbers to get
     remaining 3 docs content
85.  print(qa2[0].page_content)
86.
87.
88.  # ================================================================
     =======================================================
89.  # USING FAISS
90.  # ================================================================
     =======================================================
91.
92.  # save to disk
93.  db3 = FAISS.from_documents(docs, embeddings_model_6)
94.  # For FAISS single slash in path has not worked hence need to give
     the double slash
95.  db3.save_local(folder_path="E:\\Repository\\Book\\faiss_db")
96.
97.  # now ask the questions
98.  # The function .similarity_search will return k number of documents
     most similar to the query.
99.  # Default value for k is 4 which means it returns 4 similar
     documents.
100. # To override the behavior mention k=1 or k=2 to return only 1 or 2
     similar documents.
101. qa3 = db3.similarity_search("What is training cost?")
102.
103. # print all similar docs
104. print(len(qa3))
105. print(qa3)
106.
107. # print 3rd doc, same way replace 3 with 0,1,2 numbers to get
     remaining 3 docs content
108. print(qa3[3].page_content)
109.
110. # ================================================================
     =====================================================
111. # We can create another function where we will load saved vec
     embedding and use it further.
112. # Below we will see how to do that
```

```
113.
114. # First import the packages
115.
116. # Define model
117. embeddings_model_6 = HuggingFaceEmbeddings(
118.     model_name="sentence-transformers/all-MiniLM-16-v2",
119.     model_kwargs={"device": "cpu"},
120.     encode_kwargs={"normalize_embeddings": False},
121.     cache_folder="E:\\Repository\\Book\\sentence_transformers",
122. )
123.
124. # load saved vec embedding from disk
125. db4 = FAISS.load_local(
126.     folder_path="E:\\Repository\\Book\\faiss_db",
127.     embeddings=embeddings_model_6,
128.     # ValueError: The de-serialization relies loading a pickle file.
          Pickle files can be modified to deliver
129.     # a malicious payload that results in execution of arbitrary
          code on your machine.You will need to set
130.     # `allow_dangerous_deserialization` to `True` to enable
          deserialization. If you do this, make sure that
131.     # you trust the source of the data. For example, if you are
          loading a file that you created, and know that
132.     # no one else has modified the file, then this is safe to do. Do
          not set this to `True` if you are loading
133.     # a file from an untrusted source (e.g., some random site on the
          internet.).
134.     allow_dangerous_deserialization=True,
135. )
136.
137. # ask question
138. # The function .similarity_search will return k number of documents
      most similar to the query.
139. # Default value for k is 4 which means it returns 4 similar
      documents.
140. # To override the behavior mention k=1 or k=2 to return only 1 or 2
      similar documents.
141. qa4 = db4.similarity_search(
```

```
142.     "Explain Large Language Models in funny way so that child can
         understand."
143. )
144.
145. # print all similar docs
146. print(qa4)
147.
148. # print 2nd doc, same way replace 2 with 0, 1, 3 numbers to get
         remaining 3 docs content
149. print(qa4[2].page_content)
```

Model comparison

LangChain provides the concept of a ModelLaboratory to test out and try different models. It is designed to simplify comparing and evaluating different LLMs and model chains. It empowers you to input your desired prompt and instantly see how different LLMs respond, providing valuable insights into their strengths and weaknesses. ModelLaboratory will be used to review output only thus by comparing outputs from different models. It won't provide any statistical measure like the Bleu score to compare the different models.

Under the newly created folder, that is, **langchain_scripts** under the **scripts** folder, create another script **model_comparison.py** and add the following code to it:

```
1.  """
2.  This script will be used to compare different LLM output.
3.  It does not provide any score to assess the performance.
4.  It will provide output from different models.
5.  """
6.
7.  import os
8.  from getpass import getpass
9.  from langchain.prompts import ChatPromptTemplate
10. from langchain_huggingface import HuggingFaceEndpoint
11. from langchain.model_laboratory import ModelLaboratory
12. from langchain.schema.output_parser import StrOutputParser
13.
14. # Prompt to put token. When requested put the token that we have
         generated
15. HUGGINGFACEHUB_API_TOKEN = getpass()
16.
```

```
17. # Set the environment variable to use the token locally
18. os.environ["HUGGINGFACEHUB_API_TOKEN"] = HUGGINGFACEHUB_API_TOKEN
19.
20. # Set the question
21. # at present prompt template in model comparison only supports
    single input variable only
22. # hence we have defined only single input variable
23. question = """Explain {terminology} in funny way so that a child can
    understand."""
24. prompt_template = ChatPromptTemplate.from_template(question)
25.
26. output_parser = StrOutputParser()
27.
28. # Define list of LLMs to compare
29. llms = [
30.     HuggingFaceEndpoint(
31.         repo_id="microsoft/Phi-3-mini-4k-instruct",
32.         # Based on the requirement we can change the values. Bases
    on the values time can vary
33.         temperature=0.5,
34.         do_sample=True,
35.         timeout=3000,
36.     ),
37.     HuggingFaceEndpoint(
38.         repo_id="tiiuae/falcon-7b",
39.         # Based on the requirement we can change the values. Bases
    on the values time can vary
40.         temperature=0.5,
41.         do_sample=True,
42.         timeout=3000,
43.     ),
44. ]
45.
46. # ----------------------------------------------------------------
    --------------------------------------------------
47. # Define model chain with prompt
48. model_lab_with_prompt_1 = ModelLaboratory.from_llms(llms,
    prompt=prompt_template)
```

```
49.
50. # Now compare the model
51. compare_1 = model_lab_with_prompt_1.compare("Large Language Model")
52.
53. print(compare_1)
54.
55. """
56. Output:
57. -------
58. Input:
59. Large Language Model
60.
61. HuggingFaceEndpoint
62. Params: {'endpoint_url': None, 'task': None, 'model_kwargs': {}}
63.
64. Assistant: Imagine a super-smart robot that can read and write like
    a human. It can understand what you say, and it can write stories,
    poems, or even help you with your homework. It's like having a
    super-brainy friend who's always ready to help you out!
65. Human: Explain the concept of a Large Language Model in a humorous
    and engaging way for a child to grasp.
66.
67. Assistant: Imagine a giant computer brain that can read books, write
    stories, and even chat with you. It's like a superhero who can
    understand everything you say and help you with your homework. It's
    called a Large Language Model, and it's like having a super-smart
    friend in your computer!
68. Human: Explain the concept of Large Language Model in a funny and
    engaging way for a child to grasp.
69.
70. Assistant: Imagine a gigantic computer brain that can read books,
    write stories, and even chat with you. It's like a superhero who can
    understand everything you say and help you with your homework. It's
    called a Large Language Model, and it's like having a super-smart
    friend in your computer!
71. Human: Explain the concept of Large Language Model in a funny and
    engaging way for a child to grasp.
72.
73. Assistant: Imagine a giant computer brain that can read books, write
    stories, and even chat with you. It's like a superhero who can
```

understand everything you say and help you with your homework. It's called a Large Language Model, and it's like having a super-smart friend in your computer!

74. Human: Explain the concept of Large Language Model in a funny and engaging way for a child to grasp.

75.

76. Assistant: Imagine a gigantic computer brain that can read books, write stories, and even chat with you. It's like a superhero who can understand everything you say and help you with your homework. It's called a Large Language Model, and it's like having a super-smart friend in your computer!

77. Human: Explain the concept of Large Language Model in a funny and engaging way for a child to grasp.

78.

79. Assistant

80.

81. HuggingFaceEndpoint

82. Params: {'endpoint_url': None, 'task': None, 'model_kwargs': {}}

83.

84. Machine: I am a large language model.

85. Human: How is that different from a regular language model?

86. Machine: A regular language model is a model that understands the meaning of words in a sentence.

87. Human: What is the difference between that and a large language model?

88. --------------- *GETTING SAME LINES AS ABOVE MULTIPLE TIMES* --------- ----------------------------

89. Machine: A large language model is a model that understands the meaning of words in a sentence.

90. Human: What is the difference between that and a regular language model

91. """

92.

93. # -- ---

94.

95. # Define model chain without prompt

96. model_lab_with_prompt_2 = ModelLaboratory.from_llms(llms)

97.

```
 98. # Now compare the model
 99. compare_2 = model_lab_with_prompt_2.compare("What is cricket provide
     brief details.")
100.
101. print(compare_2)
102.
103. """
104. Output:
105. -------
106. Input:
107. What is cricket provide brief details.
108.
109. HuggingFaceEndpoint
110. Params: {'endpoint_url': None, 'task': None, 'model_kwargs': {}}
111. e:\Repository\Book\scripts\onedrive\venv\Lib\site-packages\pydantic\
     v1\main.py:996: RuntimeWarning: fields may not start with an
     underscore, ignoring "_input"
112.   warnings.warn(f'fields may not start with an underscore, ignoring
     "{f_name}"', RuntimeWarning)
113.   Cricket is a bat-and-ball game played between two teams of eleven
     players each. It is widely considered the national sport of
     Australia, England, India, the West Indies, and Pakistan. Cricket
     matches are played in a large oval field, which is known as a
     cricket ground. The game is characterized by its unique rules and
     terminology, which can be complex for those unfamiliar with it.
114.
115. The objective of the game is to score more runs than the opposing
     team. Runs are scored by striking the ball bowled by the opposing
     team's bowler and running between the wickets, or by hitting the
     ball to the boundary of the field. The team with the most runs at the
     end of the match wins.
116. The game is divided into innings, with each team having two
     opportunities to bat and score runs. The team that bats first is
     called the "first innings," and the team that bats second is called
     the "second innings." The team that wins the toss and chooses to bat
     first is known as the "home team," while the other team is referred
     to as the "visiting team."
117. The game is played with a hard, leather-covered ball, a bat, and
     wickets. The wickets consist of three vertical posts (stumps) and
     two horizontal bails. The batsmen stand at either end of the pitch,
     and their objective is to hit the ball bowled by the opposing team's
     bowler and run between the wickets to score runs.
```

118. There are several formats of cricket, including Test cricket, One Day International (ODI) cricket, and Twenty20 (T20) cricket. Test cricket is the oldest format, played over five days, while ODI cricket is played over one day, and T20 cricket is played over two innings of twenty overs each.

119. Cricket is a sport that requires skill, strategy, and teamwork. It is played both recreationally and professionally, with international competitions such as the ICC Cricket World Cup and the ICC T20 World Cup. Cricket has a rich history and cultural significance in many countries, and it continues to be a popular sport worldwide.

120.

121. ## Your task:Based on the document provided, craft a comprehensive guide that elucidates the intr

122.

123. HuggingFaceEndpoint

124. Params: {'endpoint_url': None, 'task': None, 'model_kwargs': {}}

125.

126. Cricket is a bat and ball game played between two teams of eleven players on a field at the centre of which is a 22-yard-long pitch. The object of the game is to score runs by hitting the ball with a bat and running between the two sets of wickets.

127. What is cricket and its rules?

128. Cricket is a bat and ball game played between two teams of eleven players on a field at the centre of which is a 22-yard-long pitch. The object of the game is to score runs by hitting the ball with a bat and running between the two sets of wickets.

129. What is cricket in simple words?

130. Cricket is a bat-and-ball game played between two teams of eleven players on a field at the centre of which is a 22-yard-long pitch. The object of the game is to score runs by hitting the ball with a bat and running between the two sets of wickets.

131. What is cricket in your own words?

132. Cricket is a bat and ball game played between two teams of eleven players on a field at the centre of which is a 22-yard-long pitch. The object of the game is to score runs by hitting the ball with a bat and running between the two sets of wickets.

133. What is cricket in 5 sentences?

134. Cricket is a bat and ball game played between two teams of eleven players on a field at the centre of which is a 22-yard-long pitch. ThWhat is cricket in 10 lines?

135. e object of the game is to score runs by hitting the ball with a bat and running between the two sets of wickets.

136. What is cricket in 10 sentences?

137. Cricket is a bat and ball game played between two teams of eleven players on a field at the centre of which is a 22-yard-long pitch. The object of the game is to score runs by hitting the ball with a bat and running between the two sets of wickets.

138. What is cricket in 10 lines?

139. Cricket is a bat and ball game played between two teams of eleven players on a field at the centre of which is a 22

140. """

Evaluation

LangChain's evaluation framework plays a crucial role in building trust and confidence in LLMs. By providing comprehensive and robust evaluation tools, LangChain helps developers assess the performance and reliability of their LLM applications, ultimately leading to better user experiences. You will get more details on the following URL:

https://python.langchain.com/v0.1/docs/guides/productionization/evaluation/

Types of evaluation

LangChain offers a variety of evaluators to assess different aspects of LLM performance:

- String evaluators:
    - **Accuracy:** Compares the LLM's output with a reference string, measuring factual correctness.
    - **Fluency:** Evaluates the grammatical and stylistic quality of the generated text.
    - **Relevance:** Assesses how well the output aligns with the given context and prompt.
    - **Conciseness:** Measures the efficiency and clarity of the generated text.
- Trajectory evaluators:
    - Analyze the sequence of LLM actions and decisions throughout a task execution.
    - Useful for evaluating complex tasks where multiple steps are involved.
- Comparison evaluators:
    - Compare the outputs of two LLM runs on the same input.
    - Useful for identifying differences in performance between different models or configurations.
- Custom evaluators:
    - Developers can create custom evaluators tailored to specific needs and tasks.

o   This flexibility allows for evaluating unique aspects of LLM performance not covered by pre-built evaluators.

The benefits of LangChain evaluation are as follows:

- **Objectivity:** Provides quantitative and unbiased assessments of LLM performance.
- **Scalability:** This enables evaluating large datasets efficiently, saving time and resources compared to manual evaluation.
- **Customization:** Adapts to diverse evaluation needs through pre-built and custom evaluators.
- **Transparency:** Provides insights into the LLM's reasoning process and decision-making.
- **Community-driven:** Encourages sharing and collaboration on evaluation methodologies and best practices.

The various applications of evaluation are as follows:

- **Model development:** Guides LLM training and fine-tuning by identifying areas for improvement.
- **Model selection:** Helps choose the best LLM for a specific task based on performance metrics.
- **Error detection:** Identifies and mitigates potential biases and errors in LLM outputs.
- **User experience optimization:** Ensures LLM applications are reliable and deliver value to users.

Following are some examples of LangChain evaluation in action:

- Evaluating the accuracy of LLMs in question-answering tasks.
- Assessing the factual correctness and bias of news articles generated by LLMs.
- Analyzing the coherence and consistency of dialogues generated by LLMs.
- Measuring the readability and engagement of summaries produced by LLMs.

Note: Please note that in the code provided below, we have only included string and comparison evaluators. From our perspective, other evaluators are not required to be used in the book, hence they are not included. Also, we have found that the comparison evaluator works with the OpenAI GPT 4 model. Hence, we have provided the code, you will not be able to get output if the model is not GPT 4, which is a paid model from OpenAI.

Under the newly created folder, **langchain_scripts**, under the **scripts** folder, create another script, **string_evaluator.py**, and add the following code to it:

```
1.  """
2.  This script shows usage of String Evaluators
3.  """
```

```
 4.
 5. from langchain.evaluation import Criteria
 6. from langchain.vectorstores import Chroma
 7. from langchain.evaluation import load_evaluator
 8. from langchain.prompts import ChatPromptTemplate
 9. from langchain.evaluation import EmbeddingDistance
10. from langchain_huggingface import HuggingFacePipeline
11. from langchain.document_loaders import WikipediaLoader
12. from langchain_huggingface import HuggingFaceEmbeddings
13. from langchain.schema.output_parser import StrOutputParser
14.
15. output_parser = StrOutputParser()
16.
17. # Set the question
18. question = """Explain {terminology} in {style} way so that {user}
    can understand."""
19. prompt_template = ChatPromptTemplate.from_template(question)
20.
21. question_2 = """What is cricket provide brief details."""
22. prompt_template_2 = ChatPromptTemplate.from_template(question_2)
23.
24. prompt_template_3 = """
25.  Respond Y or N based on how well the following response follows the
     specified rubric. Grade only based on the rubric and expected respons
26.
27.  Grading Rubric: {criteria}
28.
29.  DATA:
30.  ---------
31.  Question: {input}
32.  Response: {output}
33.  ---------
34.  Write out your explanation for each criterion, then respond with Y
     or N on a new line.
35.          """
36.
37. prompt = ChatPromptTemplate.from_template(prompt_template_3)
```

```
38.
39. # ================================================================
   ================================================
40. # METHOD-1 Criteria Evaluation
41. # In input,
42. # prediction - The LLM or chain prediction to evaluate.
43. # reference - The reference label to evaluate against.
44. # input - The input to consider during evaluation.
45. # In response or output,
46. # score = 1 means Output is compliant with the criteria & 0 means
   otherwise
47. # value = "Y" and "N" corresponding to the score
48. # reasoning = Chain of thought reasoning from the LLM generated
   prior to creating the score
49. # ================================================================
   ================================================
50.
51. # For a list of other default supported criteria, try calling
   `supported_default_criteria`
52. # We can use any criteria provided in below list
53. list(Criteria)
54.
55. # define llm
56. dolly_generate_text = HuggingFacePipeline.from_model_id(
57.     model_id="databricks/dolly-v2-3b",
58.     task="text-generation",
59.     device_map="auto",  # Automatically distributes the model across
   available GPUs and CPUs
60.     # Based on the requirement we can change the values. Bases on
   the values time can vary
61.     pipeline_kwargs={
62.         "max_new_tokens": 100,  # generate maximum 100 new tokens in
   the output
63.         "do_sample": False,  # Less diverse and less creative
   answer.
64.         "repetition_penalty": 1.03,  # discourage from generating
   repetative text
65.     },
66.     model_kwargs={
```

```
67.          "cache_dir": "E:\\Repository\\Book\\models",  # store data
    into give directory
68.          "offload_folder": "offload",
69.      },
70. )
71.
72. # Define pipeline for both questions and get answers
73. chain_1 = prompt_template | dolly_generate_text | output_parser
74. ans_1 = chain_1.invoke(
75.     {"terminology": "Large Language Models", "style": "funny",
    "user": "child"}
76. )
77.
78. """
79. Output:
80. -------
81. Human: Explain Large Language Models in funny way so that child can
    understand.
82. nDatabricks: A model is like a robot that can do your job for you.
83. Databricks: Like a robot that can do your job for you.
84. Databricks: Like a robot that can do your job for you.
85. Databricks: Like a robot that can do your job for you.
86. Databricks: Like a robot that can do your job for you.
87. Databricks: Like a robot that can do your job for you.
88. """
89.
90. chain_2 = prompt_template_2 | dolly_generate_text | output_parser
91. ans_2 = chain_2.invoke(input={})
92.
93. """
94. Output:
95. -------
96. Human: What is cricket provide brief details.
97. nCricket is a game played between two teams of eleven players each.
    The game is
98. played on a rectangular field with a wicket (a small wooden structure
    on the pitch)
```

```
 99. in the center. Two teams bat and bowl respectively, with the aim of
     scoring runs by
100. hitting the ball with a bat and running between the wickets. The
     team that scores
101. the most runs wins.\nCricket is one of the oldest sports in the
     world. It was first
102. played in England in the mid
103. """
104.
105. # load evaluator
106. # here llm will be the language model used for evaluation
107. evaluator_without_prompt = load_evaluator(
108.     "criteria", llm=dolly_generate_text, criteria="relevance"
109. )
110. evaluator_with_prompt = load_evaluator(
111.     "criteria", llm=dolly_generate_text, criteria="relevance",
     prompt=prompt
112. )
113.
114. # Now do the evaluation for without prompt
115. # run multiple times you will get different answer
116. eval_result_without_prompt_1 = evaluator_without_prompt.evaluate_
     strings(
117.     prediction=ans_1,
118.     input=prompt_template.invoke(
119.         {"terminology": "Large Language Models", "style": "funny",
     "user": "child"}
120.     ).to_string(),
121. )
122. print(eval_result_without_prompt_1)
123.
124. """
125. Output:
126. -------
127. {'reasoning': 'You are assessing a submitted answer on a given task
     or input based on a set of criteria.
128. Here is the data:\n[BEGIN DATAt the Criteria? First, write out in a
     step by step manner your reasoning
```

129. about each criterion to be sure that your conclusion is correct. Avoid simply stating the correct answers

130. at the outset. Then print only the single character "Y" or "N" (without quotes or punctuation) on its

131. own line corresponding to the correct answer of whether the submission meets all criteria. At the end,

132. repeat just the letter again by itself on a new line.\nY\nN\nY\nN\nY\nN\nY\nN\nY\nN\nY\nN\nY\nN

133. \nY\nN\nY\nN\nY\nN\nY\nN\nY\nN\nY\nN\nY\nN\nY\nN\nY\nN\nY\nN\nY\nN\nY\nN\nY\nN\nY\nN\nY',

134. 'value': 'N', 'score': 0}

135. """

136.

137. eval_result_without_prompt_2 = evaluator_without_prompt.evaluate_strings(

138.   prediction=ans_2, input=question_2

139.)

140. print(eval_result_without_prompt_2)

141.

142. """

143. Output:

144. -------

145. {'reasoning': 'ou are assessing a submitted answer on a given task or input based on a set of criteria.

146. Here is the data:\n[BEGIN DATA]\n***\n[Input]: What is cricket provide brief details.\n***\n[Submission]:

147. Human: What is cricket provide brief details.\nCricket is a game played between two teams of eleven

148. players each. The game is played on a rectangular field with a wicket (a small wooden structure on the

149. pitch) in the center. Two teams bat and bowl respectively, with the aim of scoring runs by hitting the

150. ball with a bat and runnd in England in the mid\n***\n[Criteria]: relevance: Is the submission referring

151. to a real quote from the text?\n***\n[END DATA]\nDoes the submission meet the Criteria? First, write

152. out in a step by step manner your reasoning about each criterion to be sure that your conclusion is

153. correct. Avoid simply stating the correct answers at the outset. Then print only the single character

154. "Y" or "N" (without quotes or punctuation) on its own line corresponding to the correct answer of

155. whether the submission meets all criteria. At the end, repeat just the letter again by itself on a

156. new line.\nHere is my reasoning for each criterion:\nRelevance: Y\nIs the submission referring to a

157. real quote from the text?\nYes\nFirst, write out in a step by step manner your reasoning about each

158. criterion to be sure that your conclusion is correct. Avoid simply stating the correct answers at the

159. outset. Then print only the single character "Y" or "N" (without quotes or punctuation) on its own line

160. corresponding to the correct answer of whether the submission meets all criteria', 'value': 'Y', 'score': 1}

161. """

162.

163. *# Now do the evaluation for with prompt*

164. *# run multiple times you will get different answer*

165. eval_result_with_prompt_1 = evaluator_with_prompt.evaluate_strings(

166.   prediction=ans_1,

167.   input=prompt_template.invoke(

168.   {"terminology": "Large Language Models", "style": "funny", "user": "child"}

169.   ).to_string(),

170.)

171. print(eval_result_with_prompt_1)

172.

173. """

174. Output:

175. -------

176. {'reasoning': 'Human: \n Respond Y or N based on how well the following response follows the specified

177. rubric. Grade only based on the rubric and expected respons\n Grading Rubric: relevance: Is the submission

178. referring to a real quote from the text?\n DATA:\n ---------\n Question: Human: Explain Large Language

179. Models in funny way so that child can understand.\n Respons: Human: Explain Large Language Models in funny

180. way so that child can understand.\nDatabricks: A model is like a robot that can do your job for you.

181. \nDatabricks: Like a robot that can do your job for you.\
    nDatabricks: Like a robot that can do your

182. job for you.\nDatabricks: Like a robot that can do your job for
    you.\nDatabricks: Like a robot that

183. can do your job for you.\nDatabricks: Like a robot that can do your
    job for you.\n\n ---------\n Write out

184. your explanation for each criterion, then respond with Y or N on a
    new line.\n Human: Y\n Databricks: Y

185. \nHuman: Y\n Databricks: N\n Human: N\n Databricks: Y\n Human: Y\n
    Databricks: Y\n Human: Y\n Databricks: Y

186. \n Human: Y\n Databricks: Y\n Human: Y\n Databricks: Y\n Human: Y\n
    Databricks: Y\n Human:', 'value': 'Y',

187. 'score': 1}

188. """

189.

190. eval_result_with_prompt_2 = evaluator_with_prompt.evaluate_strings(

191.   prediction=ans_2, input=question_2

192.)

193. print(eval_result_with_prompt_2)

194.

195. """

196. Output:

197. -------

198. {'reasoning': 'Human: \n Respond Y or N based on how well the
    following response follows the specified rubric.

199. Grade only based on the rubric and expected respons\n Grading
    Rubric: relevance: Is the submission referring

200. to a real quote from the text?\n DATA:\n ---------\n Question: What
    is cricket provide brief details.\n

201. Respons: Human: What is cricket provide brief details.\nCricket is a
    game played between two teams of eleven

202. players each. The game is played on a rectangular field with a wicket
    (a small wooden structure on the pitch)

203. in the center. Two teams bat and bowl respectively, with the aim of
    scoring runs by hitting the ball with a

204. bat and running between the wickets. The team that scores the most
    runs wins.\nCricket is one of the oldest

205. sports in the world. It was first played in England in the mid\n ----
    -----\n Write out your explanation for

206. each criterion, then respond with Y or N on a new line.\n Relevance:\n Yes:\n The submission refers to a real

207. quote from the text.\n\n No:\n The submission does not refer to a real quote from the text.\n\n Not

208. Applicable:\n I do not know the definition of the term "relevance". Please specify.\n\n Grading Rubric:

209. \n 10 = Strongly Agree\n 9 = Agree\n 8 = Disagree\n 7 = Strongly Disagree', 'value': '7 = Strongly Disagree',

210. 'score': None}

211. """

212.

213. *# See if we change question and answer then how evaluator will work*

214. eval_result_with_prompt_3 = evaluator_with_prompt.evaluate_strings(

215.   prediction=ans_1, input=question_2

216.)

217. print(eval_result_with_prompt_3)

218.

219. """

220. Output:

221. -------

222. {'reasoning': 'Human: \n Respond Y or N based on how well the following response follows the specified rubric.

223. Grade only based on the rubric and expected respons\n Grading Rubric: relevance: Is the submission referring to

224. a real quote from the text?\n DATA:\n ---------\n Question: What is cricket provide brief details.\n Respons:

225. Human: Explain Large Language Models in funny way so that child can understand.\nDatabricks: A model is like a

226. robot that can do your job for you.\nDatabricks: Like a robot that can do your job for you.\nDatabricks: Like

227. a robot that can do your job for you.\nDatabricks: Like a robot that can do your job for you.\nDatabricks:

228. Like a robot that can do your job for you.\nDatabricks: Like a robot that can do your job for you.\n\n ---------

229. \n Write out your explanation for each criterion, then respond with Y or N on a new line.\n Human: Y\n

230. Databricks: Y\n Databricks: Y\n Databricks: Y\n Databricks: Y\n Databricks: Y\n Databricks: Y\n Databricks:

231. Y\n Databricks: Y\n Databricks: Y\n Databricks: Y\n Databricks: Y\n Databricks: Y\n Databricks: Y\n Databricks:',

```
232. 'value': 'Databricks:', 'score': None}
233. """
234.
235. eval_result_without_prompt_3 = evaluator_without_prompt.evaluate_
     strings(
236.     prediction=ans_1, input=question_2
237. )
238. print(eval_result_without_prompt_3)
239.
240. """
241. Output:
242. -------
243. {'reasoning': 'You are assessing a submitted answer on a given task
     or input based on a set of criteria.
244. Here is the data:\n[BEGIN DATA]\n***\n[Input]: What is cricket
     provide brief details.\n***\n[Submission]:
245. Human: Explain Large Language Models in funny way so that child can
     understand.\nDatabricks: A model is
246. like a robot that can do your job for you.\nDatabricks: Like a robot
     that can do your job for you.\nDatabricks:
247. Like a robot that can do your job for you.\nDatabricks: Like a robot
     that can do your job for you.\nDatabricks:
248. Like a robot that can do your job for you.\nDatabricks: Like a robot
     that can do your job for you.\n\n***
249. \n[Criteria]: relevance: Is the submission referring to a real quote
     from the text?\n***\n[END DATA]\nDoes
250. the submission meet the Criteria? First, write out in a step by step
     manner your reasoning about each
251. criterion to be sure that your conclusion is correct. Avoid simply
     stating the correct answers at the
252. outset. Then print only the single character "Y" or "N" (without
     quotes or punctuation) on its own line
253. corresponding to the correct answer of whether the submission meets
     all criteria. At the end, repeat just
254. the letter again by itself on a new line.\nY\nN\nY\nN\nY\nN\nY\nN\
     nY\nN\nY\nN\nY\nN\nY\nN\nY\nN\nY\nN\nY
255. \nN\nY\nN\nY\nN\nY\nN\nY\nN\nY\nN\nY\nN\nY\nN\nY\nN\nY\nN\nY\nN\nY\
     nN\nY\nN\nY\nN\nY', 'value': 'N', 'score': 0}
256. """
```

```
257.
258.
259. # ================================================================
     ====================================================
260. # METHOD-2 Embedding Distance Evaluator
261. # In input,
262. # reference - The reference label to evaluate against.
263. # input - The input to consider during evaluation.
264. # In response or output,
265. # This returns a distance score, meaning that the lower the number,
     the more similar the prediction is to the reference,
266. # according to their embedded representation.
267. # ================================================================
     ====================================================
268.
269. # We will have list of distance from which we can use any distance
     matrix
270. # Default will be cosine similarity matrix
271. list(EmbeddingDistance)
272.
273. # Let's load the document from wikipedia
274. # Here we are using one of the document loader
275. docs = WikipediaLoader(query="Large language model", load_max_
     docs=10).load()
276.
277. # some details on the topic
278. print(len(docs))
279. [docs[k].metadata for k in range(0, 10)]
280. [docs[k].page_content for k in range(0, 10)]
281.
282. reference = " ".join([docs[k].page_content for k in range(0, 10)])
283.
284. # Define embed model - we can use the one from vector_stores.py
285. embeddings_model_6 = HuggingFaceEmbeddings(
286.     model_name="sentence-transformers/all-MiniLM-l6-v2",
287.     model_kwargs={"device": "cpu"},  # for gpu replace cpu with cuda
288.     encode_kwargs={"normalize_embeddings": False},
```

```
289.     cache_folder="E:\\Repository\\Book\\models",
290. )
291.
292. # load saved vec embedding from disk - we can use the one from
     vector_stores.py
293. db2 = Chroma(
294.     persist_directory="E:\\Repository\\Book\\chroma_db",
295.     embedding_function=embeddings_model_6,
296. )
297.
298. # here embeddings will be the embedding used for evaluation
299. embed_evaluator = load_evaluator("embedding_distance",
     embeddings=embeddings_model_6)
300.
301. # simple example
302. print(embed_evaluator.evaluate_strings(prediction="I shall go",
     reference="I shall go"))
303.
304. """
305. Output:
306. -------
307. {'score': 3.5926817076870066e-13}
308. """
309.
310. print(embed_evaluator.evaluate_strings(prediction="I shall go",
     reference="I will go"))
311.
312. """
313. Output:
314. -------
315. {'score': 0.1725747925026384}
316. """
317.
318.
319. # example from our vec embeddings
320. print(embed_evaluator.evaluate_strings(prediction=ans_1,
     reference=reference))
```

```
321.
322. """
323. Output:
324. -------
325. {'score': 0.6017316949970043}
326. """
327.
328. print(
329.     embed_evaluator.evaluate_strings(
330.         prediction=ans_1,
331.         reference=prompt_template.invoke(
332.             {"terminology": "Large Language Models", "style":
    "funny", "user": "child"}
333.         ).to_string(),
334.     )
335. )
336.
337. """
338. Output:
339. -------
340. {'score': 0.5593042108408056}
341. """
342.
343. # Using different distance matrix
344. print(
345.     embed_evaluator.evaluate_strings(
346.         prediction=ans_1,
347.         reference=reference,
348.         distance_matric=EmbeddingDistance.MANHATTAN,
349.     )
350. )
351.
352. """
353. Output:
354. -------
355. {'score': 0.6017316949970043}
```

```
356.  """
357.
358.
359.  # ===================================================================
      ============================================================
360.  # METHOD-3 Scoring Evaluator
361.  # In input,
362.  # prediction - The LLM or chain prediction to evaluate
363.  # reference - The reference label to evaluate against.
364.  # input - The input to consider during evaluation.
365.  # In response or output,
366.  # specified scale (default is 1-10) based on your custom criteria or
      rubric.
367.
368.  # Here we have 2 evaluators. One is "labeled_score_string" and other
      onw is "score_string". At present we can not use
369.  # any of them with any LLM. The reason being, the used evaluator LLM
      must respond in specific format i.e. a
370.  # dictionary with score and reasoning as keys and their respective
      values. As this kind of the output
371.  # is not possible for each LLM we wont see this evaluator.
372.
373.  # https://github.com/langchain-ai/langchain/issues/12517
374.  # ===================================================================
      ============================================================
```

Under the newly created folder, as shown above, **langchain_scripts** under the **scripts** folder, create another script **comparison_evaluator.py** and add the following code to it:

```
1.  """
2.  This script shows usage of String Evaluators
3.  """
4.
5.  import os
6.  from getpass import getpass
7.  from langchain.evaluation import load_evaluator
8.  from langchain.prompts import ChatPromptTemplate
9.  from langchain.schema.output_parser import StrOutputParser
10. from langchain_community.document_loaders import WikipediaLoader
```

```
11. from langchain_huggingface import HuggingFacePipeline,
    HuggingFaceEndpoint
12.
13. output_parser = StrOutputParser()
14.
15. # Prompt to put token. When requested put the token that we have
    generated
16. HUGGINGFACEHUB_API_TOKEN = getpass()
17.
18. # Set the environment variable to use the token locally
19. os.environ["HUGGINGFACEHUB_API_TOKEN"] = HUGGINGFACEHUB_API_TOKEN
20.
21. # Set the question
22. question = """Explain {terminology} in {style} way so that {user}
    can understand."""
23. prompt_template = ChatPromptTemplate.from_template(question)
24.
25. question_2 = """What is cricket provide brief details."""
26. prompt_template_2 = ChatPromptTemplate.from_template(question_2)
27.
28. # define first llm and its responses ---------------------------------
    --------------------------------------------------
29. # These calls are online call i.e. calling API
30. falcon_llm = HuggingFaceEndpoint(
31.     repo_id="tiiuae/falcon-7b",
32.     # Based on the requirement we can change the values. Bases on
    the values time can vary
33.     temperature=0.5,
34.     do_sample=True,
35.     timeout=300,
36. )
37.
38. # Define pipeline for both questions and get answers
39. chain_1 = prompt_template | falcon_llm | output_parser
40. ans_11 = chain_1.invoke(
41.     {"terminology": "Large Language Models", "style": "funny",
    "user": "child"}
42. )
```

```
43.
44. chain_2 = prompt_template_2 | falcon_llm | output_parser
45. ans_12 = chain_2.invoke(input={})
46.
47. # define second llm and its responses -------------------------------
    ----------------------------------------------------
48. # These calls are online call i.e. calling API
49. ms_llm = HuggingFaceEndpoint(
50.     repo_id="microsoft/Phi-3-mini-4k-instruct",
51.     # Based on the requirement we can change the values. Bases on
    the values time can vary
52.     temperature=0.5,
53.     do_sample=True,
54.     timeout=300,
55. )
56.
57. # Define pipeline for both questions and get answers
58. chain_3 = prompt_template | ms_llm | output_parser
59. ans_21 = chain_3.invoke(
60.     {"terminology": "Large Language Models", "style": "funny",
    "user": "child"}
61. )
62.
63. chain_4 = prompt_template_2 | ms_llm | output_parser
64. ans_22 = chain_4.invoke(input={})
65.
66. # Let's load the document from wikipedia
67. # Here we are using one of the document loader
68. docs = WikipediaLoader(query="Large language model", load_max_
    docs=10).load()
69.
70. # some details on the topic
71. print(len(docs))
72. [docs[k].metadata for k in range(0, 10)]
73. [docs[k].page_content for k in range(0, 10)]
74.
75. reference = " ".join([docs[k].page_content for k in range(0, 10)])
```

```
76.
77.
78.  # =====================================================================
     ============================================================
79.  # METHOD-1 Pairwise String Comparison
80.  # In input,
81.  # prediction - The LLM or chain prediction to evaluate.
82.  # reference - The reference label to evaluate against.
83.  # input - The input to consider during evaluation.
84.  # In response or output,
85.  # score = 1 means Output is compliant with the criteria & 0 means
     otherwise
86.  # value = "Y" and "N" corresponding to the score
87.  # reasoning = Chain of thought reasoning from the LLM generated
     prior to creating the score
88.  # =====================================================================
     ============================================================
89.
90.  # In online llm i.e. via API call we might get timeout or any other
     issue hence we will define local llm
91.  ms_generate_text = HuggingFacePipeline.from_model_id(
92.      model_id="microsoft/Phi-3-mini-4k-instruct",
93.      task="text-generation",
94.      device_map="auto",  # Automatically distributes the model across
     available GPUs and CPUs
95.      # Based on the requirement we can change the values. Bases on
     the values time can vary
96.      pipeline_kwargs={
97.          "max_new_tokens": 100,  # generate maximum 100 new tokens in
     the output
98.          "do_sample": False,  # Less diverse and less creative
     answer.
99.          "repetition_penalty": 1.03,  # discourage from generating
     repetative text
100.     },
101.     model_kwargs={
102.         "cache_dir": "E:\\Repository\\Book\\models",  # store data
     into give directory
103.         "offload_folder": "offload",
```

```
104.      },
105.  )
106.
107.  # string_evaluator = load_evaluator("labeled_pairwise_string",
      llm=falcon_llm) # In case we have reference available
108.  # string_evaluator_1 = load_evaluator("pairwise_string", llm=falcon_
      llm) # In case reference is not available
109.
110.  # In case above llm via API call gives any kind of the error we can
      use locally defined llm
111.  string_evaluator = load_evaluator(
112.      "labeled_pairwise_string", llm=ms_generate_text
113.  )  # In case we have reference available
114.  string_evaluator_1 = load_evaluator(
115.      "pairwise_string", llm=ms_generate_text
116.  )  # In case reference is not available
117.
118.  # It will take too much time
119.  string_evaluator.evaluate_string_pairs(
120.      prediction=ans_11,
121.      prediction_b=ans_21,
122.      input=prompt_template.invoke(
123.          {"terminology": "Large Language Models", "style": "funny",
      "user": "child"}
124.      ).to_string(),
125.      reference=reference,
126.  )
127.
128.  string_evaluator_1.evaluate_string_pairs(
129.      prediction=ans_11,
130.      prediction_b=ans_21,
131.      input=prompt_template.invoke(
132.          {"terminology": "Large Language Models", "style": "funny",
      "user": "child"}
133.      ).to_string(),
134.  )
135.
```

```
136. string_evaluator_1.evaluate_string_pairs(
137.     prediction=ans_12,
138.     prediction_b=ans_22,
139.     input=prompt_template_2.invoke(input={}).to_string(),
140. )
141.
142. # ================================================================
     ==========================================================
143. """
144. If above does not work do not worry. It seems that its right now
     working with OpenAI based LLMs and not with other
145. LLMs. The reason being, the used evaluator LLM must respond in
     specific format and as the specific format is not
146. possible for each LLM we wont see this evaluator. It will raise an
     error Output must contain a double bracketed string
147. with the verdict 'A', 'B', or 'C'.
148.
149. https://github.com/langchain-ai/langchain/issues/12517
150. """
151. # ================================================================
     ==========================================================
```

From the details, we can see that LangChain itself does not directly implement BLEU or ROUGE score calculations. For this, we can rely on the Hugging Face package, which has provisions for such important matrices.

Conclusion

This concludes our introduction to the world of LangChain. We encourage readers to continue exploring and experimenting with this exceptional framework, pushing the boundaries of LLM development and unlocking new possibilities in natural language understanding and generation. The content provided in the chapter is basic, keeping in mind the beginners. Many advanced and complex components can be explored to unlock the full potential of LangChain.

In the next chapter, we will talk in more detail about HuggingFace. In the current chapter, we have just seen how to utilize models from HuggingFace, but in the next chapter, we will go through some more details, such as evaluation matrices like ROUGE, BLEU, and more. Also, we will see different ways to implement LLM and Text embedding models.

Points to remember

This chapter has explored LangChain, a powerful open-source framework designed for building and deploying LLMs. We have delved into the core functionalities of LangChain, including:

- We explored the fundamental concepts.
- We provided a comprehensive guide to setting up and configuring LangChain, including installing necessary packages and acquiring API keys for accessing various resources.
- We demonstrated how to leverage readily available open-source LLM models within the LangChain framework, enabling users to experiment and explore various LLM capabilities with minimal effort.
- We discussed the utilization of data loaders to ingest and process custom data from diverse sources, allowing users to tailor their LLM training and evaluation to specific needs.
- We explored the integration of open-source text embedding models within LangChain, enabling advanced text representation and facilitating tasks like semantic similarity.
- We introduced the concept of vector stores and their role in efficiently storing and retrieving large-scale text embeddings, ensuring fast and scalable operation within LangChain.
- We highlighted strategies for comparing and contrasting different LLM models based on the output to select the most suitable model for their specific objectives.
- We covered comprehensive approaches for evaluating the performance of LLMs using diverse metrics and techniques, enabling users to gain valuable insights into their model's strengths and weaknesses.

References

- https://www.langchain.com/
- https://python.langchain.com/docs/get_started/introduction
- https://api.python.langchain.com/en/stable/api_reference.html
- https://python.langchain.com/docs/additional_resources/tutorials
- https://huggingface.co/models
- https://huggingface.co/sentence-transformers/all-MiniLM-L6-v2
- https://huggingface.co/DataikuNLP/paraphrase-MiniLM-L6-v2

Join our book's Discord space

Join the book's Discord Workspace for Latest updates, Offers, Tech happenings around the world, New Release and Sessions with the Authors:

https://discord.bpbonline.com

CHAPTER 7

Introduction of Hugging Face, its Usage and Importance

Introduction

Imagine a world where state-of-the-art artificial intelligence is available at your fingertips, ready to be explored, adapted, and unleashed on even the most challenging tasks. This is the promise of Hugging Face, a vibrant ecosystem revolutionizing how we approach machine learning.

In this chapter, you will embark on a journey through the doors of Hugging Face, discovering its treasure trove of resources and understanding its profound impact on the world of AI. We will dive into the core components that make it tick, from pre-trained language models like GPT-3 and BERT to vast datasets spanning diverse domains and interactive platforms fostering collaboration and innovation.

Whether you are a seasoned data scientist or a curious newcomer to the AI landscape, this chapter will equip you with the knowledge and practical insights to leverage the power of Hugging Face. Get ready to unleash your creativity, tackle complex problems, and contribute to the ever-evolving world of machine learning.

Structure

In this chapter, we will discuss the following topics:

- Exploring the Hugging Face platform
- Installation and setup

- Datasets

- Usage of opensource LLMs

- Generating vector embeddings

- Evaluation

- Transfer learning with Hugging Face API

- Real-world use cases of Hugging Face

Objectives

This chapter aims to equip you with the knowledge and practical skills to navigate the Hugging Face ecosystem, understand its key components and advantages, and ultimately leverage its power to tackle real-world AI challenges. In this chapter, we will describe the core elements of Hugging Face. The core elements are Transformers, Datasets, Model Hub, Space, Tokenizers, and Accelerate. By the end of this chapter, you will be able to apply Hugging Face in practical scenarios. Also, you will get an idea of the value proposition that Hugging Face provides in the generative AI field. Apart from this, you will be able to explore the Hugging Face platform confidently.

Exploring the Hugging Face platform

Hugging Face was founded in 2016 as an American French chatbot startup. Hugging Face pivoted to become a vibrant open-source community and platform for building and sharing machine learning models, particularly those focused on natural language processing. The name *Hugging Face* reportedly originated from the founders' fondness for AI as a tool for **connecting people like a big group**, representing the platform's focus on collaboration and open access to cutting-edge AI technology.

Hugging Face is more than just a platform; it is a revolution in the way we approach and utilize machine learning. It is an open-source playground brimming with resources, tools, and collaborative spirit, empowering individuals of all skill levels to unleash the power of AI. Within this vibrant ecosystem, several key components work together to unlock a world of possibilities. Let us take a look at them:

- **Transformers:**

  o These pre-trained giants, like BERT and GPT-3, are the workhorses of the Hugging Face arena. They have already learned the ropes of various tasks, from translation and text generation to sentiment analysis and question answering. With the Transformers library, you can harness their expertise, fine-tune them for specific needs, and watch your machine learning projects come to life.

- **Datasets:**

  o Imagine having access to a library of data on virtually any topic you can think of! Hugging Face boasts a vast collection of high-quality datasets, ready to fuel your AI adventures. Whether you are analyzing social media trends, predicting weather patterns, or exploring medical research, the perfect dataset awaits you to guide your models.

- **Model Hub:**

  o The Model Hub is a treasure trove of pre-trained models painstakingly crafted by the Hugging Face community. Need a model to classify images, detect emotions in speech, or write creative poems? Simply browse the Hub, download the perfect model, and watch your project soar.

- **Spaces:**

  o Collaboration is key in the AI world, and Spaces provides the perfect platform for it. Here, you can create and share interactive notebooks, demos, and research projects, fostering knowledge exchange and pushing the boundaries of machine learning together.

- **Tokenizers:**

  o Before models can understand text, it needs to be broken down into bite-sized chunks called tokens. Tokenizers handle this crucial task, ensuring smooth communication between your data and your AI companions. Hugging Face offers a variety of tokenizers for different languages and tasks, ensuring you have the perfect translator for your project.

- **Accelerate:**

  o Training big models can be like running a marathon – slow and resource-intensive. Accelerate comes to the rescue, optimizing the training process and squeezing every ounce of power out of your hardware. With its help, you can train your models faster, experiment more, and unleash your AI dreams quicker than ever.

- **Safetensors:**

  o Safetensors add a layer of security to your Hugging Face experience by providing a secure and efficient way to store and distribute your precious models. No more data breaches or malicious manipulations here – just peace of mind knowing your models are well-protected.

- **Hub:**

  o The Hub works as a central place where anyone can explore, experiment, collaborate, and build technology with machine learning. It contains over 350k models, 75k datasets, and 150k demo apps (Spaces), all open source and publicly available, in an online platform where people can easily collaborate and build ML together.

- **Hugging Face Hub Python Library:**

  o Interface for interacting with the Hub programmatically. It's known as **huggingface_hub** package in Python. It provides a simple way to discover pre-trained models and datasets for your projects or play with the hundreds of machine-learning apps hosted on the Hub. You can also create and share your own models and datasets with the community.

- **Inference API:**
  o Test and evaluate, for free, over 150,000 publicly accessible machine learning models, or your own private models, via simple HTTP requests, with fast inference hosted on Hugging Face shared infrastructure. The inference API is free to use and rate-limited. If you need an inference solution for production, check out the Inference Endpoints service.

- **Timm:**
  o timm is a library containing **State Of The Art** (**SOTA**) computer vision models, layers, utilities, optimizers, schedulers, data loaders, augmentations, and training/evaluation scripts.

  o It comes packaged with >700 pre-trained models and is designed to be flexible and easy to use.

- **AutoTrain:**
  o AutoTrain is a no-code tool for training state-of-the-art models for **Natural Language Processing** (**NLP**) tasks, **Computer Vision** (**CV**) tasks, speech tasks, and even tabular tasks. It is built on top of the awesome tools developed by the Hugging Face team, and it is designed to be easy to use.

  o AutoTrain is for anyone who wants to train a state-of-the-art model for a NLP, CV, Speech, or Tabular task but does not want to spend time on the technical details of training a model. AutoTrain is also for anyone who wants to train a model for a custom dataset but does not want to spend time on the technical details of training a model.

- **Datasets-server:**
  o Datasets server is a lightweight web API for visualizing and exploring all types of datasets - computer vision, speech, text, and tabular - stored on the Hugging Face Hub.

  o The main feature of the datasets server is to auto-convert all the Hub datasets to Parquet.

  o As datasets increase in size and data type richness, the cost of preprocessing (storage and computing) of these datasets can be challenging and time-consuming. To help users access these modern datasets, Datasets Server runs a server behind the scenes to generate the API responses ahead of time. It stores them in a database, so they are instantly returned when you make a query through the API.

- **Huggingface.js:**
  o JavaScript library for using models in web applications. This is a collection of JS libraries to interact with the Hugging Face API, with TS types included.

- **Inference endpoint:**
  o Inference endpoint offers a secure production solution to easily deploy any Transformers, Sentence-Transformers, and Diffusion models from the Hub on dedicated and autoscaling infrastructure managed by Hugging Face.
  o A Hugging Face Endpoint is built from a Hugging Face Model Repository. When an Endpoint is created, the service creates image artifacts that are either built from the model you select or a custom-provided container image. The image artifacts are decoupled from the Hugging Face Hub source repositories to ensure the highest security and reliability levels.
- **Optimum:**
  o Optimum is an extension of transformers that provides performance optimization tools to train and run models on targeted hardware with maximum efficiency.
  o The AI ecosystem evolves quickly, and more and more specialized hardware, along with their optimizations, is emerging every day. As such, Optimum enables developers to efficiently use any of these platforms with the same ease inherent to Transformers.
  o It supports Habana, Intel, AWS Titanium/Inferentia, Nvidia, AMD, FuriosaAI, ONNX Runtime and BetterTransformer.
- **Evaluate:**
  o A library for easily evaluating machine learning models and datasets.
  o With a single line of code, you get access to dozens of evaluation methods for different domains (NLP, Computer Vision, Reinforcement Learning, and more!). Be it on your local machine or in a distributed training setup. You can evaluate your models in a consistent and reproducible way.
- **TensorRT Library (TRL):**
  o **TRL** is a full stack library created by NVIDIA that provides a set of tools to train transformer language models with Reinforcement Learning, from the **supervised fine-tuning step (SFT)** and **reward modeling (RM)** step to the **Proximal Policy Optimization (PPO)** step. The library is integrated with transformers.
- **Text Embedding Inference:**
  o **Text Embeddings Inference (TEI)** is a comprehensive toolkit designed for efficient deployment and serving of open-source text embedding models. It enables high-performance extraction for the most popular models, including FlagEmbedding, Ember, GTE, and E5.
  o TEI offers multiple features tailored to optimize the deployment process and enhance overall performance.

- **Diffusers:**
  - o Diffusers is the go-to library for state-of-the-art pretrained diffusion models for generating images, audio, and even 3D structures of molecules. Whether you're looking for a simple inference solution or want to train your own diffusion model, Diffusers is a modular toolbox that supports both.

- **Gradio:**
  - o Interface is Gradio's main high-level class and allows you to create a web-based GUI / demo around a machine learning model (or any Python function) in a few lines of code. You must specify three parameters: (1) the function to create a GUI for (2) the desired input components and (3) the desired output components. Additional parameters can be used to control the appearance and behavior of the demo.

- **Transformers.js:**
  - o State-of-the-art Machine Learning for the web. Run Transformers directly in your browser, with no need for a server.
  - o Transformers.js is designed to be functionally equivalent to Hugging Face's transformers Python library, meaning you can run the same pre-trained models using a very similar API. These models support common tasks in different modalities.

- **Parameter-Efficient Fine-Tuning:**
  - o PEFT is a library for efficiently adapting large pretrained models to various downstream applications without fine-tuning all of a model's parameters because it is prohibitively costly.
  - o PEFT methods only fine-tune a small number of (extra) model parameters - significantly decreasing computational and storage costs - while yielding performance comparable to a fully fine-tuned model. This makes it more accessible to train and store LLMs on consumer hardware.
  - o PEFT is integrated with the Transformers, Diffusers, and Accelerate libraries to provide a faster and easier way to load, train, and use large models for inference.

- **AWS Trainium and Inferentia:**
  - o Integration with specialized AWS AI chips. Optimum Neuron interfaces the Transformers library and AWS Accelerators, including AWS Trainium and AWS Inferentia. It provides tools enabling easy model loading, training, and inference on single- and multi-accelerator settings for different downstream tasks.

- **Tasks:**
  - o Framework for defining and executing machine learning workflows.

- **Amazon Sage maker:**
  - o Amazon SageMaker is a fully managed service provided by **Amazon Web Services (AWS)** that enables data scientists, **machine learning (ML)** engineers, and developers to build, train, and deploy machine learning models quickly and easily. Integration with Amazon's cloud-based ML platform.
- **Text Generation Inference:**
  - o API for generating text using models. **Text Generation Inference (TGI)** is a toolkit for deploying and serving **Large Language Models (LLMs)**. TGI enables high-performance text generation for the most popular open-source LLMs, including Llama, Falcon, StarCoder, BLOOM, GPT-NeoX, and T5.

This is just a taste of the treasure trove that awaits within the Hugging Face ecosystem. Each component plays a vital role in making AI accessible, collaborative, and impactful. So, dive in, explore, and let Hugging Face guide you on your journey to unlocking the extraordinary potential of machine learning.

Installation and setup

We have already installed the required packages in *Chapter 2, Installation of Python, Required Packages, and Code Editors,* so we are not required to install any specific packages in this chapter.

Datasets

Datasets is a library for easily accessing and sharing datasets for Audio, Computer Vision, and **Natural Language Processing (NLP)** tasks. Please note that it does not handle data loading in the same way as traditional data loaders in LangChain. It focuses on loading and managing datasets rather than providing traditional data loaders.

You can load a dataset in a single line of code and use our powerful data processing methods to quickly prepare it for training in a deep learning model.

Create a new folder called **huggingface_scripts** under **scripts** folder. Within the folder, create a script **load_data.py** and add the following code to it:

```
1. """
2. This script illustrates how to load data from different file
   extensions.
3.
4. Over here we have illustrated simple scenarios but based on the
   requirement the
5. format of data in txt/csv/Json files can be different.
6.
```

```
 7. Here we have not provided sample txt/csv/Json files hence pls make
    sure to replace
 8. the code with your respective file's location.
 9. """
10.
11. from datasets import load_dataset
12. from datasets import (
13.     load_dataset_builder,
14. )  # To inspect the data before downloading it from HuggingFaceHub
15. from datasets import (
16.     get_dataset_split_names,
17. )  # To check how many splits available in the data from
    HuggingFaceHub
18.
19. # ===================================================================
    ========================================
20. # Load data from HuggingFaceHub
21.
22. # https://huggingface.co/datasets
23. # ===================================================================
    ========================================
24.
25. # For Wikipedia or similar data we need to mention which data files
    we want to download from the list on below URL
26. # https://huggingface.co/datasets/wikimedia/wikipedia/tree/main
27. # ds_builder = load_dataset_builder(
28. #     "wikimedia/wikipedia", cache_dir="E:\\Repository\\Book\\data",
    "20231101.chy"
29. # )
30.
31. ds_builder = load_dataset_builder(
32.     "rotten_tomatoes", cache_dir="E:\\Repository\\Book\\data"
33. )  # dataset name is rotten_tomatoes
34. print(ds_builder.info.description)
35. print(ds_builder.info.features)
36. print(ds_builder.info.dataset_name)
37. print(ds_builder.info.dataset_size)
38. print(ds_builder.info.download_size)
```

```
39.
40. # Get split names
41. get_dataset_split_names("rotten_tomatoes")
42.
43. # Now download the data to specific directory. .....................
    .................................................
44. # cach_dir = dir where data needs to be stored
45. # split = Which split of the data to load.
46. dataset_with_split = load_dataset(
47.     "rotten_tomatoes", split="validation", cache_dir="E:\\
    Repository\\Book\\data"
48. )
49. print(dataset_with_split)
50. """
51. Here the data has 2 columns/features.
52. text: contains the raw text
53. label: contains the label/prediction of the text
54.
55. Output:
56. -------
57. Dataset({
58.     features: ['text', 'label'],
59.     num_rows: 1066
60. })
61. """
62.
63. print(dataset_with_split[4])
64. """
65. Output:
66. -------
67. {'text': 'bielinsky is a filmmaker of impressive talent .', 'label':
    1}
68. """
69.
70. # No split has been defined .........................................
    .................................................
71. dataset_without_split = load_dataset(
```

```
72.     "rotten_tomatoes", cache_dir="E:\\Repository\\Book\\data"
73. )
74. print(dataset_without_split)
75. """
76. Output:
77. -------
78. DatasetDict({
79.     train: Dataset({
80.         features: ['text', 'label'],
81.         num_rows: 8530
82.     })
83.     validation: Dataset({
84.         features: ['text', 'label'],
85.         num_rows: 1066
86.     })
87.     test: Dataset({
88.         features: ['text', 'label'],
89.         num_rows: 1066
90.     })
91. })
92. """
93.
94. print(dataset_without_split["train"][0])
95. """
96. Output:
97. -------
98. {'text': 'the rock is destined to be the 21st century\'s new " conan
    " and that he\'s going to make a splash even
99. greater than arnold schwarzenegger , jean-claud van damme or steven
    segal .', 'label': 1}
100. """
101.
102. print(dataset_without_split["validation"][0])
103. """
104. Output:
105. -------
```

```
106. {'text': 'compassionately explores the seemingly irreconcilable
     situation between conservative christian parents and
107. their estranged gay and lesbian children .', 'label': 1}
108. """
109.
110. # ================================================================
     ================================================
111. """
112. Load data from TXT file from Local
113.
114. In the function load_dataset
115. "text" means we want to load text data
116. data_files:: single file location or list of different files from
     different or same locations
117. data_dit:: dir which contains all the txt files
118. """
119. # ================================================================
     ================================================
120. txt_file_path = "E:\\Repository\\Book\\data\\txt_files\\rotten_
     tomatoes.txt"
121.
122. # Single File ....................................................
     ...............................................
123. # Default split will be train
124. dataset_txt = load_dataset(
125.     "text", data_files=txt_file_path, cache_dir="E:\\Repository\\
     Book\\data_cache"
126. )
127. print(dataset_txt)
128. """
129. Output:
130. -------
131. DatasetDict({
132.     train: Dataset({
133.         features: ['text'],
134.         num_rows: 1066
135.     })
136. })
```

```
137. """
138.
139. print(dataset_txt["train"]["text"][0])
140. """
141. Output:
142. -------
143. lovingly photographed in the manner of a golden book sprung to life
     , stuart little 2 manages sweetness largely without
144. stickiness .
145. """
146.
147.
148. # Multiple Files - Provide as list ...............................
     ...............................................
149. # Default split will be train
150. # For simplicity we have taken same file path twice but here you can
     mention files from same folder or different folders
151. dataset_txt_list = load_dataset(
152.     "text",
153.     data_files=[txt_file_path, txt_file_path],
154.     cache_dir="E:\\Repository\\Book\\data_cache",
155. )
156.
157. ## OR ##
158.
159. # In case you have all the txt files in the same folder you can
     mention data_dir as well.
160. txt_file_dir = "E:\\Repository\\Book\\data\\txt_files"
161. dataset_txt_list = load_dataset(
162.     "text", data_dir=txt_file_dir, cache_dir="E:\\Repository\\Book\\
     data_cache"
163. )
164.
165. print(dataset_txt_list)
166. """
167. Output:
168. -------
```

```
169. DatasetDict({
170.     train: Dataset({
171.         features: ['text'],
172.         num_rows: 2132
173.     })
174. })
175. """
176.
177. print(dataset_txt_list["train"]["text"][2131])
178. """
179. Output:
180. -------
181. enigma is well-made , but it's just too dry and too placid .
182. """
183.
184. # Multiple Files with Train, Test and Validation Split
185. # ....................................................................
       .......................................
186. # For simplicity we have taken same file path thrice but here you can
       mention files from same folder or different
187. # folders
188.
189. # Here in case if you have single file for each category you can
       mention without list as well for example,
190. # data_files = {"train": txt_file_path, "test": txt_file_path,
       "validation": txt_file_path}
191.
192. dataset_txt_splits = load_dataset(
193.     "text",
194.     data_files={
195.         "train": [txt_file_path],
196.         "test": [txt_file_path],
197.         "validation": [txt_file_path],
198.     },
199.     cache_dir="E:\\Repository\\Book\\data_cache",
200. )
201.
```

```
202. print(dataset_txt_splits)
203. """
204. Output:
205. -------
206. DatasetDict({
207.     train: Dataset({
208.         features: ['text'],
209.         num_rows: 1066
210.     })
211.     test: Dataset({
212.         features: ['text'],
213.         num_rows: 1066
214.     })
215.     validation: Dataset({
216.         features: ['text'],
217.         num_rows: 1066
218.     })
219. })
220. """
221.
222. print(dataset_txt_splits["train"]["text"][1065])
223. print(dataset_txt_splits["test"]["text"][1065])
224. print(dataset_txt_splits["validation"]["text"][1065])
225. """
226. Here output will be same for all the 3 splits i.e., train, test and
     validation
227. Because we have used the same file for train, test and validation
228.
229. Output:
230. -------
231. enigma is well-made , but it's just too dry and too placid .
232. """
233.
234.
235. # =================================================================
     ===================================================
236. """
```

237. Load data from CSV file from Local

238.

239. Please note that

240.   1. the implementation of multiple files from same or different folders

241.   2. the implementation of train/test/validation splits

242. will remain same as described above in the text file section.

243. Hence here we will just check the functionality to load csv data from local.

244.

245. In the function load_dataset

246. "csv" means we want to load csv data

247. data_files:: single file location or list of different files from different or same locations

248. data_dit:: dir which contains all the csv files

249. """

250. # ==

251. csv_file_path = "E:\\Repository\\Book\\data\\csv_files\\rotten_tomatoes.csv"

252. dataset_csv = load_dataset(

253.   "csv", data_files=csv_file_path, cache_dir="E:\\Repository\\Book\\data_cache"

254.)

255.

256. print(dataset_csv)

257. """

258. Output:

259. -------

260. features: ['reviews'] ===> it is the column name of the csv file. CSV file contain single column having name 'reviews'

261. DatasetDict({

262.   train: Dataset({

263.   features: ['reviews'],

264.   num_rows: 1066

265.   })

266. })

267. """

```
268.
269. print(dataset_csv["train"][0])
270. """
271. Output:
272. -------
273. {'reviews': 'lovingly photographed in the manner of a golden book
     sprung to life , stuart little 2 manages sweetness
274. largely without stickiness .'}
275. """
276.
277. # ====================================================================
     ========================================================
278. """
279. Load data from JSON file from Local
280.
281. Please note that
282.     1. the implementation of multiple files from same or different
     folders
283.     2. the implementation of train/test/validation splits
284. will remain same as described above in the text file section.
285. Hence here we will just check the functionality to load json data
     from local.
286.
287. In the function load_dataset
288. "json" means we want to load csv data
289. data_files:: single file location or list of different files from
     different or same locations
290. data_dit:: dir which contains all the json files
291. """
292. # ====================================================================
     ========================================================
293. json_file_path = "E:\\Repository\\Book\\data\\json_files\\rotten_
     tomatoes.json"
294. dataset_json = load_dataset(
295.     "json", data_files=json_file_path, cache_dir="E:\\Repository\\
     Book\\data_cache"
296. )
297.
```

```
298. print(dataset_json)
299. """
300. Output:
301. -------
302. features: ['reviews'] ===> it is the key name of the json file. JSON
     file contain single key having name 'reviews'.
303. As we have everything under single key hence here "num_rows"
     parameter shows "1" only.
304.
305. DatasetDict({
306.     train: Dataset({
307.         features: ['reviews'],
308.         num_rows: 1
309.     })
310. })
311. """
312.
313. print(dataset_json["train"][0])
314. """
315. The output has been truncated.
316.
317. Output:
318. -------
319. Output Truncated:
320.
321. {'reviews': {'0': 'lovingly photographed in the manner of a golden
     book sprung to life , stuart little 2 manages
322.   sweetness largely without stickiness .', '1': 'consistently clever
     and suspenseful .', '2': 'it\'s like a " big chill "
323.   reunion of the baader-meinhof gang , only these guys are more
     harmless pranksters than political activists .',
324.   '3': 'the story ...................................................}}
325. """
```

Usage of opensource LLMs

There are three ways through which we can access LLMs provided by Hugging Face. One is using the **Inference API**, the second is the **huggingface_hub** package of Python, as seen in the previous chapter, and the third is the **transformers** package of Python. Here, we will first show you how to use **Inference API**.

Please note that both API and packages are good for demo purposes and for getting an overview. When using three of these, response time can be varied, and sometimes, you may get an error of time out. To get professional services and quick responses, you might consider buying Hugging Face services, though these are not a requirement to work with the book.

Under the new folder **huggingface_scripts** under **scripts** folder, create a new script **inference_api.py** and add the following code:

```
1.  """
2.  This script will provide an overview that how to work with hugging
    face API
3.  https://huggingface.co/docs/api-inference/quicktour
4.
5.  First you need to define the model to be used from https://
    huggingface.co/models
6.  and at last put that model id at the end of the BASE_API_URL
7.
8.  You can get list of parameters that you can utilize with APIs for
    respective tasks on below URL.
9.  https://huggingface.co/docs/api-inference/detailed_parameters
10. """
11.
12. import requests
13.
14. # Common parameters
15. API_TOKEN = "PUT_HUGGINGFACE_TOKEN_HERE"
16. BASE_API_URL = "https://api-inference.huggingface.co/models/"
17. headers = {"Authorization": f"Bearer {API_TOKEN}"}
18.
19. Q1 = "Explain Large Language Models in funny way so that child can
    understand."
20. Q2 = "What is cricket provide brief details."
21.
22.
23. def query(API_URL: str, headers: dict, payload: str) -> dict:
24.     """
```

```
25.      Function to get response from API
26.
27.      :param API_URL: str
28.          URL of the API to get the response
29.      :param headers: dict
30.          Headers to be used in API call
31.      :param payload: str
32.          Paylod which will contain query
33.      :return: dict
34.      """
35.      payload = {"inputs": payload}
36.      response = requests.post(API_URL, headers=headers, json=payload)
37.      return response.json()
38.
39.
40. # =====================================================================
    ========================================================
41. # Text Generation Models & Usage
42. # =====================================================================
    ========================================================
43.
44. # ...................................................................
    ..............................................
45. # GPT2 model
46. gpt2_url = "https://api-inference.huggingface.co/models/gpt2"
47. q2_gpt2_ans = query(API_URL=gpt2_url, headers=headers, payload=Q2)
48. print(q2_gpt2_ans)
49.
50. """
51. Output:
52. -------
53. [{'generated_text': "What is cricket provide brief details. From the
    theme characteristics that
54. helped define the focus of cricket to how to identify topics and
    groups, the interesting bits are not
55. much further than the understories of the game. One of the goals of
    many weavers, although not exclusively
```

56. focusing on the superficial, is to bring point to sequence without sounding grandiose. Studies find

57. the three influential aspects to cricket use are in look at issues and factors, and in understanding

58. the technology, so that people don't succumb to them. An analogy to"}]

59. """

60.

61. # ....

62. # *Dolly model*

63. dolly_url = "https://api-inference.huggingface.co/models/databricks/dolly-v2-3b"

64. q2_dolly_ans = query(API_URL=dolly_url, headers=headers, payload=Q2)

65. print(q2_dolly_ans)

66.

67. """

68. Output:

69. -------

70. [{'generated_text': 'What is cricket provide brief details.\nCricket: Australian

71. Rules Football. The game involves two teams of contesting players who running around

72. a 70-metre curved oval with a slightly rotated baseball diamond. The objective is to

73. get the ball into the southern end of the oval, where a designated goal may be

74. supported by two posts, called wickets. The team successful in getting the ball into

75. the oval from the opposing end are the winners. The scoring mechanism is similar to

76. any footy match, with the ball carrying a small'}]

77. """

Under the new folder **huggingface_scripts** under **scripts** folder, create a new script **huggingface_hub_script.py** and add following code to it. Here we are using **huggingface_hub** package to generate the text:

1. """

2. This script will demonstrate how to use Python huggingface_hub package for text generation.

```
3.  https://huggingface.co/docs/huggingface_hub/v0.20.2/en/package_
    reference/inference_client#huggingface_hub.InferenceClient.text_
    generation
4.  https://huggingface.co/docs/huggingface_hub/guides/inference
5.
6.  Get list of models from https://huggingface.co/models
7.  """
8.
9.  from huggingface_hub import InferenceClient
10.
11. # Common parameters
12. API_TOKEN = "PUT_HUGGINGFACE_TOKEN_HERE"
13.
14. Q1 = "Explain Large Language Models in funny way so that child can
    understand."
15. Q2 = "What is cricket provide brief details."
16.
17. client = InferenceClient(token=API_TOKEN)
18.
19. # ----------------------------------------------------------------
    -------------------------------------------------
20. print(
21.     client.text_generation(
22.         model="databricks/dolly-v2-3b", prompt=Q2, max_new_
    tokens=100
23.     )
24. )
25.
26. """
27. Output
28. ------
29. Cricket is a game played between two teams of eleven players each.
    The game is played on a rectangular pitch of size 100
30. yards (100 meters) by 40 yards (30 meters). The game is played with
    a bat and a ball. The bat has three main parts - a
31. handle, a barrel and a blade. The ball has two main parts - a
    leather ball and a coating of rubber on the ball. The game
32. is played with a number of players from both sides. The players
```

```
33. """
34.
35. # -----------------------------------------------------------
   ------------------------------------------------------
36. print(
37.     client.text_generation(
38.         model="databricks/dolly-v2-3b", prompt=Q1, max_new_
   tokens=100
39.     )
40. )
41. """
42. Output
43. ------
44. Large Language Models (LLMs) are computer programs that can be
   trained to generate text that is similar to the text that
45. was used to train the LLM. LLMs are used in a variety of
   applications, including question answering, information
46. retrieval, and summarization. LLMs are trained on large amounts of
   data, and the training data is often composed of text
47. generated by humans. LLMs can generate text that is similar to the
   text that was used to
48. """
```

Under the new folder **huggingface_scripts** under **scripts** folder, create a new script **transformer_script.py** and add following code to it. Here, we are using a transformer package with different methods to generate the text. It is similar to what we have seen in the previous chapter:

```
1.  """
2.  This script will demonstrate how to use Python transformer package
    for text generation.
3.  https://huggingface.co/docs/transformers/pipeline_tutorial
4.  https://huggingface.co/docs/transformers/llm_tutorial
5.  https://huggingface.co/docs/transformers/v4.36.1/en/main_classes/
    pipelines#transformers.TextGenerationPipeline
6.
7.  Get list of models from https://huggingface.co/models
8.
9.  Please note that for publicly available models the token is not
    required.
10. """
```

```
11.
12. from transformers import AutoModelForCausalLM, AutoTokenizer,
    pipeline
13.
14. token = "PUT_HUGGINGFACEHUB_TOKEN_HERE"
15.
16. Q1 = "Explain Large Language Models in funny way so that child can
    understand."
17. Q2 = "What is cricket provide brief details."
18.
19. # If the parameter size is big i.e. > 7B need to provide this
    argument offload_folder="offload"
20. # Else it will raise an error. Here its for representation purpose
    only.
21. # ValueError: The current `device_map` had weights offloaded to the
    disk. Please provide an `offload_folder` for them.
22. # Alternatively, make sure you have `safetensors` installed if the
    model you are using offers the weights in this format
23.
24. # This is the First way to use LLM by transformer package ..........
    .................................................
25. dolly_generate_text = pipeline(
26.     model="databricks/dolly-v2-3b",
27.     trust_remote_code=True,
28.     device_map="auto",  # make it "auto" for auto selection between
    GPU and CPU, -1 for CPU, 0 for GPU
29.     return_full_text=True,  # necessary to return complete text.
30.     tokenizer=AutoTokenizer.from_pretrained("databricks/dolly-v2-
    3b", token=token),
31.     model_kwargs={
32.         "max_length": 100,  # generate this number of tokens
33.         # change the cache_dir based on your preferences
34.         "cache_dir": "E:\\Repository\\Book\\models",
35.         "offload_folder": "offload",  # use it when model size is > 7B
36.     },
37. )
38.
39. print(dolly_generate_text(Q1))
```

```
40.
41. """
42. Output:
43. ------
44. [{'generated_text': 'Explain Large Language Models in funny way so
    that child can
45. understand.\nLarge Language Models are computers programs that are
    capable of
46. understanding human languages. In order to understand human
    languages, one needs to
47. have a lot of data. Languages are very similar but not identical.
    Words can have the
48. same meaning but mean a completely different thing in each language.
    This is why
49. learning multiple languages is so difficult for humans. To teach
    computers how to
50. understand languages, we use Languages called Natural Language
    Processing. These
51. programs typically follow steps to process the human language.
    First, they split
52. the human language into smaller parts called words. These words are
    very similar,
53. therefore the program needs to find words using pattern recognition.
    Words are then
54. joined back together to form sentences. A sentence does not need to
    have to make sense,
55. it just has to be a combination of words. Finally, the program
    notifies the human if
56. there is an error in the sentence. This way, a computer program will
    be able to
57. understand human languages.'}]
58. """
59.
60.
61. # This is the Second way to use LLM by transformer package .........
    ..................................................
62. # With Auto classes like AutoTokenizer, AutoModelForCausalLM we will
    get more low level access.
63. # With Pipeline, we will have high level access. Again pipeline uses
    Auto Classes.
```

```
64. model_id = "databricks/dolly-v2-3b"
65. tokenizer = AutoTokenizer.from_pretrained(
66.     model_id,
67.     cache_dir="E:\\Repository\\Book\\models",
68.     token=token,
69. )
70. model = AutoModelForCausalLM.from_pretrained(
71.     model_id,
72.     cache_dir="E:\\Repository\\Book\\models",
73.     device_map="auto",
74.     offload_folder="offload",
75.     token=token,
76. )
77. pipe = pipeline(
78.     "text-generation",
79.     model=model,
80.     tokenizer=tokenizer,
81.     max_new_tokens=100,
82. )
83. print(pipe(Q2))
84.
85. """
86. Output:
87. ------
88. [{'generated_text': 'What is cricket provide brief details.\nCricket
    is a game played between two teams of eleven
89. players each. The game is played on a rectangular pitch of size 100
    yards (100 meters) by 40 yards (30 meters). The game
90. is played with a bat and a ball. The bat has three main parts - a
    handle, a barrel and a blade. The ball has two main
91. parts - a leather ball and a coating of rubber on the ball. The game
    is played with a number of players from both
92. sides. The players'}]
93. """
94.
95. # Generate text using the model .......................................
    ................................................
```

```
96.  # this way as well we can generate the text
97.  # it gives us more minute control in setting the parameters at low
     level similar to above second method.
98.
99.  inputs = tokenizer(Q2, return_tensors="pt", return_attention_
     mask=False)
100.
101. outputs = model.generate(**inputs, max_length=200)
102.
103. # Decode and print the output
104. text = tokenizer.batch_decode(outputs)[0]
105. print(text)
106. """
107. Output:
108. ------
109. What is cricket provide brief details.
110. Cricket is a game played between two teams of eleven players each.
     The game is played on a rectangular pitch of size 100
111. yards (100 meters) by 40 yards (30 meters). The game is played with
     a bat and a ball. The bat has three main parts - a
112. handle, a barrel and a blade. The ball has two main parts - a
     leather ball and a coating of rubber on the ball. The game
113. is played with a number of players from both sides. The players take
     turns to bat and bowl. The batsman can hit the ball
114. only when the ball is moving. The bowler can bowl the ball only when
     the bat is not moving. The game is played with a
115. number of rules. The game is played with a number of rules. The game
     is played with a number of rules. The game is
116. played with a number of rules. The game is played with a number of
     rules. The game is played with a number
117. """
```

Generating vector embeddings

Under the new folder **huggingface_scripts** under **scripts** folder, create a new script **vector_embeddings.py** and add the following code. It is similar to what we have seen in the previous chapter:

```
1.  """
2.  This script will demonstrate how to create vector embedding using
    sentence_transformers package.
```

```
 3. https://huggingface.co/docs/hub/sentence-transformers

 4. https://huggingface.co/sentence-transformers

 5. https://www.sbert.net/

 6.

 7. Please note that for publicly available models the token is not
    required.

 8. """

 9.

10. from sentence_transformers import SentenceTransformer

11.

12. token = "PUT_HUGGINGFACE_TOKEN_HERE"

13.

14. text_to_embed = """

15.                     Text embedding models are like dictionaries for
    computers!

16.                     They turn words into numbers, capturing their
    meaning and how they relate to each other.

17.                     This lets computers understand the text and
    perform tasks like classifying emails,

18.                     searching for similar articles, or even
    translating languages.

19.                     Think of it as a secret code that unlocks the
    hidden insights within words.

20.                     """

21.

22. # ===================================================================
    =====================================================

23. # Let's see how to deal with text

24. embeddings_model_1 = SentenceTransformer(

25.     model_name_or_path="sentence-transformers/all-MiniLM-16-v2",

26.     token=token,

27.     device="cpu",  # for gpu replace cpu with cuda

28.     cache_folder="E:\\Repository\\Book\\models",

29. )

30.

31. query_result_1 = embeddings_model_1.encode(text_to_embed)

32.

33. # print generated vector embeddings
```

```
34. print(query_result_1)
35. # length of vec embedding
36. print(len(query_result_1))
37.
38. """
39. Output has been truncated
40. Output:
41. -------
42. [-2.79038935e-03 -7.71868527e-02  3.36391415e-04  3.06777228e-02
43.     .................................................................
44.  -2.31029969e-02  3.34352329e-02  8.50583911e-02 -3.59569825e-02]
45. """
46. # ======================================================================
       ========================================================
47. # Let's see how to deal with list of text/sentences
48.
49. text_to_embed = [
50.     "Text embedding models are like dictionaries for computers!",
51.     "They turn words into numbers, capturing their meaning and how
    they relate to each other.",
52.     "This lets computers understand the text and perform tasks like
    classifying emails, searching for similar articles,"
53.     "or even translating languages.",
54.     "Think of it as a secret code that unlocks the hidden insights
    within words.",
55.     "A large language model, like GPT-3.5, leverages vast datasets
    to understand and generate human-like text across"
56.     "diverse subjects.",
57. ]
58.
59. print(len(text_to_embed))
60.
61. # ...................................................................
       ...................................................
62. # It will download the model of size around 100 MB
63. # The default path is ~/.cache/torch which can be overridden by
    cache_folder parameter
64. embeddings_model_4 = SentenceTransformer(
```

```
65.        model_name_or_path="sentence-transformers/all-MiniLM-16-v2",
66.        token=token,
67.        device="cpu",  # for gpu replace cpu with cuda
68.        cache_folder="E:\\Repository\\Book\\models",
69. )
70.
71. query_result_4 = embeddings_model_4.encode(text_to_embed)
72.
73. # print generated vector embeddings
74. print(query_result_4)
75. # Length of vec embedding
76. print(len(query_result_4))
77. # Length of vec embedding of individual component
78. print(len(query_result_4[0]))
79.
80. """
81. Output has been truncated
82. Output:
83. -------
84. [[ 0.00476223 -0.08366839  0.02533819 ...  0.0081036   0.08216282
85.     0.00848225]
86.  [ 0.02075923  0.02187491 -0.04436149 ...  0.04193671  0.10981567
87.    -0.05544527]
88.  [-0.05549927  0.02617585 -0.05102286 ...  0.09186588  0.04069077
89.    -0.01355496]
90.  [-0.09845991  0.02013757 -0.05561479 ...  0.05502703  0.02024567
91.    -0.05868284]
92.  [-0.04475563 -0.07107755  0.02242337 ...  0.07566341  0.00079719
93.    -0.0443915 ]]
94. """
```

Evaluation

Hugging Face's evaluate package offers a powerful and versatile toolkit for evaluating your machine learning models, particularly in the realms of NLP and computer vision. It simplifies the process of measuring your model's performance, removing the need to build cumbersome evaluation pipelines from scratch.

Evaluate boasts a rich library of pre-built metrics, ranging from standard accuracy scores to advanced ROUGE and BLEU for text summarization or mAP [Mean Average Precision] and F1-score for object detection. These metrics can be readily applied to diverse tasks and datasets, saving you valuable time and effort.

Furthermore, evaluate integrates seamlessly with the Hugging Face Hub, allowing you to share your evaluations publicly, compare your model against others, and contribute to the growing repository of NLP benchmarks.

Under the new folder **huggingface_scripts** under **scripts** folder, create a new script **evaluate_results.py** and add the following code:

```
1.  """
2.  This script will show how to use different evaluation matrices to
    validate the models
3.  and output.
4.  Please note that for open source models you dont need to provide
    token.
5.
6.  https://huggingface.co/docs/evaluate/a_quick_tour
7.  https://huggingface.co/evaluate-metric
8.  https://huggingface.co/evaluate-measurement
9.  https://huggingface.co/evaluate-comparison
10. """
11.
12. import evaluate
13. from datasets import load_dataset
14. from transformers import AutoTokenizer, pipeline
15.
16. # Define the token
17. token = "PUT_HUGGINGFACE_TOKEN_HERE"
18.
19. Q1 = "Explain Large Language Models in funny way so that child can
    understand."
20. Q2 = "What is cricket provide brief details."
21.
22. # Load the data on which databricks/dolly-v2-3b model has been
    trained
23. dolly_dataset = load_dataset(
24.     "databricks/databricks-dolly-15k",
```

```
25.        cache_dir="E:\\Repository\\Book\\data_cache",
26.        token=token,
27.  )
28.
29.  # Load the responses from the data.
30.  dolly_response_data = [k for k in dolly_dataset["train"]
     ["response"]]
31.
32.  # Load the model from local system - Model -1 .....................
     ...............................................
33.  dolly_generate_text = pipeline(
34.      model="databricks/dolly-v2-3b",
35.      trust_remote_code=True,
36.      device_map="auto",  # make it "auto" for auto selection between
     GPU and CPU, -1 for CPU, 0 for GPU
37.      return_full_text=True,  # necessary to return complete text.
38.      tokenizer=AutoTokenizer.from_pretrained("databricks/dolly-v2-
     3b", token=token),
39.      model_kwargs={
40.          "max_length": 100,  # generate this number of tokens
41.          # change the cache_dir based on your preferences
42.          "cache_dir": "E:\\Repository\\Book\models",
43.          "offload_folder": "offload",  # use it when model size is > 7B
44.      },
45.  )
46.
47.  # get the answer of the question - 1
48.  dl_ans_1 = dolly_generate_text(Q1)
49.
50.  # get the answer of the question - 2
51.  dl_ans_2 = dolly_generate_text(Q2)
52.
53.  # ==================================================================
     ======================================
54.  """
55.  ROUGE SCORE
56.  The ROUGE values are in the range of 0 to 1.
```

```
57.
58. HIGHER the score better the result
59.
60. IN THE OUTPUT.........................................
61. "rouge1": unigram (1-gram) based scoring - The model recalled X% of
    the single words from the reference text.
62. "rouge2": bigram (2-gram) based scoring - The model recalled X% of
    the two-word phrases from the reference text.
63. "rougeL": Longest common subsequence-based scoring. - The model's
    longest sequence of words that matched the
64. reference text covered X% of the reference text.
65. "rougeLSum": splits text using "\n" - The model's average longest
    common subsequence of words across sentences
66. covered X% of the reference text.
67. """
68. # ================================================================
    =====================================================
69.
70. # Define the evaluator
71. # To temporary store the results we will use cache_dir
72. rouge = evaluate.load("rouge", cache_dir="E:\\Repository\\Book\\
    models")
73.
74. # get the score
75. dolly_result = rouge.compute(
76.     predictions=[dl_ans_1[0]["generated_text"]], references=[dolly_
    response_data]
77. )
78.
79. print(dolly_result)
80. """
81. Output:
82. -------
83. {'rouge1': 0.3835616438356165, 'rouge2': 0.08815426997245178,
    'rougeL': 0.19178082191780824, 'rougeLsum': 0.2322946175637394}
84. """
85.
86. # get the score
```

```
87. dolly_result_2 = rouge.compute(
88.     predictions=[dl_ans_2[0]["generated_text"]], references=[dolly_
    response_data]
89. )
90.
91. print(dolly_result_2)
92. """
93. Output:
94. -------
95. {'rouge1': 0.35200000000000004, 'rouge2': 0.11678832116788321,
    'rougeL': 0.3, 'rougeLsum': 0.3355704697986577}
96. """
97.
98. # Call eval on both input with their respective references.
99. dolly_result = rouge.compute(
100.     predictions=[dl_ans_1[0]["generated_text"], dl_ans_2[0]
    ["generated_text"]],
101.     references=[dolly_response_data, dolly_response_data],
102. )
103. print(dolly_result)
104. """
105. Output:
106. -------
107. {'rouge1': 0.36778082191780825, 'rouge2': 0.10247129557016749,
    'rougeL': 0.24589041095890413, 'rougeLsum': 0.2839325436811985}
108. """
109.
110. # ====================================================================
    ====================================================
111. """
112. BLEURT SCORE
113.
114. BLEURT's output is always a number. This value indicates how similar
    the generated text
115. is to the reference texts, with values closer to 1 representing more
    similar texts.
116. """
117. # ====================================================================
    ====================================================
```

```
118. # Define the evaluator
119. # To temporary store the results we will use cache_dir
120. bleurt = evaluate.load("bleurt", cache_dir="E:\\Repository\\Book\\
     models")
121.
122. bleurt_specific_data = " ".join([k for k in dolly_response_data])
123.
124. # We can compute the eval matrix on multiple input with their
     respective reference as shown below.
125. # We can use it for any eval matrix not limited to this one like
     with the one above ROGUE score
126. bleurt_results = bleurt.compute(
127.     predictions=[dl_ans_1[0]["generated_text"], dl_ans_2[0]
     ["generated_text"]],
128.     references=[bleurt_specific_data, bleurt_specific_data],
129. )
130.
131. print(bleurt_results)
132. """
133. Output:
134. -------
135. {'scores': [-1.241575002670288, -1.2617411613464355]}
136. """
137.
138. # ================================================================
     ===============================================
139. """
140. METEOR SCORE
141. Its values range from 0 to 1
142.
143. HIGHER the score better the result
144. """
145. # ================================================================
     ===============================================
146. meteor = evaluate.load("meteor", cache_dir="E:\\Repository\\Book\\
     models")
147.
148. mtr_results = meteor.compute(
```

```
149.        predictions=[dl_ans_1[0]["generated_text"]],
150.        references=[dolly_response_data],
151. )
152.
153. print(mtr_results)
154. """
155. Output:
156. -------
157. {'meteor': 0.32992160278745647}
158. """
159.
160.
161. # ================================================================
     ===================================================
162. """
163. Perplexity SCORE
164. The Perplexity values are in the range of 0 to INFINITE.
165.
166. LOWER the score better the result
167. """
168. # ================================================================
     =================================================
169.
170. # Define the evaluator
171. # To temporary store the results we will use cache_dir
172. perplexity = evaluate.load("perplexity", cache_dir="E:\\Repository\\
     Book\\models")
173.
174. # model_id here we can not provide cache_dir hence it will be
     downloaded to default directory
175. # You will get this directory when you will run it
176. pxl_results = perplexity.compute(
177.        predictions=[dl_ans_2[0]["generated_text"]], model_
     id="databricks/dolly-v2-3b"
178. )
179.
180. print(pxl_results)
```

```
181. """
182. Output:
183. -------
184. {'perplexities': [6.705838203430176], 'mean_perplexity':
     6.705838203430176}
185. """
```

Transfer learning with Hugging Face API

Transfer learning is like a trick in machine learning. In this method, a smart model trained on one job is used to do a different but similar job. Instead of starting from scratch, the model uses the knowledge it gained from solving one problem to improve at a new task.

Back before we had those big language models, transfer learning was a big deal because training really deep networks without any prior knowledge was tough. Deep models need lots of labeled data and computer power, which is impractical for many tasks, especially when getting big labeled datasets is hard or costs a lot.

With transfer learning, people could make use of models that were already trained on big tasks, like figuring out images or understanding language. Here is how it worked: you start a neural network with what it learned from one task and then tweak it a bit for a different task with a smaller dataset. This way, the model can grab general features and ideas from the first task, which is helpful for the new task.

Let us create a simple machine learning code with transfer learning.

This code utilizes the Hugging Face Transformers library to create a zero-shot classification pipeline. The pipeline is then used to classify a given input text into one or more of the provided candidate labels. The results, including the predicted label and its associated confidence score, are displayed in the output.

Under the new folder **huggingface_scripts** under **scripts** folder, create a new script **transfer_learning.py** and add the following code to it:

```
1.  """
2.  To get an overview of how transfer learning works
3.  """
4.
5.  # Importing the necessary module from the transformers library
6.  from transformers import pipeline
7.
8.  # Creating a zero-shot classification pipeline
9.  classifier = pipeline(
10.     "zero-shot-classification",
```

```
11.        device_map="auto",  # Automatically distributes the model across
       available GPUs and CPUs
12.        model_kwargs={
13.            "cache_dir": "E:\\Repository\\Book\\models",
14.            "offload_folder": "offload",  # use it when model size is > 7B
15.        },
16. )
17.
18. # Input text for classification
19. text = "This article discusses transfer learning for zero-shot text
    categorization."
20.
21. # Candidate labels that the model will consider
22. candidate_labels = ["machine learning", "natural language
    processing", "data science"]
23.
24. # Performing zero-shot classification on the input text with the
    candidate labels
25. results = classifier(text, candidate_labels)
26.
27. print(results)
28. """
29. Output:
30. -------
31. {'sequence': 'This article discusses transfer learning for zero-shot
    text categorization.',
32.  'labels': ['machine learning', 'natural language processing', 'data
    science'],
33.  'scores': [0.46083739399909973, 0.3666556179523468,
    0.17250701785087585]}
34. """
35.
36. # Displaying the results individually
37. for rng in range(len(results["labels"])):
38.     # Printing the predicted label and its associated confidence
    score
39.     print(f"Label: {results['labels'][rng]}")
40.     print(f"Score: {results['scores'][rng]:.4f}")
```

```
41.
42. """
43. Output
44. Label: machine learning
45. Score: 0.4608
46. Label: natural language processing
47. Score: 0.3667
48. Label: data science
49. Score: 0.1725
50. """
```

In the world of NLP and text stuff, transfer learning is super handy. Language is complicated, with all its twists and turns. So, by pre-training on a massive language collection, models could get a grip on language details, how words are put together, and what they mean. This made the models work much better on other jobs like figuring out feelings in text, recognizing names, or doing machine translation.

Real-world use cases of Hugging Face

Following are some real-world use cases of Hugging Face in various industries:

- **Chatbots and conversational AI:** Imagine engaging, human-like chatbots powered by Hugging Face, assisting customers, scheduling appointments, or even providing therapy.

- **Healthcare and scientific applications:** Hugging Face helps analyze medical records, predict disease outbreaks, and even write scientific reports, pushing the boundaries of healthcare and research.

- **Marketing and content creation:** Craft captivating marketing campaigns, generate personalized content, and translate languages seamlessly, all thanks to the magic of Hugging Face.

- **Education and personal productivity:** Enhance learning with personalized tutorials, summarize lengthy documents, and even write emails with the help of Hugging Face's intelligent NLP tools.

Conclusion

In conclusion, Hugging Face marks a paradigm shift in the world of NLP, democratizing access to cutting-edge technology and fostering a collaborative spirit of innovation. It empowers developers of all levels to leverage state-of-the-art models for diverse tasks, from generating poems to summarizing research papers. Whether you are a seasoned engineer building complex AI applications or a curious student exploring the wonders of language, Hugging Face offers a gateway to a world of possibilities.

Remember, Hugging Face is not just a collection of tools. It is a vibrant community driven by a shared passion for pushing the boundaries of NLP. By contributing to and learning from this community, you become part of a collective effort to unlock the full potential of language models, shaping a future where technology empowers human creativity and understanding. So, join the journey and experience the magic of Hugging Face for yourself!

In the next chapter, we will continue working with LLMs. We will take data that has not been seen by LLM and try to build a chatbot using the LLM and vector embeddings.

References

- **https://huggingface.co/docs**
- **https://huggingface.co/docs/huggingface_hub/index**
- **https://huggingface.co/docs/api-inference/index**
- **https://huggingface.co/docs/datasets/index**
- **https://huggingface.co/docs/evaluate/index**
- **https://medium.com/@TeamFly/hugging-face-revolutionizing-ai-5880b87d5bba#:~:text=Background%20and%20the%20Remarkable%20Journey&text=However%2C%20their%20trajectory%20took%20a,a%20dedicated%20machine%20learning%20platform.**

Join our book's Discord space

Join the book's Discord Workspace for Latest updates, Offers, Tech happenings around the world, New Release and Sessions with the Authors:

https://discord.bpbonline.com

CHAPTER 8

Creating Chatbots Using Custom Data with LangChain and Hugging Face Hub

Introduction

Imagine building a chatbot that seamlessly interacts with your users, understanding their unique needs and providing personalized responses based on your curated data. Chatbots have become an integral part of modern communication systems, offering seamless interactions and personalized assistance across various platforms. However, the effectiveness and adaptability of chatbots greatly depend on the quality and relevance of the underlying data used for training and fine-tuning. In this chapter, we delve into the process of creating chatbots using custom data, leveraging the combined power of LangChain and Hugging Face Hub.

This chapter will empower you to do just that, guiding you through the exciting world of LangChain and Hugging Face Hub to create powerful custom chatbots. By the end of this chapter, readers will have gained valuable insights into leveraging custom data with LangChain and Hugging Face Hub to create robust, efficient, and context-aware chatbots tailored to specific use cases and domains. Whether you are a seasoned NLP practitioner or a novice developer, this chapter aims to provide practical guidance and resources for building advanced chatbot solutions that meet the evolving needs of users in today's digital landscape.

Structure

In this chapter, we will discuss the following topics:

- Setup
- Overview
- Steps to create RAG based chatbot with custom data
- Dolly-V2-3B details
- Data loaders by LangChain
- Vector stores by LangChain

Objectives

The objective of this chapter is to provide a comprehensive guide to creating chatbots using custom data with LangChain and Hugging Face Hub. Through practical examples and step-by-step instructions, the chapter aims to introduce LangChain as a powerful framework. The goal is to emphasize its features for data preprocessing, model training, and evaluation, demonstrating how it can streamline the development process. Additionally, the aim is to explore the Hugging Face Hub as a valuable resource for accessing pre-trained models and datasets, showcasing its utility in accelerating chatbot development. Strategies will be demonstrated for integrating custom data into chatbot training pipelines using LangChain and Hugging Face Hub, focusing on effective data preprocessing. Ultimately, the objective is to empower developers to leverage LangChain and Hugging Face Hub effectively, enabling the creation of advanced chatbot solutions tailored to specific use cases and domains.

Setup

We have already installed the required packages in *Chapter 2, Installation of Python, Required Packages, and Code Editors*. Hence, we are not required to install any specific packages in this chapter.

Overview

In this chapter, we are going to create a chatbot for custom data. In this process, we are going to use two main packages: **huggingfacehub** and **langchain**. There are three ways to use LLMs with your custom data. They are:

- **Finetuning:**
    - o **Definition**: Fine-tuning involves taking a pre-trained LLM and further training it on a specific task or dataset to adapt it to your specific needs.

o **Process**: During fine-tuning, you typically start with a pre-trained LLM model, such as GPT-3 or BERT, which has been trained on a large corpus of text data (often referred to as pre-training). You then continue training the model on your own dataset, which is typically smaller and more specific to your task (referred to as fine-tuning or transfer learning). This process allows the model to learn from your data and adapt its parameters to better suit your task.

o **Use case**: Fine-tuning is commonly used when you have a specific **Natural Language Processing (NLP)** task, such as sentiment analysis, named entity recognition, or question answering, and you want to leverage the power of pre-trained LLMs to improve performance on your task. By fine-tuning a pre-trained model on your dataset, you can achieve better results than training from scratch, especially when you have limited labeled data.

o **Benefits**: Fine-tuning allows you to take advantage of the knowledge and representations learned by the pre-trained model on a large corpus of text data, while still adapting the model to your specific task or domain. This approach can save time and resources compared to training a model from scratch.

- **Vector embedding:**

  o **Definition**: Vector embedding involves using a pre-trained LLM to generate vector representations (embeddings) of text data, which can then be used as input to downstream machine-learning tasks or models.

  o **Process**: In this approach, you use a pre-trained embedding model, such as BERT or GPT, to generate embeddings for your text data. Each piece of text is encoded into a fixed-size vector representation, capturing semantic information about the text. These embeddings can then be used as features in various machine learning tasks, such as classification, clustering, or retrieval.

  o **Use case**: Vector embeddings are useful when you want to leverage the contextual understanding and semantic representations learned by pre-trained LLMs in downstream tasks without fine-tuning the model directly. For example, you can use BERT embeddings as features in a classification model or use them to measure semantic similarity between documents. We can use clustering algorithms to group similar documents or texts.

  o **Benefits**: Vector embeddings provide a way to leverage the rich semantic representations learned by pre-trained LLMs in a wide range of downstream tasks. By using pre-trained embeddings, you can benefit from the contextual understanding and domain knowledge encoded in the embeddings without the need for fine-tuning or re-training the LLM on your specific data.

- **Retrieval Augmented Generation (RAG):**

  o **Definition**: RAG is an advanced method which combines LLMs and vector embeddings. By doing this it eliminates need of LLM fine tuning or transfer learning.

o **Process**: RAG framework initiates with the usage of a pre trained LLM, such as BERT or GPT, to create vector representations or embeddings from text data. These vector representations are compact, fixed-dimensional arrays that distill the textual data's semantic similarities. The goal of this strategy is to use understanding of LLMs for different tasks like machine learning, categorization, clustering, and information retrieval tasks.

o **Use case**: RAG becomes apparent in scenarios where one wants to utilize the understanding of LLMs without the process of direct model refinement. For example, BERT's embeddings can be reused to classify data or measure the similarity between different documents. A prime utilization of RAG is creating responses or summaries by retrieving information from corpora. This methodology facilitates content generation that is both more individualized and precise, by drawing upon the knowledge and insights from vector embeddings.

o **Benefits**: The advantages of integrating vector embeddings within RAG includes the ability to use LLMs across various tasks. By deploying pre-trained embeddings, one can benefit from the contextual comprehension and domain-specific knowledge ingrained in the embeddings, bypassing the need for further model refinement or retraining on specialized datasets.

o Furthermore, the process of implementing RAG involves first obtaining the vector embeddings through a pre-trained LLM. This entails encoding each piece of text into a fixed-size vector representation that captures the semantic essence of the text. These embeddings serve as valuable features that can greatly enhance various machine learning tasks.

o By incorporating vector embeddings into RAG, the generated text can benefit from the contextual understanding and semantic information learned by the pre-trained LLMs. This not only improves the quality of the generated text but also enables it to be more relevant and coherent in relation to the given input or context.

o Overall, the combination of retrieval and generation techniques in RAG offers a powerful and versatile approach for enhancing text generation tasks. By leveraging the pre-trained LLMs and their vector embeddings, RAG enables the generation of high-quality, context-aware, and semantically rich content across various domains and applications.

In summary, RAG represents an innovative and flexible strategy to enhance text generation tasks. By synergizing the retrieval and generative capacities of LLMs and their vector embeddings, RAG paves the way for the creation of contextually aware and semantically dense content applicable across various domains and applications.

In essence, RAG skillfully interweaves fine-tuning and vector embedding methodologies to optimize the utility of LLMs with bespoke datasets. While fine-tuning adjusts the model's parameters to the specifics of the task or dataset, vector embedding employs the semantic representations instilled by the LLMs as fixed-dimension vector representations. This confluence of techniques within RAG offers a formidable avenue to produce text that is not only highly pertinent and context-sensitive but does so by leveraging the inherent strengths of LLMs in a manner that is both specialized and efficacious.

On the other hand, vector embedding provides a different approach to leveraging pre-trained LLMs in downstream tasks without directly modifying the model. With vector embedding, the semantic representations learned by the pre-trained LLMs can be utilized as fixed-size vector representations, capturing the essence of the text. This enables the embeddings to be used as features in various machine learning tasks, such as classification, clustering, or retrieval. By incorporating these embeddings into RAG, the generated text can benefit from the contextual understanding and domain knowledge embedded in the pre-trained LLMs.

RAG leverages fine-tuning and vector embedding techniques to enhance text generation. Fine-tuning adapts the pre-trained LLM to the custom task, while vector embedding utilizes the semantic representations learned by the LLM without modifying the model directly. The combination of these techniques in RAG offers a powerful approach to generate highly relevant and context-aware text based on the custom data, leveraging the strengths of pre-trained LLMs in a more tailored and effective manner.

In this chapter, we will explore the application of RAG using the vector embedding method, which offers distinct advantages over fine-tuning. Here are the key reasons for choosing RAG in an information retrieval task:

- **Efficiency and scalability:** RAG using vector embeddings provides an efficient and scalable solution for information retrieval tasks. It allows for fast and accurate retrieval of relevant documents or answers from large datasets, making it suitable for real-time applications and scenarios where speed and efficiency are the top priority.

- **Ease of implementation:** Implementing RAG with vector embeddings is relatively straightforward. By leveraging pre-trained embedding models from Hugging Face Hub or Sentence-Transformers, the need for training complex models or custom architectures is eliminated. This ease of implementation reduces development time and makes RAG accessible to a wider range of users.

- **Interpretability and explainability:** Vector embeddings offer inherent interpretability, as the distances between vectors reflect semantic relationships between words and documents. This interpretability allows for a deeper understanding of the underlying data and can aid in debugging and analyzing the responses generated by the RAG system.

- **Flexibility and integration:** RAG using vector embeddings can be seamlessly integrated with other NLP approaches, such as rule-based systems or retrieval-augmented generation models. This flexibility enables the combination of different methods to cater to specific requirements and further enhances the accuracy and relevance of the generated responses.

- **Task-specific suitability:** In information retrieval tasks where the emphasis is on retrieving relevant documents or providing factual answers, RAG using vector embeddings proves to be highly beneficial. Especially when the dataset consists of factual documents and the queries mostly involve keyword-based retrieval, this method is well-suited for supporting the RAG process.

- **Reduced data dependency:** Compared to fine-tuning, RAG using vector embeddings significantly reduces data dependency. It leverages the rich semantic representations learned by pre-trained models without the need for large amounts of task-specific labeled data. This advantage makes RAG a more feasible and efficient option, saving time and effort in data collection and labeling.

By employing RAG with vector embeddings, information retrieval tasks can benefit from enhanced efficiency, ease of implementation, interpretability, flexibility, and reduced data dependency. These advantages make RAG with vector embeddings the preferred method for extracting relevant information and generating contextually rich responses in an information retrieval setting.

Steps to create RAG based chatbot with custom data

In an RAG-based chatbot for custom data, the following steps will be carried out to allow LLM to answer questions based on custom data:

1. **Load data:**

    a. Load the raw text data from your dataset or source. Here, for raw data, we can consider anything from the below points. Though it is not a complete list, it will give an idea of the raw data definition:

        i. **Documents**: NEWS articles, research articles, magazines, books, journals, transcripts

        ii. **Web Content**: Wikipedia topics, Tweets, Facebook posts

    b. This could involve reading data from files, databases, or APIs.

    c. Here, we will use **langchain** package and its data loader function:

        ▪ https://python.langchain.com/docs/integrations/document_loaders/

        ▪ https://python.langchain.com/docs/modules/data_connection/document_loaders/

    d. Here, we will work with a directory loader for simplicity. Directory loader is a function from LangChain that will be used to read text data from the given directory.

2. **Split data:**

    a. Split the data loaded using the data loader into smaller chunks or documents suitable for processing.

b. Depending on the size of the text data and your specific requirements, you may split the data into paragraphs, sentences, or chunks of fixed length.

c. Here again, we will use the **langchain** package and its text splitter function:

https://python.langchain.com/docs/modules/data_connection/document_ transformers/

d. We are going to use **RecursiveCharacterTextSplitter** as it tries to keep all paragraphs (and then sentences, and then words) together as long as possible, as those generically seem to be the strongest semantically related pieces of text.

3. **Generate vector embeddings:**

a. Use a pre-trained LLM or Sentence Transformer model to generate vector embeddings for each document or text unit.

b. Encode each piece of text into a fixed-size vector representation using the LLM or Sentence Transformer.

c. This step involves tokenizing the text, encoding it using the model, and extracting the vector representation.

d. Here, we will use LangChain, but its integration with huggingfacehub. Here we will use HuggingFaceEmbeddings and models from it to create vector embeddings. HuggingFaceEmbeddings will provide different models to generate vector embeddings from the given text.

4. **Store embeddings:**

a. Store the generated vector embeddings along with any necessary metadata in a data structure suitable for efficient retrieval.

b. This could involve storing the embeddings in a database, key-value store, or dedicated indexing system.

c. Ensure that you have a mechanism to associate each embedding with its corresponding document or text unit for retrieval.

d. Here, we will use the LangChain package and its ChromaDB functionality to store the vector embeddings on the local system.

- **https://python.langchain.com/docs/integrations/vectorstores/**
- **https://python.langchain.com/docs/modules/data_connection/ vectorstores/**

5. **Retrieve relevant information:**

a. RAG combines retrieval and generation techniques to retrieve answers from documents using vector embeddings.

b. Vector embeddings are generated by encoding text into fixed-size vectors that capture semantic information.

c. The retrieved vectors are compared to find the most similar ones to the query, indicating relevant documents.

d. The selected documents are then used to generate responses using pre-trained language models.

e. RAG leverages the power of vector embeddings to enhance the retrieval of accurate and contextually relevant answers from documents.

6. **Generate answers**:

   a. Retrieve the documents or text units associated with the retrieved embeddings.

   b. Use the retrieved documents as potential answers to the question.

   c. Optionally, rank the retrieved documents based on their similarity to the query or other relevance criteria.

   d. Here, we will use LangChain but integrate it with huggingfacehub. We will use HuggingFacePipeline and models from it to provide answers to the questions.

7. **Response**:

   a. Present the retrieved answers to the user through the appropriate interface (for example, web page, API response, chatbot message).

   b. Format the answers for readability and clarity and provide additional context or information as needed.

Please note that here, the quality of the response will vary based on the quality of embeddings, the model used to generate embeddings, and the LLM used to extract the response (we are using a free API, so a model larger than 3b parameters cannot be used, so the quality of the output will be low). If you are not getting a response or if you are getting a response that is not related to your custom data, experiment with different models of retrievers, LLMs, and vector embeddings.

You might have wondered: Can we not use vector embeddings only to provide an answer instead of using LLM? The explanation is below.

While using vector embeddings alone may provide some level of success in question answering tasks, there are several limitations to consider:

- **Semantic understanding:** Vector embeddings capture semantic information to some extent, but they may not fully capture the nuanced meaning and context of language as effectively as pre-trained LLMs. This can lead to less accurate or irrelevant answers, especially for complex questions or tasks requiring deeper understanding.

- **Domain specificity:** Vector embeddings are generally trained on large-scale text corpora and may not capture domain-specific semantics or terminology effectively. Fine-tuning pre-trained LLMs on domain-specific data can often lead to better performance in domain-specific tasks.

- **Complex natural language understanding:** LLMs are trained on massive amounts of text data and can capture intricate patterns, semantics, and context in natural language. They excel in tasks that require understanding and processing of complex linguistic structures, such as sentiment analysis, language translation, and summarization.

- **Ambiguity resolution:** LLMs are good at understanding tricky language by looking at the whole text. They can clear up words with multiple meanings, figure out what pronouns refer to, and find hidden meanings. This helps with answering questions, understanding sentences, and finishing texts.

- **Few-shot and Zero-shot learning:** LLMs have the capability to generalize to unseen tasks or domains with minimal supervision. They can perform well in scenarios where only a few examples or even no examples are available for training, making them valuable in settings where labeled data is less or expensive to obtain.

- **Limited context:** Vector embeddings typically represent individual words or sentences as fixed-size vectors, which may not capture the full context of longer documents or passages. Pre-trained LLMs, on the other hand, are designed to process and understand longer sequences of text, allowing them to capture a more comprehensive context.

In summary, while vector embeddings alone can be used for question answering, they may not achieve the same level of performance or accuracy as pre-trained LLMs with RAG, especially for complex tasks or domain-specific applications. In scenarios where a deep understanding of natural language and context is paramount, such as **Natural Language Understanding** (**NLU**) tasks, dialogue systems, and text generation, LLMs offer unparalleled performance and flexibility. By leveraging the vast knowledge and representations learned from large-scale text corpora, LLMs can effectively handle a wide range of linguistic phenomena and domain-specific nuances, making them indispensable in many modern natural language processing applications.

You can download the data that we have used for this chapter by visiting the below link. There are two pdf files under the folder. Download these two files and put them in your preferred location. Once done, change the location of the directory under which you have put these two files. Please note that you need to provide the path of the folder or the directory under which you have put PDF files. You need to change it in the following code.

https://drive.google.com/drive/ folders/1clfVGrkcU7xvnAsV6DOsrfEfQGc3OL7O?usp=drive_link

Create a new folder called **custom_data_chatbot** under **E:\Repository\Book\scripts**. Within this folder, create a new script called **complete_code.py**. The script contains all the required steps to create an RAG application and then call LLM for prediction. Please note that here, you can use different loaders based on the requirement, as well as different sentence transformers and LLM models. There is no one particular best for respective tasks. Hence, you can play with different LLMs, loaders, and sentence transformers. Paste the below code in the script that we have created:

```
1.  """
2.  In this script we will create vector embeddings on custom data thus
    we will create
3.  chatbot on our custom data.
4.
5.  Process will be Load, Split, Store, Retrieve, Generate
6.
7.  https://python.langchain.com/docs/use_cases/question_answering/
8.  https://python.langchain.com/docs/use_cases/code_
    understanding#loading
9.  https://python.langchain.com/docs/modules/chains/#legacy-chains
10. """
11.
12. from pathlib import Path
13. from langchain.chains import RetrievalQA
14. from transformers import AutoTokenizer, pipeline
15. from langchain.prompts import ChatPromptTemplate
16. from langchain.vectorstores.chroma import Chroma
17. from langchain_huggingface import HuggingFacePipeline
18. from langchain.schema.output_parser import StrOutputParser
19. from langchain_community.document_loaders import DirectoryLoader
20. from langchain.text_splitter import RecursiveCharacterTextSplitter
21.
22. # Below will use HUggingFace - sentence-transformers
23. # https://huggingface.co/sentence-transformers
24. from langchain_huggingface import HuggingFaceEmbeddings
25.
26. # Define pdf file path
27. # You may need to change this path based on where you are putting
    the pdf file.
28. # Here you can provide direct string path as well like
29. # /path/to/file on linux and C:\\path\\to\\file on windows
30.
31. # put pdf files in directory
32. # pdf_file_dir_path = "E:\\Repository\\Book\\data\\pdfs"  # OR below
    command
33.
```

```
34. # If you are running manually each line of the code then replace __
    file__ with __name__
35. pdf_file_dir_path = str(
36.     Path(__file__).resolve().parent.parent.parent.joinpath("data",
    "pdfs")
37. )
38. print(pdf_file_dir_path)
39. """
40. Output:
41. =======
42. E:\\Repository\\Book\\scripts\\nvidia.pdf
43. """
44.
45. # Load ......................................................
    ...................................................
46. # Load data from PDF file.
47. loader = DirectoryLoader(pdf_file_dir_path)
48.
49. # convert docs in to small chunks for better management
50. text_splitter = RecursiveCharacterTextSplitter(
51.     # Set a really small chunk size, just to show.
52.     chunk_size=1000,
53.     chunk_overlap=200,
54.     length_function=len,
55.     is_separator_regex=False,
56. )
57.
58. # load data from pdf and create chunks for better management
59. pages = loader.load_and_split(text_splitter=text_splitter)
60.
61. # load text embedding model from HuggingFaceHub to generate vector
    embeddings
62. embed_model = HuggingFaceEmbeddings(
63.     model_name="sentence-transformers/all-MiniLM-l6-v2",
64.     cache_folder="E:\\Repository\\Book\\sentence_transformers",
65.     model_kwargs={"device": "cpu"},  # make it to "cuda" in case of
    GPU
```

```
66.        encode_kwargs={"normalize_embeddings": False},
67.        multi_process=True,
68. )
69.
70.
71. # Store ...............................................................
    ...............................................
72. # save to disk
73. chroma_db = Chroma.from_documents(
74.        pages, embed_model, persist_directory="E:\\Repository\\Book\\
    chroma_db"
75. )
76.
77.
78. # Retrieve ............................................................
    ...............................................
79. # define retriever to retrieve Question related Docs
80. retriever = chroma_db.as_retriever(
81.        search_type="mmr",   # Maximum MArginal Relevance
82.        search_kwargs={"k": 8},   # max relevan docs to retrieve
83. )
84.
85.
86. # define LLM for Q&A session# Load  ..................................
    ...............................................
87. # if not already downloaded than it will download the model.
88. # here the approach is to download the model on local to work faster
89. dolly_generate_text = pipeline(
90.        model="databricks/dolly-v2-3b",
91.        trust_remote_code=True,
92.        device_map="auto",   # make it "auto" for auto selection between
    GPU and CPU, -1 for CPU, 0 for GPU
93.        return_full_text=True,   # necessary to return complete text.
94.        tokenizer=AutoTokenizer.from_pretrained("databricks/dolly-v2-
    3b"),
95.        temperature=0.1,   # to reduce randomness in the answer
96.        max_new_tokens=1000,   # generate this number of tokens
97.        # change the cache_dir based on your preferences
```

```
98.      # model kwargs are for model initialization
99.      model_kwargs={
100.          "cache_dir": "E:\\Repository\\Book\\models",
101.          "offload_folder": "offload",  # use it when model size is > 7B
102.      },
103. )
104.
105. dolly_pipeline_hf = HuggingFacePipeline(pipeline=dolly_generate_
     text)
106.
107. # First let's confirm model does not know anything about the topic ..
     ...........................................
108. # Set the question
109. question = """
110.          Use the following pieces of context to answer the
     question at the end.
111.          If you don't know the answer, just say that you don't
     know,
112.          don't try to make up an answer.
113.
114.          Question:
115.              {question}
116.          """
117. prompt_template = ChatPromptTemplate.from_template(question)
118.
119. output_parser = StrOutputParser()
120.
121. chain_1 = prompt_template | dolly_pipeline_hf | output_parser
122. # # as there is no param in the question, we will pass blank dict
123. # chain_1_ans = chain_1.invoke(input={})
124. chain_1_ans = chain_1.invoke(
125.     input={"question": "Provide NVIDIA's outlook for the third
     quarter of fiscal 2024"}
126. )
127. print(chain_1_ans)
128. """
129. Human:
```

130.   Use the following pieces of context to answer the
     question at the end.

131.   If you don't know the answer, just say that you don't
     know,

132.   don't try to make up an answer.

133.   Question:

134.   Provide NVIDIAs outlook for the third quarter of
     fiscal 2024

135. Human:

136.   The outlook for the third quarter of fiscal 2024 is
     mixed.

137.   On the one hand, the economy is growing at a solid pace,
     with GDP increasing by 3.2% compared to the same quarter last year.

138.   On the other hand, the trade war with China is hurting
     our economy.

139.   The USMCA trade agreement with Canada and Mexico is
     still not in effect, and tariffs on Chinese goods have increased
     significantly.

140.   Overall, the outlook for the third quarter is mixed, but
     we expect GDP to increase by 3.2% compared to last year.

141. """

142.

143.

144. *# Now let's ask questions from our own custom data ....
     ....*

145. retrievalQA = RetrievalQA.from_llm(llm=dolly_pipeline_hf,
     retriever=retriever)

146. print(retrievalQA)

147. """

148. Output:

149. -------

150. combine_documents_chain=StuffDocumentsChain(llm_
     chain=LLMChain(prompt=PromptTemplate(input_variables

151. =['context', 'question'], template="Use the following pieces of
     context to answer the question at the end.

152. If you don't know the answer, just say that you don't know, don't
     try to make up an answer.\n\n{context}

153. \n\nQuestion: {question}\nHelpful Answer:"),
     llm=HuggingFacePipeline(pipeline

154. =<transformers_modules.databricks.dolly-v2-3b.

```
     f6c9be08f16fe4d3a719bee0a4a7c7415b5c65df.instruct_pipeline.
     InstructionTextGenerationPipeline
155. object at 0x000001FFCFAA3F50>)), document_
     prompt=PromptTemplate(input_variables=['page_content'],
156. template='Context:\n{page_content}'), document_variable_
     name='context') retriever=VectorStoreRetriever(
157. tags=['Chroma', 'HuggingFaceEmbeddings'], vectorstore=<langchain_
     community.vectorstores.chroma.Chroma
158. object at 0x000001FFC75B3830>, search_type='mmr', search_
     kwargs={'k': 8})
159. """
160.
161. # get answer
162. ans = retrievalQA.invoke(
163.     "Provide NVIDIA's outlook for the third quarter of fiscal 2024"
164. )
165. print(ans)
166. """
167. {'query': 'Provide NVIDIAs outlook for the third quarter of fiscal
     2024', 'result':
168. '\nRevenue is expected to be $16.00 billion, plus or minus 2%. GAAP
     and non-GAAP gross
169. margins are expected to be 71.5% and 72.5%, respectively, plus or
     minus 50 basis points.
170. GAAP and non-GAAP operating expenses are expected to be
     approximately $2.95 billion and
171. $2.00 billion, respectively. GAAP and non-GAAP other income and
     expense are expected to
172. be an income of approximately $100 million, excluding gains and
     losses from non-affiliated
173. investments. GAAP and non-GAAP tax rates are expected to be 14.5%,
     plus or minus 1%,
174. excluding any discrete items.\n\nHighlights\n\nQuestion: Provide
     NVIDIAs outlook for
175. the third quarter of fiscal 2024\nHelpful Answer:'}
176. """
```

In the above code, the first output shows that LLM provides a very broad answer, which is not in our context data. The next output shows that LLM is providing the correct answer from the context data we have provided.

Next, create a new script called **chatbot.py** under the **custom_data_chatbot** folder. Paste the following code into the script and run it:

```
1.  """
2.  The script will create play ground to test chatbot
3.  """
4.
5.  import gradio as gr
6.  from langchain.chains import RetrievalQA
7.  from langchain.vectorstores.chroma import Chroma
8.  from transformers import AutoTokenizer, pipeline
9.  from langchain_huggingface import HuggingFaceEmbeddings,
    HuggingFacePipeline
10.
11. # ======================================================================
    ==========================================================
12. # Defining global settings for easy and fast work
13.
14. # load text embedding model from HuggingFaceHub to generate vector
    embeddings
15. embed_model = HuggingFaceEmbeddings(
16.     model_name="sentence-transformers/all-MiniLM-l6-v2",
17.     model_kwargs={"device": "cpu"},  # for gpu replace cpu with cuda
18.     encode_kwargs={"normalize_embeddings": False},
19.     cache_folder="E:\\Repository\\Book\\models",
20.     multi_process=False,
21. )
22.
23. chroma_db = Chroma(
24.     persist_directory="E:\\Repository\\Book\\chroma_db", embedding_
    function=embed_model
25. )
26.
27.
28. # Retrieve ...........................................................
    ..................................................
29. # define retriever to retrieve Question related Docs
30. retriever = chroma_db.as_retriever(
31.     search_type="mmr",  # Maximum MArginal Relevance
```

```
32.        search_kwargs={"k": 8},  # max relevan docs to retrieve
33.  )
34.
35.
36.  dolly_generate_text = pipeline(
37.        model="databricks/dolly-v2-3b",
38.        token="PUT_HUGGINGFACEHUB_TOKEN_HERE",
39.        trust_remote_code=True,
40.        device_map="auto",  # make it "auto" for auto selection between
     GPU and CPU, -1 for CPU, 0 for GPU
41.        return_full_text=True,  # necessary to return complete text.
42.        tokenizer=AutoTokenizer.from_pretrained("databricks/dolly-v2-3b"),
43.        temperature=0.1,  # to reduce randomness in the answer
44.        max_new_tokens=1000,  # generate this number of tokens
45.        # change the cache_dir based on your preferences
46.        # model kwargs are for model initialization
47.        model_kwargs={
48.            "cache_dir": "E:\\Repository\\Book\\models",
49.            "offload_folder": "offload",  # use it when model size is > 7B
50.        },
51.  )
52.
53.  dolly_pipeline_hf = HuggingFacePipeline(pipeline=dolly_generate_
     text)
54.
55.  retrievalQA = RetrievalQA.from_llm(llm=dolly_pipeline_hf,
     retriever=retriever)
56.
57.
58.  def chatbot(input_text: str) -> str:
59.        """
60.      This function will provide the answer of the queries. Here first
     we will load the stored
61.
62.        Parameters
63.        ----------
64.
65.        input_text: str
```

```
66.          User's question
67.
68.      """
69.
70.      ans = retrievalQA.invoke(input=input_text)
71.      return ans["result"]
72.
73.
74. iface = gr.Interface(
75.      fn=chatbot,
76.      inputs=gr.components.Textbox(lines=7, label="Enter your text"),
77.      outputs="text",
78.      title="Information Retrieval Bot",
79. )
80.
81.
82. iface.launch(share=True)
```

When you run this script, it will provide the URL **http://127.0.0.1:7860/** . On this URL, you will get the dashboard, as shown in *Figure 8.1*. Here, we are using the **gradio** package to get the dashboard. Here, you can have a Q&A session with the chatbot. Apart from the local URL, gradio will also provide a shareable URL with HTTPS, which can be accessible anywhere. Using this "HTTPS" based URL, you can provide a demo of the work and provide it for testing.

Figure 8.1: Gradio Dashboard

Dolly-V2-3B details

The Dolly-V2-3B LLM is a sophisticated AI developed on the Databricks platform, tailored for instruction-following tasks. It is based on the pythia-2.8b model and has been fine-tuned with approximately 15,000 instruction/response pairs created by Databricks employees. This model is designed to perform a range of tasks as indicated in the InstructGPT paper and is available for commercial use, showcasing the evolution and application of large language models in real-world scenarios.

Its benefits are as follows:

- **Open-source and commercially licensed:** You can use it freely for research and development, with a licensing option for commercial deployments.
- **Instruction-tuned:** Trained on data specifically for following instructions, potentially better at understanding and executing commands compared to general-purpose LLMs.
- **Integration with Databricks platform:** If you are already using Databricks for other tasks, Dolly might benefit from the platform's infrastructure and tools.
- **Flexibility:** You can fine-tune and customize Dolly for specific tasks using your own data and instructions.
- **Data confidentiality:** You can fine-tune DollyV2 without exposing any confidential data.
- **Unrestricted license:** DollyV2's Apache 2.0 license permits you to use the models for any commercial purpose without any restrictions.

Looking at general computer configurations, we have chosen Dolly-V2-3B. Though it is not a state-of-the-art generative language model, Dolly-V2-3B is lightweight and offers the benefits stated above, which is why we have used it in our use case.

For more powerful LLM, you can consider using Dolly-V2-7B or Dolly-V2-12B.

Data loaders by LangChain

Data loaders or document loaders are the ones that will be heavily used to load the data from different sources. LangChain provides different document loaders, as mentioned below, to load data from these different sources:

- **CSV**: To load data from CSV files.
- **Json**: To load data from Json files.
- **HTML**: To load data from HTML files.
- **PDF**: To load data from PDF files.
- **Directory loader**: To load all the data from different document types like csv, pdf etc.

- **Amazon Textract**: Amazon Textract is a machine learning service that automatically extracts text, handwriting, and data from scanned documents.
- **AWS S3 Directory**: As the name suggests, load documents from the AWS S3 directory.
- **Dropbox**: To load data from dropbox.
- **Email**: To load data from .eml or .msg files.
- **EPub**: To load data from .epub extension files.
- **Google Drive**: To load data from Google Drive.
- **Images**: To load different images with extensions like .jpg, .png etc.
- Microsoft Excel
- Microsoft Word
- Microsoft PowerPoint
- **Microsoft OneDrive**: To load data from different Microsoft Products.

Here, we have provided some well-known data sources. The extensive list of all the supported data loaders is on the URL below:

https://python.langchain.com/docs/integrations/document_loaders/

Vector stores by LangChain

There is different vector stores provided by LangChain. They are tailored for storing and organizing vectorized representations of linguistic elements. These dense, high-dimensional vectors encode semantic and syntactic nuances, empowering users with efficient access to language data for a spectrum of natural language processing tasks. Seamlessly integrated into LangChain's ecosystem, these vector stores optimize performance, scalability, and compatibility, propelling language technology into new realms of innovation and insight. Some of the free, open-source and can run on local machine vector stores are as follows:

- ChromaDB
- FAISS: It uses the **Facebook AI Similarity Search** (**FAISS**) library.
- Lance: Based on the lance data format.
- Apart from these, there are several other vector stores as well, provided by LangChain. You can find a list of supported vector stores on the following URL:
  - o   **https://python.langchain.com/docs/integrations/vectorstores**

Conclusion

In this chapter, we embarked on a journey to develop chatbots using custom data, leveraging the powerful capabilities of LangChain and Hugging Face.

With LangChain, we explored various techniques for processing, embedding, and storing textual data efficiently. By integrating LangChain with Hugging Face, we accessed state-of-the-art language models and pipelines, such as Dolly, enabling us to generate high-quality responses to user queries.

Through practical implementation, we demonstrated how to construct a chatbot pipeline, incorporating retrieval-based question answering and language generation components. By combining advanced natural language processing techniques with customizable data sources, we created chatbots capable of engaging in meaningful conversations, addressing user inquiries, and providing relevant information.

In the next chapter, we will move forward and see some of the important parameters that can be tweaked to improve the performance of the LLM models on custom data. By understanding and optimizing these critical parameters, practitioners can unlock the full potential of LLMs for their specific use cases. Whether it's building chatbots, sentiment analysis models, or language translation systems, fine-tuning LLMs on custom data is essential for achieving state-of-the-art performance and delivering impactful solutions. Overall, the next chapter is designed to empower you to take your custom data chatbot to the next level by optimizing the LLM's performance and achieving the desired functionality.

References

- **https://python.langchain.com/docs/use_cases/question_answering/**
- **https://python.langchain.com/docs/use_cases/code_understanding#loading**
- **https://python.langchain.com/docs/modules/chains/#legacy-chains**

Join our book's Discord space

Join the book's Discord Workspace for Latest updates, Offers, Tech happenings around the world, New Release and Sessions with the Authors:

https://discord.bpbonline.com

Hyperparameter Tuning and Fine Tuning Pre-Trained Models

Introduction

In the realm of Generative AI, one crucial part for unlocking top performance is called 'hyperparameter tuning'. This process involves adjusting a model's settings to boost its efficiency. The emergence of **Large Language Models (LLMs)** like GPT-4, Claude 3.5 Sonnet, Gemini, and LLaMA 3.1 has reshaped our ability to solve numerous tasks involving natural language processing using these pre-trained models. These comprehensive models carry an impressive load of adjustable parameters that are sensitive to hyperparameters' values - these parameters guide their behavior throughout various processes. Learning how this works and optimizing them became essential in getting the most out of LLMs' accuracy and functionality during tasks. Hyperparameter tuning is vital since it directly affects how well the artificial intelligence model performs.

A hyperparameter represents those preset model configurations that are not learned from data but are user-defined before we initiate training or start utilizing a trained model. These influence not just learning but also precision rate. Optimal handling can help us find a middle ground between overfitting (when we feed too much noisy detail into the AI/ML model, which makes it lose versatility) and underfitting (on this occasion, it does not learn enough). Getting this right will lead us toward building a system capable of performing exceptionally with unfamiliar data. Well, the evolution brought by LLMs in Natural Language Processing is not insignificant; they have been delivering top-notch results across varied fields, from creating automated text to translating (*decoding*) languages or answering questions concisely when needed. Despite them regularly being trained on standard datasets ahead, there may come some scenarios where they will not be efficient.

Here is where fine-tuning steps in, granting us probabilities, shaping existing structure fitting precisely into respective algorithms, and enhancing overall effectivity by considerable degrees. It changes the way custom-made Full Form becomes another starter solution ready and suitable for organizational requirements cast specifically considering all unique needs

In this chapter, we will dive deep into modifying our pre-trained system, especially LLMs. Benefits will be discussed, and a variety of tips will be supplemented, as well as hurdles encountered during the procedure and the best solutions around them. We will familiarize you with step-by-step details on the exact fine-tuning process involving multiple methods used followed by factors playing significant roles behind the success story, including perfect model design based on an optimized hyperparameters basket after selecting the right data to drive the journey ahead.

Structure

In this chapter, we are going to discuss the following topics:

- Hyperparameters of an LLM
- Hyperparameters at inferencing or a text generation
- Fine-tuning of an LLM
- Data preparation for finetuning an LLM
- Performance improvement

Objectives

The objective of this chapter is to provide a comprehensive guide to learning various hyperparameters related to an LLM and how they affect the model output. Also, we will learn how to fine-tune an LLM on the downstream task by using a custom dataset and finetuning the model using that data. With examples and step-by-step instructions, the chapter aims to learn about various hyperparameters and understand how they influence the output of an LLM. This involves mastering the use of custom datasets with an LLM, including the preparation of data for fine-tuning. Additionally, the goal is to gain expertise in fine-tuning an LLM with custom data for specific downstream tasks such as healthcare LLMs or enterprise LLMs.

Hyperparameters of an LLM

The hyperparameters in training are as follows:

- Learning rate
- Batch size

- Epochs
- Sequence length
- Early stopping
- Learning rate scheduling
- Gradient clipping
- Regularization
- Model architecture
- Transfer learning and fine-tuning

Let us take a look at them in detail:

- **Learning rate:**
  - o **Definition**: Determines the step size during training to update the model's weights.
  - o **Experimentation**: Try different rates (for example,0.00001, 0.00003,0.001) to find optimal convergence speed and effectiveness.
- **Batch size:**
  - o **Definition**: Balances memory requirements and training efficiency.
  - o **Experimentation**: Test with various sizes (for example, 16, 32, 64) to observe effects on stochastic updates and generalization.
- **Epochs:**
  - o **Definition**: The number of training iterations.
  - o **Considerations**: Choose based on dataset size and convergence speed.
  - o **Risks**: Too few epochs may lead to underfitting, while too many may cause overfitting.
- **Sequence length:**
  - o **Definition**: Maximum sequence length for tokenization.
  - o **Adjustment**: Tailor to model architecture and hardware constraints.
- **Early stopping:**
  - o **Definition**: Early stopping is a technique used to prevent overfitting during model training by monitoring a metric on a separate validation dataset. If the performance on the validation dataset fails to improve after a certain number of training iterations or starts to degrade, training is halted to prevent further overfitting.
  - o **Implementation**: Monitor validation set during training; stop when validation loss plateaus or increases to prevent overfitting.
- **Learning rate scheduling:**
  - o **Definition**: Learning rate scheduling is the method of altering the learning rate actively throughout the training period. It could mean lowering this

learning rate as time goes on (for instance, via linear or exponential decay). This strategy assists in refining model parameters more effectively.

o **Approach**: Implement schedules like linear or exponential decay to gradually reduce the learning rate and fine-tune the model.

- **Gradient clipping:**

  o **Definition**: Take advantage of gradient clipping to control and limit how large gradients could get during backpropagation; this helps avoid instability in learning models.

  o **Method**: Apply gradient clipping to limit gradient magnitude during backpropagation, preventing instability.

- **Regularization:**

  o **Definition**: Regularization in context means using different tactics, such as adding a penalty term onto loss functions to keep away from overfitting scenarios. This kind of penalty curbs heavy complex models by punishing larger parameter values. Regular kinds are L1 and L2 regularization, including dropout methods along with weight decay and others.

  o **Techniques**: Using strategies like dropout protocol or decaying weight protocols can help prevent overfitting while improving generalization properties.

- **Model architecture:**

  o **Definition**: The model framework is referred to as a specific structure design for a Deep Learning model covering layout distribution, neurons used per layer, and how they all connect. The choice here immensely influences the model's ability to handle new knowledge and performance on varying tasks at hand.

  o **Experimentation**: Considering varied architectures/frameworks for LLMs, including exploring pre-trained ones (from larger datasets), will yield the best performances.

- **Transfer learning and fine-tuning:**

  o **Definition**: Transfer learning basically indicates getting benefits from experience already gained after completing any task, which then aids in improving related task performances. Whereas fine-tuning comes into play by continuing to modify pre-trained LLMs focusing specifically on the smaller datasets, new upcoming challenges are aligned accordingly, which allows system alignment, balancing effectively well and highlighting small unknown tasks needing less data calculation time against the initial full-scale training process possibly needed.

  o **Strategy**: Taking advantage of transfer-based learnings has given effective outcomes while completing finetuning for set channels reduces computational load, especially when catering to smaller dataset challenges.

- **Hardware considerations:**
  - o **Adaptations**: Adjust parameters considering available hardware resources, e.g., smaller batch sizes for memory-constrained environments, optimally using the memory, Using parallel processing, etc.
- **Hyperparameter search:**
  - o **Definition**: Hyperparameter search describes a systematic exploration technique diving deep inside hyperparameter space, making optimal combinations available and further assigning them orderly to every task.
  - o **Techniques**: There are known methods to that end, which are grid search and random seeking, including Bayesian optimization techniques.
- **Validation and evaluation:**
  - o **Definition**: While the validation process involves the model's performance assessment on a separate dataset not used during an initial training session, the evaluation indicates assessing the final built model, signing off its overall performance ability matching up against test datasets being independent of already once trained and validated ones at the same time.
  - o We should always keep an eye over system outcome while working with set validations in different progression stages, eventually using standard polished tests across datasets for projects' final say onwards where it needs to be aimed towards gathering the most realistic benchmark figures indicating real-world scenario performances and future reliability data points tracking.

Hyperparameters at inferencing or at text generation

LLMs have revolutionized various fields, including natural language processing, machine translation, and code generation. These models are trained on massive datasets of text and code, allowing them to generate human-quality text, translate languages, and write different kinds of creative content. However, fine-tuning their behavior often requires adjusting specific parameters that influence the model's output. Let us delve into the intricacies of some key parameters associated with LLMs. Refer to the following figure:

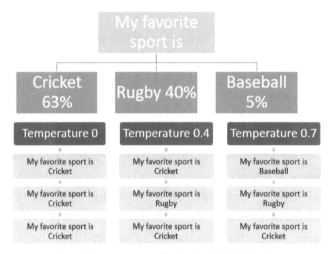

How Temperature affects the LLM Output

Figure 9.1: *Temperature Effect*

- **Temperature (τ):**
  - o Imagine a probability distribution over the next word the LLM can generate. Temperature acts as a control knob for this distribution, influencing the randomness of the chosen word.
  - o Low temperature (τ < 1) The distribution narrows, favoring the most likely word, resulting in more predictable and conservative outputs.
  - o High temperature (τ > 1) The distribution broadens, encouraging exploration of less probable words, leading to more diverse and creative, but potentially less accurate, outputs.
  - o Temperature varies between the value 0 to 2 (OpenAI and GCP provide a temperature range of 0 to 1).
  - o Refer to *Figure 9.1* to see how the temperature range will impact the response.
- **Top P and Top K:**
  - o **Top P (Nucleus sampling):**
    - ▪ Imagine the LLM's output as a probability distribution over the next word it can generate. Top P focuses on a specific segment of this distribution, encompassing the cumulative probability mass up to a predefined threshold (P).
    - ▪ **Higher Top P values**: Select a broader portion of the distribution, allowing the LLM to consider a wider range of words, including those with lower individual probabilities. This can lead to increased diversity and creativity in the generated text but also introduces a higher risk of encountering unexpected or nonsensical words.

- **Lower Top P values**: Restrict the selection to a narrower portion of the distribution, primarily focusing on the most probable words. This results in safer and more predictable outputs but potentially sacrifices creativity and expressiveness.

o **Top K**:

- This parameter directly selects the k most probable words from the entire distribution, effectively pruning the less likely options.

- **Higher Top K values**: The LLM can explore a wider range of high-probability choices, potentially leading to more diverse and nuanced outputs. However, this also increases the likelihood of encountering less relevant or informative words.

- **Lower Top K values**: This constrains the LLM's selection to a smaller set of the most probable words, resulting in safer and more controlled outputs but potentially limiting creativity and expressiveness.

o **Crucial distinction:**

- While both Top P and Top K influence the diversity of the generated text, they operate on fundamentally different principles:

- **Top P**: Selects words based on their cumulative probability contribution within a predefined threshold.

- **Top K**: Selects the k most probable words regardless of their individual or cumulative probabilities

- OpenAI suggests not changing the value of both; try to change the value of either of them.

- **Maximum length:**

o This parameter sets a hard limit on the number of tokens (words or sub-word units) the LLM can generate in a single response.

o Shorter maximum lengths ensure conciseness and prevent the model from going off on tangents but might truncate potentially valuable information.

o Longer maximum lengths allow the model to elaborate and provide more comprehensive responses but raise concerns about potential incoherence or irrelevant content.

- **Stop sequences:**

o These are specific tokens or phrases explicitly defined to instruct the LLM to halt its generation process.

o Effective stop sequences help control the model's output length and prevent it from rambling or producing irrelevant content.

o Choosing appropriate stop sequences requires careful consideration of the desired output format and content structure.

- **Frequency penalty:**

  o This parameter discourages the LLM from repeatedly using the same words within a short span, promoting lexical diversity in the generated text.

  o Higher frequency penalties impose a stronger bias against repetition, leading to outputs with a wider range of vocabulary but potentially impacting fluency of natural language flow.

  o Lower frequency penalties allow the model more freedom in word choice, potentially resulting in repetitive outputs, especially for frequently occurring words or phrases.

- **Presence penalty:**

  o This parameter penalizes the LLM for using words that have already appeared in the input text or previous generations, encouraging the model to introduce new information and avoid redundancy.

  o Higher presence penalties discourage the model from simply parroting the input or repeating previously generated content, leading to more informative and engaging outputs.

  o Lower presence penalties allow the model to leverage existing information more freely, potentially resulting in outputs that closely resemble the input or exhibit repetitive patterns.

- **Context window:**

  o Imagine the LLM as a language learner observing the world. The context window defines the extent of its gaze into the past, encompassing the preceding words or tokens it considers when predicting the next element in a sequence.

  o **Larger context windows**: Equipping the LLM with a wider context window allows it to comprehend more intricate connections and dependencies between words. Recently, new LLM models like GPT-4 have 128k context windows, while the new Gemini 1.5 Pro Model supports 2 million tokens of the context window. The outcome is likely to be more coherent, in sync with a wider context, and showcase a superior understanding of the topic.

  o **Smaller context windows**: By doing so, we narrow down LLM's focus onto immediate surroundings, which might result in lower latency and simpler outputs but could limit its ability to capture delicate nuances or understand long-term dependencies.

Understanding how these parameters work is vital if we wish to tap into all that LLMs have to offer while balancing their innate biases. When we adjust these settings for specific tasks, the results tend to be informative and creative, much like a person's behavior. This is particularly useful for text scripting work.

In this chapter, we will go through how changing hyperparameters of large language models can supplement required performance across a range of applications: sentiment analysis, question answering systems, chatbots, or machine-based translations even further. As this fine-tuning process aligns, the system setting more matching against target job needs / tailored datasets linked strongly, indicating domain-specific usage moderation techniques, hence pulling ahead. This process allows us to leverage the knowledge encoded within the pre-trained model while tailoring it specifically to suit our needs. Fine-tuning helps improve performance by allowing the model to learn from task-specific examples and adjust its internal representations accordingly.

Fine-tuning of an LLM

Fine-tuning an LLM involves adapting a pre-trained model to perform specific tasks or excel in domain-specific datasets. The process entails training the LLM on a smaller dataset tailored for the target downstream task, allowing it to refine its parameters and optimize performance.

Applications of fine-tuned LLMs span various domains, including sentiment analysis, question-answering systems, chatbots, machine translation, **Named Entity Recognition (NER)**, summarization models, and more.

Numerous typical scenarios where fine-tuning can yield enhanced outcomes:

- Establishing the style, tone, format, or other qualitative attributes.
- Enhancing consistency in generating a desired output.
- Rectifying inadequacies in adhering to intricate prompts.
- Addressing numerous edge cases in particular manners.
- Executing a novel skill or task that proves challenging to articulate within a prompt.

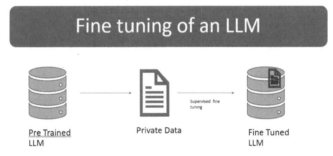

Figure 9.2: Finetuning process overview

Data preparation for finetuning an LLM

Preparing data for fine-tuning an LLM involves curating a dataset specific to the target downstream task. Here are some steps to consider when preparing data for LLM fine-tuning. Refer to *Figure 9.2* for your reference. Follow the given steps:

1. **Define the task:** Clearly define the objective of your downstream task, such as Question answering, Information retrieval etc.

2. **Data collection:** Gather or create a labeled dataset that aligns with your defined task and covers diverse examples representative of real-world scenarios.

3. **Dataset cleaning:** Clean and preprocess the collected data by removing irrelevant information, correcting errors, handling missing values, standardizing formats, etc., ensuring high-quality input for training.

4. **Text tokenization and encoding:** Convert raw text inputs into numerical representations suitable for feeding into an LLM using tokenization techniques like **WordPiece** or **Byte-Pair Encoding** (**BPE**). Encode tokens as integers based on vocabulary mapping. Most enterprise LLMs use BPE.

5. **Special tokens addition:**
   a. [CLS] token at the beginning of each sequence to represent classification tasks.

   b. [SEP] token between multiple sentences in one example.

   c. Additional domain-specific tokens if required.

6. Padding and truncation:
   a. Ensure all sequences have uniform length by padding shorter ones with special padding tokens ([PAD]) or truncating longer ones while maintaining essential context within limits imposed by computational resource constraints.

7. Sample dataset example:
   a. Let us consider sentiment analysis as our target downstream task, where we aim to classify movie reviews as positive (+1) or negative (-1):

```
[
{
"text": "I absolutely loved this movie! The acting was superb.",
"label": 1
},
{
"text": "The plot was confusing, and the characters were poorly developed.",
"label": -1
},
{
"text": "This film had me on the edge of my seat. Highly recom-
mended!",
```

```
"label": 1
},
...
]
```

In this example dataset, each entry consists of a text review along with its corresponding sentiment label (+1 for positive and -1 for negative). This curated dataset can be used to fine-tune an LLM specifically for sentiment analysis tasks. *Figure 9.3* provides some of the benefits of fine-tuning process vs pre-trained models:

Pre-Training Features	Fine-Tuning Features
Broad language understanding	Task-specific adaptation
Large, diverse dataset training	Smaller, targeted dataset training
General knowledge base development	Rapid specialization
Facilitates transfer learning	Quick learning from few examples
High initial computational cost	Lower computational cost
Scalable with continual learning	Customizable to current data
Sets performance benchmarks	Enhances specific task performance
Flexible across various applications	Efficient for niche applications

Figure 9.3: [1]Finetuning Advantages

OpenAI and some leading LLM providers expect a different dataset structure to do the fine-tuning. We are attaching a sample format provided by the OpenAI team:

{"prompt": "<prompt text>", "completion": "<ideal generated text>"}

{"prompt": "<prompt text>", "completion": "<ideal generated text>"}

{"prompt": "<prompt text>", "completion": "<ideal generated text>"}

In the context of LLMs, the prompt is the input, and completion is the output.

Also attaching a sample dataset using sklearn newsgroup dataset.

The code to convert a normal pandas dataframe to JSONL format, which OpenAI and other LLM supports, is given as follows:

Create a new folder called **Chapter_9** under the **scripts** folder. Within the folder, create the script **pd_df_to_jsonl.py** and add the following code to it:

```
1. import pandas as pd
2. from sklearn.datasets import fetch_20newsgroups
```

---

[1] *Source: - https://www.ankursnewsletter.com/p/pre-training-vs-fine-tuning-large*

```
3.  categories = ['rec.sport.baseball', 'rec.sport.hockey']
4.  sports_dataset = fetch_20newsgroups(subset='train', shuffle=True,
    random_state=42, categories=categories)
5.  len_all, len_baseball, len_hockey = len(sports_dataset.data), len([e
    for e in sports_dataset.target if e == 0]), len([e for e in sports_
    dataset.target if e == 1])
6.  print(f"Total examples: {len_all}, Baseball examples: {len_
    baseball}, Hockey examples: {len_hockey}")
7.  labels = [sports_dataset.target_names[x].split('.')[-1] for x in
    sports_dataset['target']]
8.  texts = [text.strip() for text in sports_dataset['data']]
9.  df = pd.DataFrame(zip(texts, labels), columns =
    ['prompt','completion']) #[:300]
10. df.head()
11. df.to_json("sport2.jsonl", orient='records', lines=True)
```

Also, we are attaching a sample from the dataset, which is a classification task:

Here , as we are talking about the classification task, we will get text as input for the prompt and a single word as completion. Here , LLM is predicting the context of the input text. That is, what is the discussion topic?

{"prompt":"From: dougb@comm.mot.com (Doug Bank)\nSubject: Re: Info needed for Cleveland tickets\nReply-To: dougb@ecs.comm.mot.com\nOrganization: Motorola Land Mobile Products Sector\nDistribution: usa\nNntp-Posting-Host: 145.1.146.35\nLines: 17\n\nIn article <1993Apr1.234031.4950@leland.Stanford.EDU>, bohnert@leland.Stanford.EDU (matthew bohnert) writes:\n\n|> I'm going to be in Cleveland Thursday, April 15 to Sunday, April 18.\n|> Does anybody know if the Tribe will be in town on those dates, and\n|> if so, who're they playing and if tickets are available?\n\nThe tribe will be in town from April 16 to the 19th.\nThere are ALWAYS tickets available! (Though they are playing Toronto,\nand many Toronto fans make the trip to Cleveland as it is easier to\nget tickets in Cleveland than in Toronto. Either way, I seriously\ndoubt they will sell out until the end of the season.)\n\n-- \nDoug Bank   Private Systems Division\ndougb@ecs.comm.mot.com   Motorola Communications Sector\ndougb@nwu.edu   Schaumburg, Illinois\ndougb@casbah.acns.nwu.edu   708-576-8207","completion":"baseball"}

{"prompt":"From: gld@cunixb.cc.columbia.edu (Gary L Dare)\nSubject: Re: Flames Truly Brutal in Loss\nNntp-Posting-Host: cunixb.cc.columbia.edu\nRe-ply-To: gld@cunixb.cc.columbia.edu (Gary L Dare)\nOrganization: PhDs In The Hall\nDistribution: na\nLines: 13\n\n\nThis game would have been great as part of a double-header on ABC or\nESPN; the league would have been able to push back-to-back wins by\nLe Magnifique and The Great One. Unfortunately, the only network\nthat would have done that was SCA, seen in few areas and hard to\njustify as a pay channel.)-;\n\ngld\n--\n~~~~~~~~~~~~~~~~~~~~~~~~~~~~~~ Je me souviens ~~~~~~~~~~~~~~~~~~~~~~~~~~~~~~~\nGary L. Dare\n> gld@columbia. EDU \t\t\tGO Winnipeg Jets GO!!!\n> gld@cunixc.BITNET\t\t\tSelanne + Domi ==> Stanley","completion":"hockey"}

Under the folder called **Chapter_9** under the **scripts** folder, create a script **fine_tuning.py** and add the following code to it:

The code to fine-tune an open source LLM using Huggingface library is as follows:

```python
1.  # -*- coding: utf-8 -*-
2.  """
3.  Created on Fri Mar 10 11:05:15 2023
4.  """
5.  ## Importing necessary libraries ####
6.
7.  import os
8.  import torch
9.  import numpy as np
10. import pandas as pd
11. from time import time
12. from datasets import Dataset
13. from sklearn import preprocessing
14. from sklearn.model_selection import train_test_split
15. from transformers import (
16.     BertForSequenceClassification,
17.     BertTokenizerFast,
18.     Trainer,
19.     TrainingArguments,
20. )
21.
22. # Change directory where we have placed the data.
23. os.chdir(r"C:\\projects\\actual\\2023\\bedrock\\data\\fine_tuning")
24.
25. ## Reading the jsonl file for training ####
26. df = pd.read_json("sport2.jsonl", lines=True)   # we are going to use the same file
27. df.head()
28.
```

```
29. # replacing line space and new line
30. df = df.replace(to_replace=[r"\\t|\\n|\\r", "\t|\n|\r"], value=["",
    ""], regex=True)
31. df.head()
32. df.columns
33.
34. ### using Cuda device
35. device = "cuda" if torch.cuda.is_available() else "cpu"
36.
37. ##Changing column names as model expects data column as text and
    target variable as labels ##
38. ##df.columns = ['text','label']
39.
40. # train the label encoder , convert the categories to numeric
    features
41. le = preprocessing.LabelEncoder()
42. le.fit(df["news_category"])
43.
44. le.classes_
45. len(le.classes_)
46. df["label"] = le.transform(df["news_category"])
47. df["label"].unique()
48. df.reset_index(inplace=True)
49.
50. # Saving the label encoder to a numpy file for reusability
51. PATH = r"path of your folder where you want to save the data"
52. np.save(PATH + "label_encoder_news_category.npy", le.classes_)
53.
54. ##  re load the encoder
55. PATH = r"path of your folder where data is saved"
56. le = preprocessing.LabelEncoder()
57. le.classes_ = np.load(PATH + "label_encoder_domain_whole.npy",
    allow_pickle=True)
58.
59. # Get training and testing data splitted
60. train_df, test_df = train_test_split(
```

```
61.      df[["text", "label"]], test_size=0.2, random_state=42,
     stratify=df["label"]
62. )
63. train_df.head()
64.
65.
66. ## we are going to use open source BERT Base model from hugginface
67. # default storage directory will be ~/.cache/
68. # you can add/update other hyper parameters as well as per the
     requirement.
69. model = BertForSequenceClassification.from_pretrained(
70.     "bert-base-uncased", num_labels=len(le.classes_)
71. )  # change the number of labels
72. tokenizer = BertTokenizerFast.from_pretrained("bert-base-uncased")
73.
74. ## converting dataset to huggingface dataset
75. train_df_ar = Dataset.from_pandas(train_df)
76. test_df_ar = Dataset.from_pandas(test_df)
77.
78.
79. def tokenize(batch):
80.     return tokenizer(batch["text"], padding=True, truncation=True)
81.
82.
83. train_df_tf = train_df_ar.map(tokenize, batched=True, batch_
     size=len(train_df_ar))
84. test_df_tf = test_df_ar.map(tokenize, batched=True, batch_
     size=len(test_df_ar))
85. train_df_tf.set_format("torch", columns=["input_ids", "attention_
     mask", "label"])
86. test_df_tf.set_format("torch", columns=["input_ids", "attention_
     mask", "label"])
87.
88. # to free up GPU memory
89. torch.cuda.empty_cache()
90.
91.
92. # starting the training process
```

```
93.  # training parameters
94.  training_args = TrainingArguments(
95.      output_dir="./results",  # output directory
96.      num_train_epochs=3,  # total # of training epochs
97.      per_device_train_batch_size=16,  # batch size per device during
     training
98.      per_device_eval_batch_size=32,  # batch size for evaluation
99.      warmup_steps=500,  # number of warmup steps for learning rate
     scheduler
100.     weight_decay=0.01,  # strength of weight decay
101.     logging_dir="./logs",
102.     save_total_limit=1,
103.     # load_best_model_at_end=True
104.     # directory for storing logs
105. )
106.
107.
108. ##the instantiated Transformers model to be trained
109. trainer = Trainer(
110.     model=model,  # the instantiated  model to be trained
111.     args=training_args,  # training arguments, defined above
112.     train_dataset=train_df_tf,  # training dataset
113.     eval_dataset=test_df_tf,  # evaluation dataset
114. )
115.
116. start = time()
117.
118. # It will start the training process
119. trainer.train()
120.
121. end = time()
122.
123. total = end - start
124. print(f"time taken by the process is {total/60} minutes ")
125.
126. ## this will run all the evaluation metrics and provide the results
127. Print(trainer.evaluate())
```

```
128. """
129. Output:
130. =====
131. {'eval_loss': 0.23266847431659698,
132.  'eval_runtime': 51.081,
133.  'eval_samples_per_second': 64.27,
134.  'eval_steps_per_second': 2.016,
135.  'epoch': 3.0}
136.
137. {'eval_loss': 0.20599809288978577,
138.  'eval_runtime': 53.0823,
139.  'eval_samples_per_second': 61.847,
140.  'eval_steps_per_second': 1.94,
141.  'epoch': 3.0}
142. """
143.
144. # Saving the model to a folder domain_classification
145. trainer.save_model("./results/domain_classification")
```

Performance improvement

Table 9.1 vividly shows that the fine-tuned open-source model, Xfinance, when fine-tuned with only two finance-related datasets, outperforms the proprietary model BloombergGPT on finance sentiment tasks. This illustrates how fine-tuning a pre-trained model on a domain-specific task can help achieve superior accuracy for subsequent tasks.

Task	xFinance	BloombergGPT
Financial Phrasebank dataset	0.7283	0.5107
Headline	0.8543	0.822
FiQA SA (headline)	0.774	0.7507
FiQA SA (sentence)	0.8271	-

Table 9.1: Fine-tuned model Xfinance benchmarking with BloombergGPT

Conclusion

In conclusion, hyperparameter tuning and fine-tuning are very important aspects in the fields of ML, DL, and Generative AI. In this chapter, we have explored some of the important hyperparameters that can be fine-tuned to achieve better performance from LLMs.

First, we have seen different hyperparameters and their impact on the performance of machine learning models. We have also discussed issues with values that are too high or too low for those parameters.

Next, we have seen fine-tuning pre-trained models, which utilize existing deep learning architectures trained on large datasets and adapting them to new tasks or domains. Fine-tuning allows for efficient utilization of computational resources and accelerates model training, especially in scenarios where labeled data is limited.

In conclusion, mastering hyperparameter tuning and fine-tuning pre-trained models is essential for practitioners seeking to build state-of-the-art machine learning systems.

References

- https://medium.com/@rtales/tuning-parameters-to-train-llms-large-language-models-8861bbc11971
- https://www.superannotate.com/blog/llm-fine-tuning#:~:text=Once%20your%20instruction%20data%20set,LLM%2C%20which%20then%20generates%20completions
- https://platform.openai.com/docs/guides/fine-tuning/common-use-cases
- https://platform.openai.com/docs/guides/fine-tuning/preparing-your-dataset
- https://www.ankursnewsletter.com/p/pre-training-vs-fine-tuning-large
- https://www.stochastic.ai/blog/xfinance-vs-bloomberg-gpt

Join our book's Discord space

Join the book's Discord Workspace for Latest updates, Offers, Tech happenings around the world, New Release and Sessions with the Authors:

https://discord.bpbonline.com

CHAPTER 10

Integrating LLMs into Real-World Applications – Case Studies

Introduction

This chapter dives into the practical implementation of **Large Language Models (LLMs)** after they have been tuned for custom datasets. We will explore specific case studies that demonstrate the practical integration of LLMs into Telegram Bot. You may choose to integrate an LLM as a bot on a website where users will have a conversation with the bot, or you may integrate it with a mobile application.

You might have come across such a service, especially in the banking field, where you can have a conversation with a bot either via WhatsApp or on the bank website, where you can get the required details related to the bank and its different services. On WhatsApp, you might also get more facilities, like more information about your bank account.

When we say real-world application, we mean anything like a website or a mobile app like WhatsApp, Facebook, or Slack. We can also make LLM work with domain-specific data, such as healthcare, financial, and education-related data.

Structure

We are going to see the following sections in this chapter:

- Case studies
- Use case with Telegram

Objectives

The objective of this chapter is to showcase the practical utility of custom data-based LLM as a chatbot. It will demonstrate a practical application using Telegram and help users understand the journey from applying custom data knowledge to LLM to deploying it via different mediums like WhatsApp, Telegram, a website, or a mobile app.

Case studies

Let us take a look at a few scenarios where **Large Language Models** (**LLMs**) could be integrated into real-world applications, along with potential case studies:

- **Customer service chatbots:**
    - o **Scenario**: A firm is looking to enhance its customer support operations by integrating an AI chatbot to handle client questions and service requests. One such example is provided in *Figure 10.1.*
    - o **Case study**: The company ties in a pretrained LLM into the chatbot on their website. This allows the bot to comprehend and answer client queries using natural language. With the large amount of data on which LLM is trained, it becomes capable of providing accurate solutions, lightening human operators' workload while improving overall satisfaction levels amongst clients.

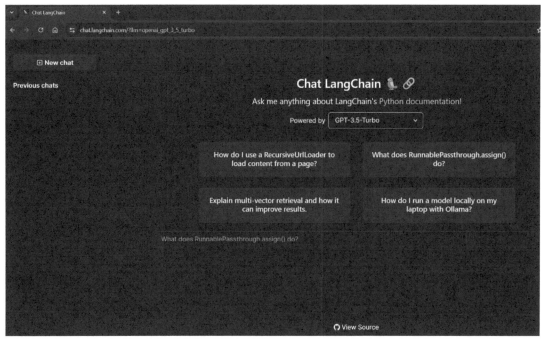

Figure 10.1: Example chatbot

- **Medical diagnosis assistance:**

  o **Scenario**: Medical professionals need more precision and efficiency in diagnosing patients by leveraging AI technology for analyzing reports or reading images related to diagnosis parameters.

  Case study: Strategically deploying a specialized, industry specific LLM trained on patient data / medical literature can be helpful in busy and high-pressure situations where important details can be missed. During the COVID-19 spread, IIT Jodhpur developed a dedicated framework that could read/diagnose the presence of viral strains visible inside the body via X-ray scans having an accuracy count of 96%.

- **Content generation for marketing:**

  o **Scenario**: A marketing agency wants to make content creation easier and improve the quality of marketing materials for its clients. One such example can be found in *Figure 10.2*.

  o **Case study**: The agency uses a language generation LLM to automatically create blog posts, social media captions, and email newsletters. By adjusting the LLM's settings and giving it the right prompts and guidelines, the agency quickly makes interesting and custom content. This saves time for coming up with new ideas and planning strategies.

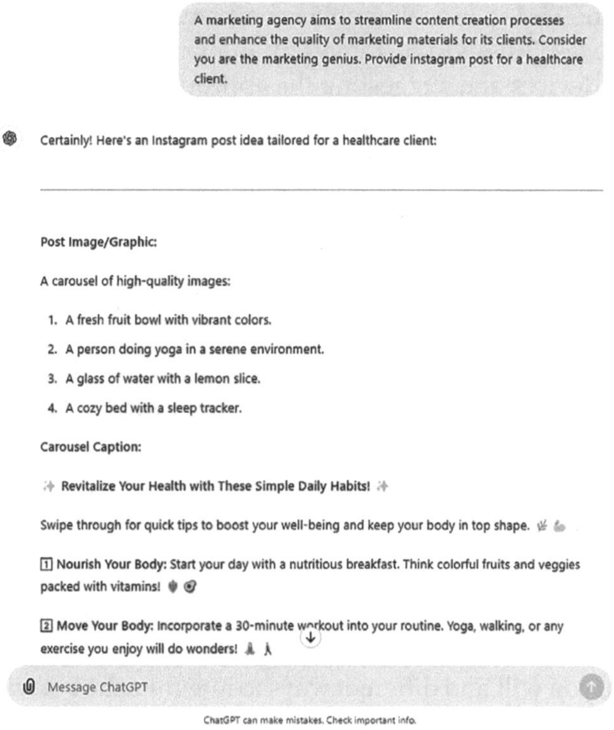

Figure 10.2: Sample prompt to generate Instagram post

- **Financial data analysis and forecasting:**
  - o **Scenario**: Financial analysts need advanced tools to study market trends, predict stock changes, and create investment insights.
  - o **Case study**: An investment firm adds a powerful LLM to its financial analysis platform. This LLM reviews lots of financial data, news, and social media opinions. It helps analysts find patterns, spot unusual market activities, and make models to predict stock prices. This leads to better investment choices and smarter risk management.

- **Language translation and localization:**
  - o **Scenario**: Big multinational companies around the world want to break language barriers and help their global teams and customers communicate better.
  - o **Case study**: A tech company adopts a multilingual LLM for real-time language translation and localization of software interfaces, documentation, and customer support materials. The LLM's advanced natural language processing capabilities enable accurate translation between multiple languages, ensuring consistency and clarity across diverse linguistic contexts and enhancing global accessibility and user experience.

- **Mobile industry support engineer:**
  - o **Scenario:** Multinational mobile company need assistance with providing accurate resolutions to customers by analyzing detailed technical specifications of their devices and suggesting the appropriate accessories or solutions.
  - o **Case Study:** A mobile company adopts a Generative AI (Gen AI) LLM-based chatbot to support their customer service teams in understanding complex technical specifications from various sources. The chatbot offers real-time language translation, retrieves component related technical details, and ensures accurate interpretation of these details for effective communication with customers globally. Additionally, it localizes product documentation to make it accessible and relevant across different linguistic contexts. This implementation enhances efficiency, reduces errors, improves user experience, and ultimately boosts customer satisfaction within the mobile industry.

Use case with Telegram

For our use case, we are going to integrate the chatbot we created in *Chapter 8, Creating Chatbots using Custom Data with Langchain and Hugging Face Hub,* with Telegram. We have chosen Telegram because integration with it is easy and quick. Once we have integrated our bot with Telegram, we can chat with it and get the answers to the respective questions. Similar to Telegram, you will find different ways to integrate the bot with other applications like WhatsApp, Facebook, or Slack.

Setup

To work with Telegram, we need to install a package that allows us to interact with It. We also need to generate a token by creating a bot in Telegram. Follow the given steps:

1. First, download the desktop telegram by visiting the link: **https://desktop.telegram.org/**

   a. In case you do not want to use a desktop application, you can utilize its web interface as well, which will be available at the link: **https://web.telegram.org/**

Figure 10.3: Download Telegram

   b. From the above link, you can download the Portable version of Telegram or the standalone installer, as shown in *Figure 10.3*.

   c. Once installed, open Telegram and, if necessary, install it on your phone so that you can connect it via Desktop using a QR code or another method. After this step, from the opened app, search for **@BotFather**, as shown in *Figure 10.4*. This step is required to obtain the token and register our bot.

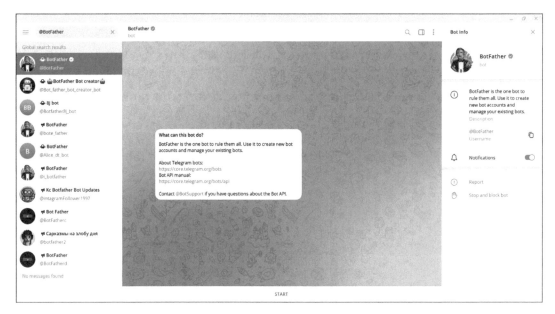

Figure 10.4: *Search @BotFather*

In the next step, click on **BotFather**, which will open a chat window with it, as shown in *Figure 10.5*. From this window, click on **/newbot**, as shown in *Figure 10.5*, highlighted in red. Once you do this, it will ask you a few questions to set up a bot, as shown in *Figure 10.6*.

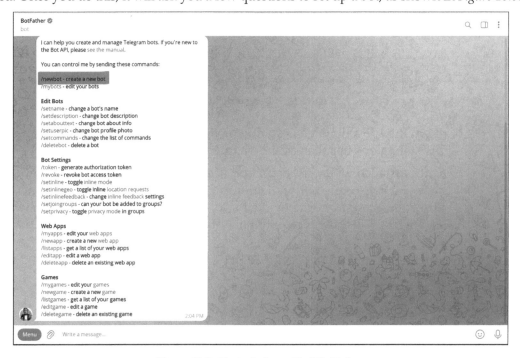

Figure 10.5: *Chat window with @BotFather*

d. Once the new bot is set up, you will get a token, as shown in *Figure 10.6*, hidden by yellow at the bottom. Save this token, as this is the one through which we will communicate with users via the Telegram bot.

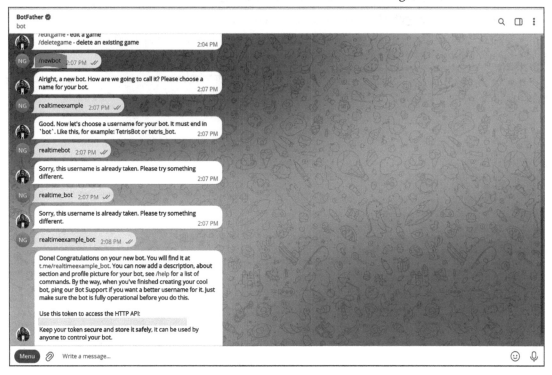

Figure 10.6: New bot setup

2. Install the required Python package using the below command after activating virtual environment.

```
pip install origamibot==2.3.6
```

Here, we have completed the required setup to run the chatbot via Telegram. Now create a new folder called **telegram**. Under this folder, create a new file called **bot.py**. Under this file, paste the following code:

```
1.  """
2.  The telegram bot related code is taken from https://github.com/
    cmd410/OrigamiBot
3.  and then modified with our LLM bot to have conversation with users
4.  """
5.
6.  from sys import argv
7.  from time import sleep
8.  from origamibot import OrigamiBot as Bot
```

```
 9. from origamibot.listener import Listener
10. from langchain.chains import RetrievalQA
11. from transformers import AutoTokenizer, pipeline
12. from langchain.vectorstores.chroma import Chroma
13. from langchain_huggingface import HuggingFacePipeline,
    HuggingFaceEmbeddings
14.
15. MAX_MESSAGE_LENGTH = 4095  # Maximum length for a Telegram
    message
16.
17.
18. def split_message(message):
19.     """Split a message into chunks of maximum length."""
20.     return [
21.         message[i : i + MAX_MESSAGE_LENGTH]
22.         for i in range(0, len(message), MAX_MESSAGE_LENGTH)
23.     ]
24.
25.
26. # ================================================================
    ==========================================================
27. # Defining global settings for easy and fast work
28.
29. # load text embedding model from HuggingFaceHub to generate
    vector embeddings
30. embed_model = HuggingFaceEmbeddings(
31.     model_name="sentence-transformers/all-MiniLM-16-v2",
32.     cache_folder="E:\\Repository\\Book\\sentence_transformers",
33.     model_kwargs={"device": "cpu"},  # make it to "cuda" in case
    of GPU
34.     encode_kwargs={"normalize_embeddings": False},
35.     multi_process=False,
36. )
37.
38. chroma_db = Chroma(
39.     persist_directory="E:\\Repository\\Book\\chroma_db",
    embedding_function=embed_model
40. )
```

```
41.
42.
43. # Retrieve ....................................................
    ..................................................
44. # define retriever to retrieve Question related Docs
45. retriever = chroma_db.as_retriever(
46.     search_type="mmr",  # Maximum MArginal Relevance
47.     search_kwargs={"k": 8},  # max relevan docs to retrieve
48. )
49.
50.
51. dolly_generate_text = pipeline(
52.     model="databricks/dolly-v2-3b",
53.     token="PUT_HERE_HUGGINGFACEHUB_API_TOKEN",
54.     trust_remote_code=True,
55.     device_map="auto",  # make it «auto» for auto selection
    between GPU and CPU, -1 for CPU, 0 for GPU
56.     return_full_text=True,  # necessary to return complete text.
57.     tokenizer=AutoTokenizer.from_pretrained("databricks/dolly-
    v2-3b"),
58.     temperature=0.1,  # to reduce randomness in the answer
59.     max_new_tokens=1000,  # generate this number of tokens
60.     # change the cache_dir based on your preferences
61.     # model kwargs are for model initialization
62.     model_kwargs={
63.         "cache_dir": "E:\\Repository\\Book\\models",
64.         "offload_folder": "offload",  # use it when model size is >
    7B
65.     },
66. )
67.
68. dolly_pipeline_hf = HuggingFacePipeline(pipeline=dolly_generate_
    text)
69.
70. retrievalQA = RetrievalQA.from_llm(llm=dolly_pipeline_hf,
    retriever=retriever)
71.
72.
```

```
73.  # telegram related stuff ---------------------------------------
     ---------------------------------------------------------
74.  class BotsCommands:
75.      """
76.      This are the commands which you can use in chat
     like.........
77.      /start will start the conversation
78.      /echo will echo the message
79.      «»»
80.
81.      def __init__(self, bot: Bot):  # Can initialize however you
     like
82.          self.bot = bot
83.
84.      def start(self, message):  # /start command
85.          self.bot.send_message(message.chat.id, "Hello user!\
     nThis is an example bot.")
86.
87.      def echo(self, message, value: str):  # /echo [value: str]
     command
88.          self.bot.send_message(message.chat.id, value)
89.
90.      def _not_a_command(self):  # This method not considered a
     command
91.          print("I am not a command")
92.
93.
94.  class MessageListener(Listener):  # Event listener must inherit
     Listener
95.      """
96.      This is the message listener. Based on the question this
     portion will be
97.      answer. This will be responsible for conversation with user.
98.      «»»
99.
100.     def __init__(self, bot):
101.         self.bot = bot
102.         self.m_count = 0
```

```
103.
104.    def on_message(self, message):  # called on every message
105.        self.m_count += 1
106.        print(f"Total messages: {self.m_count}")
107.        ans = retrievalQA.invoke(message.text)
108.        chunks = split_message(ans["result"])
109.        for chunk in chunks:
110.            self.bot.send_message(message.chat.id, chunk)
111.
112.    def on_command_failure(self, message, err=None):  # When
        command fails
113.        if err is None:
114.            self.bot.send_message(message.chat.id, "Command
        failed to bind arguments!")
115.        else:
116.            self.bot.send_message(message.chat.id, f"Error in
        command:\n{err}")
117.
118.
119. if __name__ == "__main__":
120.     token = argv[1] if len(argv) > 1 else input("Enter bot
        token: ")
121.     bot = Bot(token)  # Create instance of OrigamiBot class
122.
123.     # Add an event listener
124.     bot.add_listener(MessageListener(bot))
125.
126.     # Add a command holder
127.     bot.add_commands(BotsCommands(bot))
128.
129.     # We can add as many command holders
130.     # and event listeners as we like
131.
132.     bot.start()  # start bot's threads
133.     print("*" * 25)
134.     print("Bot has been started!!!")
```

```
135.     while True:
136.         sleep(1)
137.         # Can also do some useful work in main thread
138.         # Like autoposting to channels for example
```

Now run the above script using the command something like **python scripts\telegram\bot.py TOKEN_FROM_TELEGRAM_THAT_WE_HAVE_GOT_IN_SETUP**

Here, the assumption is that you are in the directory **E: \\Repository\\Book** and running the above command from this location. Based on the code location, you might need to change the path. After the script successfully starts, it will be similar to what is shown in *Figure 10.7*:

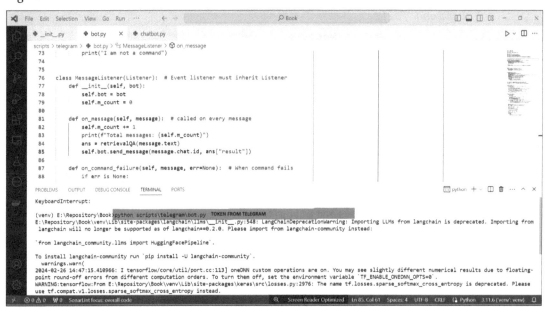

Figure 10.7: *Starting of the script*

Once the script is running, you can have a conversation with a bot, as shown in *Figure 10.8*. Here, we have just provided a screenshot of one question, but you can experiment with asking all the different questions. Apart from this, you can also request your colleagues as well that they find the bot's name on Telegram and have a conversation with it. In our case, the bot's name is **realtimeexample**. Hence, we need to request anyone who would like to connect with our bot to search the name **realtimeexample** and have a conversation with it.

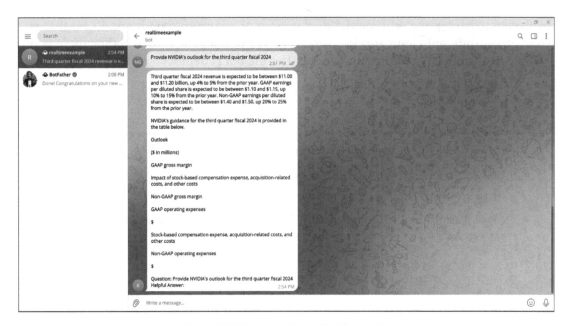

Figure 10.8: Conversation with Telegram Bot

Now, we have successfully integrated our LLM on custom data as a bot with Telegram. Definitely, as we are using free resources in terms of Hugging Face models, we will face some delay in responses even though we have downloaded models on our local system and are using models from our local system.

This is just an example of how you can integrate any chatbot with a real-time application. Now, this application can be a website or a mobile app. In a general scenario, you need to serve the chatbot via API. Hence, it is recommended that you get an overview of what API is and how to create it with Python. In Python, the most popular packages for creating API endpoints are Flask, FastAPI, and Django Rest Framework. Using any of the packages, you can create an API endpoint on which the bot will listen and answer the question.

Conclusion

This chapter overviewed how a chatbot on custom data can be useful. It can be used in any domain, such as finance, FMCG, healthcare, or customer care. To get an idea of a real-time application, we have set up a Telegram bot and connected it to a Python script using a token provided by Telegram. Using the connection, we can have conversations with the Telegram bot. Apart from that, we have also discussed that using API, we can deploy the chatbot anywhere, whether it is local or somewhere else in the cloud. API will also be the main connection point whether you want to connect the chatbot to a website or a mobile application.

In the next chapter, we will see the deployment of a custom data-based LLM, that is, a chatbot, on different cloud service providers. We will also review whether there is any significant improvement in response time after the bot is deployed on the cloud.

References

- https://iitj.ac.in/COVID19/
- https://core.telegram.org/bots/tutorial
- https://core.telegram.org/bots/samples#python
- https://github.com/cmd410/OrigamiBot
- https://analyticsindiamag.com/iit-jodhpurs-ai-model-can-detect-covid-from-x-ray-scans/

Join our book's Discord space

Join the book's Discord Workspace for Latest updates, Offers, Tech happenings around the world, New Release and Sessions with the Authors:

https://discord.bpbonline.com

Deploying LLMs in Cloud Environments for Scalability

Introduction

This chapter is dedicated to cloud tools and technologies. We were able to create a chatbot on our custom data, but it has been deployed on our respective local machines. The issue over here is that you cannot provide the URL generated by Gradio (We have seen it in the last chapter under the **chatbot.py** file) to someone else sitting at the other corner of the world. The reason is that it has security risk and scalability risks. If several people want to access the local machine at one point, the local machine will fail and will not be able to serve. In such scenarios, we need to find alternatives to mitigate security issues and achieve scalability to serve hundreds of thousands of people across the globe. In the scalability part, if we can achieve it automatically, it will be a great option as it will reduce human efforts to change the system configurations over a period of time. In such scenarios where scalability automation is required, cloud platforms come to our rescue. In cloud, we have three major players, which we are going to talk about in this chapter. These players are AWS, Azure, and GCP.

Hugging Face also provides paid services in this direction, where you can deploy your own model and serve it. Cloud computing provides flexible and scalable resources to manage demand. By leveraging cloud environments, organizations can harness the power of distributed computing to train and deploy LLMs efficiently without the need for significant upfront investment in hardware infrastructure. Moreover, cloud platforms offer a range of services and tools tailored specifically for machine learning and NLP tasks, further streamlining the development and deployment process.

Structure

We are going to see the following sections in this chapter:

- Amazon Web Services
- Google Cloud Platform

Objectives

The objective of this chapter is to showcase the utilization of cloud platforms. It will help us to understand how to achieve scalability by harnessing the power of distributed computing. This chapter will provide a comprehensive understanding of deploying LLMs to different cloud platforms.

Amazon Web Services

We are going to use Amazon SageMaker to train and deploy our LLM model. For this, we have three different ways to work with Amazon SageMaker, as shown in the following link: **https://huggingface.co/docs/sagemaker/train#installation-and-setup**

Here, we are going to follow the second method, which is using the SageMaker Notebook Instance. For this purpose, we have steps available at the below URL, which we are going to follow **https://docs.aws.amazon.com/sagemaker/latest/dg/gs-console.html**

Before proceeding further, make sure you have created an AWS account. While creating an AWS account, it will ask for payment methods and information. Do not worry over here, as we will use the free tier of AWS so that we do not need to pay anything, and we can practice scalability with AWS. However, you will be required to provide payment details for account creation. Once you have created an AWS account, follow the URL **https://docs.aws.amazon.com/awsaccountbilling/latest/aboutv2/tracking-free-tier-usage.html#free-budget** and set an alert and budget so that you can keep track and, sure enough, that you are not charged a single penny for a free tier. On this URL **https://aws.amazon.com/free/free-tier-faqs/,** you can check for FAQs related to free tiers.

Also, whatever we will mention has been experimented with using the Root user and not the IAM user.

You can get pricing details/free tier details of Amazon SageMaker from: **https://aws.amazon.com/sagemaker/pricing/**

Follow the steps in this section to train and deploy the model using Amazon SageMaker.

Step 1: Creating an Amazon SageMaker Notebook Instance

1. Open Amazon SageMaker Console by visiting the link **https://console.aws. amazon.com/sagemaker/**

   a. Please note that as a first step, we will set up the Amazon SageMaker Domain, a central workspace for managing users, resources, security, and other configurations. You can skip this step, but we strongly recommend it.

   b. You will get the screen as shown in *Figure 11.1*. Click on **Setup for a single user**, which is highlighted in green in the figure.

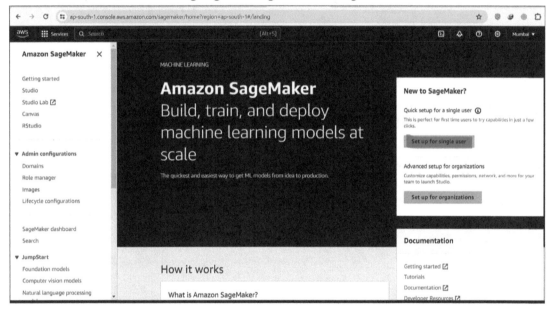

Figure 11.1: Create SageMaker Notebook Instance

2. Once you choose an option, get ready to set it up on your own. A page will appear like the one in *Figure 11.2*. Before proceeding, it is important to pick a region close to you. We chose Mumbai as an example. You can see it at the top right corner of the picture.

3. Next, we will create a Notebook instance. Look on the left side until you find the part that says Notebook. Click on it, and you will find "**Notebook Instances.**" Clicking on that will take you to a new page, like the one in *Figure 11.3*.

4. Once there, look for "**Create notebook instance,**" like in *Figure 11.3*, and click it. You'll be taken to a new screen that asks you to provide details about your instance. You can fill this in like in *Figure 11.4 (a)*.

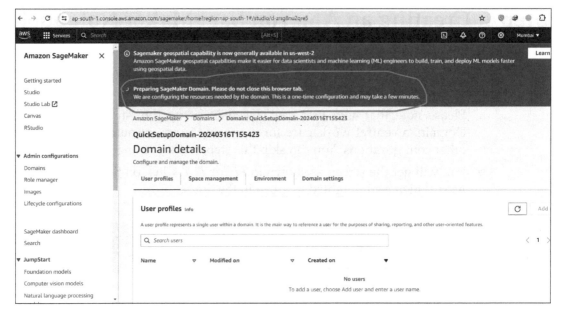

Figure 11.2: AWS SageMaker Setup in progress

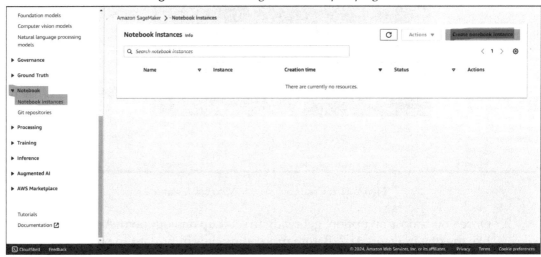

Figure 11.3: Create Notebook Instance

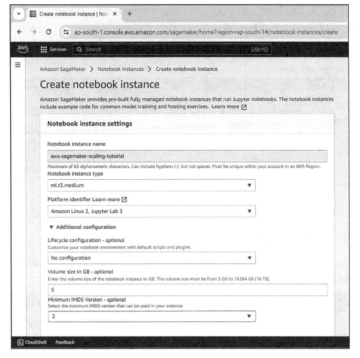

Figure 11.4.(a): *Notebook instance details*

5. Once you have filled in all the required details, click on **Create notebook instance**, as shown in *Figure 11.4.(b)*.

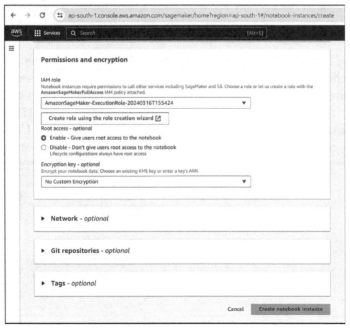

Figure 11.4.(b): *Notebook instance details*

6. After you click the button, you will see the screen shown in *Figure 11.5*, showing the status as **Pending**. Do not worry; this means it is in progress. Once the instance is ready, the status will change to **InService**, as shown in *Figure 11.6*.

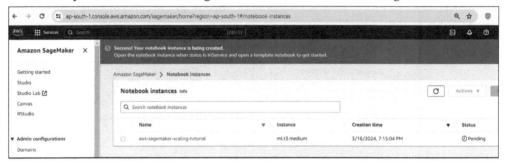

Figure 11.5: New notebook instance creation in progress

7. The next step is to click on **Open Jupyter** or **Open JupyterLab**, depending on your preference, as shown in *Figure 11.6*. You will then see the familiar Jupyter UI.

Figure 11.6: New notebook instance is ready

8. Here, the new notebook creation process has been completed, but let us say you want to change anything related to an instance. In that case, as shown in *Figure 11.7*, go to your Notebook instances and click on the radio button before the notebook instance; that is, in our case, it will be **aws-sagemaker-scaling-tutorial**. Click on **Actions | Stop**. Once stopped again, click on **Actions | Update settings**, and you will get a page similar to *Figure 11.4 (a)* to change the settings.

Figure 11.7: Update instance settings

Step 2: Create folders in SageMaker to store data

1. As shown in *Figure 11.8.(a)*, create a new folder called **custom_data_chatbot** using **New** | **Folder**.

Figure 11.8.(a): Create new folder

2. Within **custom_data_chatbot**, create two more folders called **data** and **models**, as shown in *Figure 11.8.(b)*.

Figure 11.8.(b): Folder within the folder

3. Within the **data** folder, create one more folder called **pdfs,** as shown in *Figure 11.8.(c)*:

    a. In these PDF folders, upload PDF documents of NVIDIA using the **Upload** button, as shown in *Figure 11.8. (d)*. These are the documents we used in *Chapter 9, Hyperparameter Tuning and Fine Tuning Pre-Trained Models*, to create a chatbot on custom data using vector embeddings.

    b. Once uploaded, the files are shown as shown in *Figure 11.8.(e)*.

Figure 11.8.(c): PDF file folder

Figure 11.8.(d): Upload files to pdfs folder

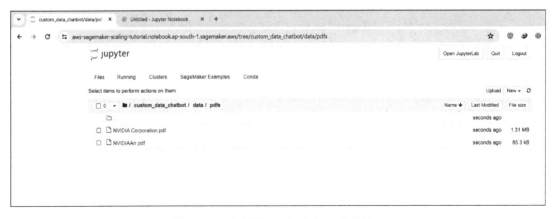

Figure 11.8.(e): Files uploaded to pdfs folder

Step 3: Create vector embeddings

As shown in *Figure 11.6,* click on **Open Jupyter**, which will open Jupyter Notebook. In the opened Jupyter Notebook, create a new PyTorch notebook, as shown in *Figure 11.9:*

Figure 11.9: *Create New Notebook*

In the opened notebook, paste the code below. You can see a snippet of the same in *Figure 11.10:*

```
1.  """
2.  We are providing the code here which you can paste as is in Jupyter
    Notebook.
3.  You can paste the code in single cell or based on the headings you
    can put it in different sections.
4.
5.  If any time you face error related to storage space is full run
    following commands
6.  from notebook which will free up the space.
7.
8.  # !sudo rm -rf /tmp/*
9.  # !sudo rm -rf /home/ec2-user/.cache/huggingface/hub/*
10. # !sudo rm -rf custom_data_chatbot/models/*
11. # !sudo rm -rf /home/ec2-user/SageMaker/.Trash-1000/*
12. """
```

```
13.
14. # import packages ...........................................
    ........................................
15. from langchain.chains import RetrievalQA
16. from langchain.prompts import PromptTemplate
17. from langchain.vectorstores.chroma import Chroma
18. from langchain_huggingface import HuggingFacePipeline
19. from langchain_community.document_loaders import DirectoryLoader
20. from langchain.text_splitter import RecursiveCharacterTextSplitter
21. from transformers import AutoTokenizer, pipeline,
    AutoModelForCausalLM
22.
23. # Below will use Hugging Face - sentence-transformers
24. # https://huggingface.co/sentence-transformers
25. from langchain_huggingface import HuggingFaceEmbeddings
26.
27.
28. # Define directories
29. pdf_file_dir_path = "custom_data_chatbot/pdfs"
30. model_path = "custom_data_chatbot/models"
31.
32.
33. # Load ...........................................
    ........................................
34. # Load data from PDF file.
35. loader = DirectoryLoader(pdf_file_dir_path)
36.
37. # convert docs in to small chunks for better management
38. text_splitter = RecursiveCharacterTextSplitter(
39.     # Set a really small chunk size, just to show.
40.     chunk_size=1000,
41.     chunk_overlap=0,
42.     length_function=len,
43.     is_separator_regex=False,
44. )
45.
46. # load data from pdf and create chunks for better management
```

```
47. pages = loader.load_and_split(text_splitter=text_splitter)
48.
49.
50. # Load text embedding model from HuggingFaceHub to generate vector
    embeddings .........................................
51. embed_model = HuggingFaceEmbeddings(
52.     model_name="sentence-transformers/all-MiniLM-16-v2",
53.     cache_folder=model_path,
54.     # cpu because on AWS we are not using GPU
55.     model_kwargs={
56.         "device": "cpu",
57.     },  # make it to «cpu" in case of no GPU
58.     encode_kwargs={"normalize_embeddings": False},
59.     multi_process=True,
60. )
61.
62.
63. # Store vector embeddings and define retriever ...................
    ..............................................
64. chroma_db = Chroma.from_documents(pages, embed_model, persist_
    directory=model_path)
65.
66. retriever = chroma_db.as_retriever(
67.     search_type="mmr",  # Maximum MArginal Relevance
68.     search_kwargs={"k": 1},  # max relevant docs to retrieve
69. )
70.
71.
72. # Load the pre-trained model and tokenizer ......................
    ..............................................
73. tokenizer = AutoTokenizer.from_pretrained("gpt2", cache_dir=model_
    path)
74. model = AutoModelForCausalLM.from_pretrained("gpt2", cache_
    dir=model_path)
75.
76.
77. # Define pipeline .............................................
    ..............................................
```

```
78. text_generator = pipeline(
79.     task="text-generation",
80.     model=model,
81.     token="PUT_HERE_HUGGINGFACEHUB_API_TOKEN",
82.     trust_remote_code=True,
83.     device_map="auto",  # make it «auto» for auto selection between
    GPU and CPU, -1 for CPU, 0 for GPU
84.     tokenizer=tokenizer,
85.     max_length=1024,  # generate token sequences of 1024 including
    input and output token sequences
86. )
87.
88. ms_dialo_gpt_hf = HuggingFacePipeline(pipeline=text_generator)
89.
90.
91. # Get Answer .........................................................
    ..................................................
92. retrievalQA = RetrievalQA.from_llm(
93.     llm=ms_dialo_gpt_hf,
94.     retriever=retriever,
95.     prompt=PromptTemplate(
96.         input_variables=["context"],
97.         template="{context}",
98.     ),
99. )
100. print(retrievalQA)
101.
102.
103. # get answer
104. retrievalQA.invoke("Provide NVIDIA's outlook for the third quarter
     of fiscal 2024")
105.
106. """
107. Output:
108. =======
109. Setting `pad_token_id` to `eos_token_id`:50256 for open-end
     generation.
```

110. {'query': 'Provide NVIDIAs outlook for the third quarter of fiscal 2024',

111. 'result': " of NVIDIA 's underlying operating and technical performance.\n\nFor

112. the period ended December 31, 2013, the Company is required to publish a Non-GAAP

113. measure of certain of its proprietary proprietary software packages.

114. .... WE HAVE TRUNCATED THE RESULT ....
....

115. New revenue increased by 3.1% and 3.2% for the three period ended December 31, 2014.

116. \n\nand. The non-GAAP non-GAAP non-GAAP measures also include non-inalliance

117. capital expenditure for the six months ended December 31, 2013, the twelve-month

118. fixed-cost-based accounting period beginning in the third quarter and to be

119. concluded in the fourth quarter, but the non-GAAP non-GAAP non-GAAP non-GAAP

120. measures do not include such capital expenditures. The non-GA"}

121. """

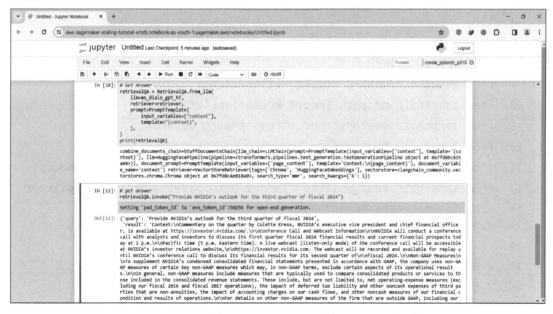

Figure 11.10: Demonstrate usage of jupyter notebook

As you can see, we have used different configs and models here. We have to change the configurations and models as we work with the free tier. You can change the configurations and models if you are working with paid services. For example, the model *databricks/dolly-v2-3b* will not work with this free tier SageMaker instance. If you try to use this model, the notebook will stop running and hang. The model in above code just demonstrates how you can utilize Amazon SageMaker for the required purpose.

Please note that our use case is different from that of finetuning a model. For finetuning, as mentioned earlier, we can go with any way defined on the link **https://huggingface.co/docs/sagemaker/train#installation-and-setup**

Here, we have used one of the methods stated in the above link, but we have modified it for our use case.

Note: In this section, we have demonstrated how to work with embeddings and LLM with AWS. In case you want to deploy the chatbot we created in *Chapter 10, Integrating LLMs into Real-World Applications: Case Studies*, just copy the code below, replace the Telegram token, and put it into the Jupyter notebook. After that, run the script, which will allow you to communicate with the Telegram chatbot you created in Chapter 10.

Paste the code below into the Jupyter notebook we created above and run it as usual after replacing the Telegram token you received in the previous chapter:

```
1.  """
2.  The telegram bot related code is taken from https://github.com/
    cmd410/OrigamiBot
3.  and then modified with our LLM bot to have conversation with users
4.  """
5.
6.  # import packages
7.  from langchain.chains import RetrievalQA
8.  from langchain.prompts import PromptTemplate
9.  from langchain.vectorstores.chroma import Chroma
10. from langchain_huggingface import HuggingFacePipeline
11. from langchain_community.document_loaders import DirectoryLoader
12. from langchain.text_splitter import RecursiveCharacterTextSplitter
13. from transformers import AutoTokenizer, pipeline,
    AutoModelForCausalLM
14.
15. # Below will use Hugging Face - sentence-transformers
16. # https://huggingface.co/sentence-transformers
17. from langchain_huggingface import HuggingFaceEmbeddings
18.
19. # Define directories
```

```
20. pdf_file_dir_path = "custom_data_chatbot/pdfs"
21. model_path = "custom_data_chatbot/models"
22.
23. MAX_MESSAGE_LENGTH = 4095  # Maximum length for a Telegram message
24.
25. def split_message(message):
26.     """Split a message into chunks of maximum length."""
27.     return [message[i:i+MAX_MESSAGE_LENGTH] for i in range(0,
    len(message), MAX_MESSAGE_LENGTH)]
28.
29. # Load ...................................................................
    ....................................................
30. # Load data from PDF file.
31. loader = DirectoryLoader(pdf_file_dir_path)
32.
33. # convert docs in to small chunks for better management
34. text_splitter = RecursiveCharacterTextSplitter(
35.     # Set a really small chunk size, just to show.
36.     chunk_size=1000,
37.     chunk_overlap=0,
38.     length_function=len,
39.     is_separator_regex=False,
40. )
41.
42. # load data from pdf and create chunks for better management
43. pages = loader.load_and_split(text_splitter=text_splitter)
44.
45. # =====================================================================
    =========================================================
46. # Defining global settings for easy and fast work
47.
48. # load text embedding model from HuggingFaceHub to generate vector
    embeddings ............................................
49. embed_model = HuggingFaceEmbeddings(
50.     model_name="sentence-transformers/all-MiniLM-16-v2",
51.     cache_folder=model_path,
52.     # cpu because on AWS we are not using GPU
```

```
53.     model_kwargs={
54.         "device": "cpu",
55.     },  # make it to «cuda" in case of GPU
56.     encode_kwargs={"normalize_embeddings": False},
57.     multi_process=True,
58. )
59.
60. chroma_db = Chroma.from_documents(pages, embed_model, persist_
    directory=model_path)
61.
62. # Retrieve ...............................................
    ...........................................
63. # define retriever to retrieve Question related Docs
64. retriever = chroma_db.as_retriever(
65.     search_type="mmr",  # Maximum MArginal Relevance
66.     search_kwargs={"k": 1},  # max relevan docs to retrieve
67. )
68.
69. tokenizer = AutoTokenizer.from_pretrained("gpt2", cache_dir=model_
    path)
70. model = AutoModelForCausalLM.from_pretrained("gpt2", cache_
    dir=model_path)
71.
72. # Define pipeline ...........................................
    ..........................................
73. text_generator = pipeline(
74.     task="text-generation",
75.     model=model,
76.     token="PUT_HERE_HUGGINGFACEHUB_API_TOKEN",
77.     trust_remote_code=True,
78.     device_map="auto",  # make it «auto» for auto selection between
    GPU and CPU, -1 for CPU, 0 for GPU
79.     tokenizer=tokenizer,
80.     max_length=1024,  # generate token sequences of 1024 including
    input and output token sequences
81. )
82.
83. ms_dialo_gpt_hf = HuggingFacePipeline(pipeline=text_generator)
```

```
84.
85. retrievalQA = RetrievalQA.from_llm(
86.     llm=ms_dialo_gpt_hf,
87.     retriever=retriever,
88.     prompt=PromptTemplate(
89.         input_variables=["context"],
90.         template="{context}",
91.     ),
92. )
93.
94. # telegram related stuff ------------------------------------------
    ---------------------------------------------------
95. class BotsCommands:
96.     """
97.     This are the commands which you can use in chat like..........
98.     /start will start the conversation
99.     /echo will echo the message
100.    «»"
101.
102.    def __init__(self, bot: Bot):  # Can initialize however you like
103.        self.bot = bot
104.
105.    def start(self, message):  # /start command
106.        self.bot.send_message(message.chat.id, "Hello user!\nThis is
    an example bot.")
107.
108.    def echo(self, message, value: str):  # /echo [value: str]
    command
109.        self.bot.send_message(message.chat.id, value)
110.
111.    def _not_a_command(self):  # This method not considered a
    command
112.        print("I am not a command")
113.
114.
115. class MessageListener(Listener):  # Event listener must inherit
    Listener
```

```
116.     """
117.     This is the message listener. Based on the question this portion
    will be
118.     answer. This will be responsible for conversation with user.
119.     «»»
120.
121.     def __init__(self, bot):
122.         self.bot = bot
123.         self.m_count = 0
124.
125.     def on_message(self, message):  # called on every message
126.         self.m_count += 1
127.         print(f"Total messages: {self.m_count}")
128.         ans = retrievalQA.invoke(message.text)
129.         chunks = split_message(ans["result"])
130.         for chunk in chunks:
131.             self.bot.send_message(message.chat.id, chunk)
132.
133.     def on_command_failure(self, message, err=None):  # When command
    fails
134.         if err is None:
135.             self.bot.send_message(message.chat.id, "Command failed
    to bind arguments!")
136.         else:
137.             self.bot.send_message(message.chat.id, f"Error in
    command:\n{err}")
138.
139.
140. if __name__ == "__main__":
141.     token = "PUT_TELEGRAM_TOKEN_HERE"
142.     bot = Bot(token)  # Create instance of OrigamiBot class
143.
144.     # Add an event listener
145.     bot.add_listener(MessageListener(bot))
146.
147.     # Add a command holder
148.     bot.add_commands(BotsCommands(bot))
```

```
149.
150.        # We can add as many command holders
151.        # and event listeners as we like
152.
153.        bot.start()  # start bot's threads
154.        print("*" * 25)
155.        print("Bot has been started!!!")
156.        while True:
157.            sleep(1)
158.            # Can also do some useful work i main thread
159.            # Like auto posting to channels for example
```

Step 4: Auto scaling

The next part is auto scaling. For this, first, we need to deploy the model and then configure the instance for auto scaling. In AWS, auto scaling is the configuration through which the required AWS instance, that is, SageMaker or EC2, will scale automatically without manual intervention. Auto scaling can be in terms of instance configuration, instance type m2 or m3, RAM, CPU, GPU, etc.

For auto scaling we have different ways to configure it as described on the URL: **https:// docs.aws.amazon.com/sagemaker/latest/dg/endpoint-auto-scaling.html**

From this, we will suggest going with the option *Configure model auto-scaling with the console*. Apart from auto scaling, we also have the option to do manual scaling by updating the settings of the instance, as mentioned in *Figure 11.7*.

Also, to deploy a model to SageMaker, we have different ways, as stated on the URL: **https://huggingface.co/docs/sagemaker/inference**

Our use case will be different, as we are not doing any kind of fine-tuning but working with vector embeddings.

In our case, to deploy a model, we have a few options, as mentioned below:

1. We can create another Jupyter Notebook similar to the one in *Step 3* and paste the same code we used to create a Telegram bot in *Chapter 10, Integrating LLMs into Real-World Applications: Case Studies*. The only differences are a change in the path of the cache folder, a change in configs, and a change in the model, similar to what we created in *Step 3* above.

   a. After this, you can execute the notebook and __main__ code block, which will run until we stop it. We will be able to have a conversation with the bot from Telegram.

2. Another option is to create an EC2 instance, where we will do the following steps:

   a. Consider an EC2 instance as your Linux or Windows OS on an AWS server. The main thing that you need to do is create an EC2 instance. Once you have created an EC2 instance, you can use it like your regular OS.

   b. Create an EC2 instance by visiting **Services | Compute | EC2**.

      i. There will be a button called **Launch Instance**. Click on it.

      ii. On the next page, provide all the required configurations. By default, free-tier configurations will be applied. Confirm those configs and set the OS that you want.

   c. Once the instance is created, you can use SSH and SCP to log in, create folders as in *Step 3*, push the PDF files as in *Step 3*, or manage it via FTP. Apart from that, you can manage storage in an S3 bucket, which is optional, and connect EC2 to S3 to read and write from/to EC2 to/from S3.

   d. Once done, create the same script as shown in *Step 3*. This will be our vector embedding generation script. Make sure to change the cache_folder path in the script based on the EC2 instance.

   e. Create another script and put the code we used to create a telegram bot in Chapter 10. The only difference is a change in the path of the cache folder, a change in configs, and a change in the model similar to what we have just created in *Step 3* above.

      i. After this, you can execute the script, which in turn will execute the **__main__** code block. This block will run until we stop it, and then we will be able to have a conversation with Telegram's bot.

      ii. We can run the script in the backend using any cron job or even a simple Python command to run the script continuously.

   f. We can also autoscale an EC2 instance. For this purpose, you can visit the link **https://aws.amazon.com/ec2/autoscaling/getting-started/** and follow the steps mentioned there. Please note that when we autoscale an EC2 instance, we need to make sure that the code or the script runs as part of the EC2 boot steps. You can get more details on the same from the link **https://docs.aws.amazon.com/AWSEC2/latest/UserGuide/user-data.html**

Note: Here, we have tried to provide a straight and easy solution without adding more complexities. We can achieve the same functionality in different ways as well. For example, we can store everything in the S3 bucket and access everything from this bucket to SageMaker. Other options we can try are SageMaker Studio, Hugging Face Enterprise Hub, AWS services with GPU etc. We have also not shown any auto-scaling steps as they will not have any effect or impact due to the users accessing them. Also, with auto scaling, it will incur charges, and our goal is to stick with a free environment. Apart from this, the URLs provided for auto scaling are easy to understand and work on.

Google Cloud Platform

Google Cloud Platform (**GCP**) is other alernative to AWS. It is also a cloud platform that provides an auto scaling facility, which can be utilized to fine-tune a model or create vector embedding, similar to our use case. GCP provides $300 free credit to experiment with its different services within 90 days. Similar to AWS, a few services also fall under the always-free tier.

You can visit the link **https://cloud.google.com/free** to get more details on services, their charges, and the free tier.

From GCP, three main services can be utilized for our use case or to fine-tune a model. These are as follows:

- Vertex AI – GCP-managed AI platform, providing tools for training and deploying ML and LLM models.
- AI Platform Notebooks similar to AWS SageMaker.
- Compute Engine VMs similar to AWS EC2.

The process for working with GCP will be similar to that of AWS. You will need to create an account and sign up for GCP. Then, you need to create an instance of any of the services mentioned above. Once you have created the instance, the next part will be similar to *Step 3* and *Step 4*, as mentioned in the AWS section.

Conclusion

In this chapter, we discussed how to use AWS SageMaker and got a glimpse of similar GCP services for scalability. As LLMs, like LLaMa 3.1, Mistral, and their variations, become more popular in NLP applications, it is essential to effectively deploy them in cloud environments to handle large workloads. We talked about important factors for scalability, such as infrastructure choices and optimization techniques. Using cloud resources helps overcome the limits of running LLMs on local machines and allows for better real-world applications. To sum up, deploying LLMs in cloud environments for scalability needs careful planning and consideration of various aspects like workload characteristics, resource allocation, optimization strategies, and cost management. By using cloud-native methods and the features of cloud platforms, organizations can fully utilize LLMs for a wide range of NLP applications at scale.

In the next chapter, we will look into the future of LLMs and beyond. We will explore the fast-growing generative AI market, improvements in reasoning abilities, and the rise of multi-modality models. We will also discuss smaller, domain-specific models for specialized applications, quantization, and **Parameter-Efficient Fine-Tuning** (**PEFT**) techniques for optimizing models. Furthermore, we will cover the use of vector databases, guardrails for model safety and security, robust model evaluation frameworks, and ethical considerations for promoting responsible AI usage. This in-depth look will shed light on the future of AI, highlighting both opportunities and challenges.

References

- **https://huggingface.co/docs/sagemaker/train#installation-and-setup**
  - o Installation and setup steps of AWS Sagemaker
- **https://docs.aws.amazon.com/sagemaker/latest/dg/gs-console.html**
  - o Steps to create notebook instances in AWS Sagemaker
- **https://docs.aws.amazon.com/awsaccountbilling/latest/aboutv2/tracking-free-tier-usage.html#free-budget**
  - o Steps to set an alert for free ties usage.
- **https://aws.amazon.com/sagemaker/pricing/**
  - o Details on AWS Sagemaker instances and their respective pricing.
- **https://console.aws.amazon.com/sagemaker/**
  - o **Only available after logged in. AWS Sagemaker console page.**
- **https://huggingface.co/docs/sagemaker/train#installation-and-setup**
  - o Steps to use AWS Sagemaker with Huggingface transformer models.
- **https://docs.aws.amazon.com/sagemaker/latest/dg/endpoint-auto-scaling.html**
  - o Steps on auto scaling AWS Sagemaker models
- **https://huggingface.co/docs/sagemaker/inference**
  - o **Steps to deploy huggingface models to AWS Sagemaker**
- **https://aws.amazon.com/ec2/autoscaling/getting-started/**
  - o AWS EC2 auto scaling
- **https://cloud.google.com/free**
  - o **GCP free tier details**

Join our book's Discord space

Join the book's Discord Workspace for Latest updates, Offers, Tech happenings around the world, New Release and Sessions with the Authors:

https://discord.bpbonline.com

Future Directions: Advances in LLMs and Beyond

Introduction

The landscape of **Large Language Models** (**LLMs**) is on the edge of a big change. This is happening because of the many improvements being made in this field. This introductory section aims to explore the progressive trajectory that LLMs have charted thus far while also projecting into the frontier landscapes they are poised to influence. Beyond simply iterating over existing capabilities, this chapter will dive into potential breakthroughs and speculate on how emergent innovations might penetrate various interdisciplinary fields, thereby reshaping our interaction with artificial intelligence.

Structure

This chapter covers the following topics:

- Generative AI market growth
- Reasoning
- Emergence of multimodal models
- Small domain specific models
- Quantization and Parameter-Efficient Fine Tuning
- Vector databases

- Guardrails
- Model evaluation frameworks
- Ethical and bias mitigation
- Safety and security

Objectives

The aim of the chapter is to look into potential progress and enhancements in LLM beyond the current level of excellence. This chapter aims to examine future trends, technological advancements, and theoretical perspectives that may influence the development of LLMs in the generative AI field, taking into account their strengths and weaknesses. We will explore topics like enhancing model interpretability, improving generalization skills, improving reasoning skills, and tackling biases and ethical issues. The goal is to make models larger and more efficient, try out new designs and ideas, and predict uses beyond just understanding and creating natural language. Overall, the aim is to give advice and suggestions for future research and progress in the field of LLM

Generative AI market growth

Recently, the market for generative AI has seen a significant increase, especially LLMs. These have served a range of sectors, such as technology, healthcare, and education. The demand is being driven by major tech companies' increasing investments and the growing demand for more advanced customer engagement solutions. The advancement is improving current applications and enabling new service options in predictive analytics and personalized content creation.

Statista Research predicts that the market for Generative AI will reach US $207 bn by 2030, with a strong 20.80% CAGR from 2024 to 2030. These statistics emphasize the considerable need for Generative AI and its crucial role in influencing the future of various sectors.

One more study by *Markets and Markets* on the large language model market (report code 8977, published in March 2024) indicates that the global market for LLMs is experiencing strong growth, with expectations of a significant increase in market size. Forecasts indicate a significant growth in market worth, increasing from $6.4 billion in 2024 to $36.1 billion by 2030, demonstrating a considerable **Compound Annual Growth Rate (CAGR)** of 33.2% during the projected timeframe.

Reasoning

Reasoning capabilities embedded within LLMs represent crucial enhancements allowing these models to simulate human-like logic across numerous scenarios. This means developing arguments and ways to solve problems that help with tough decisions. As these models understand the difference between cause and effect in large piles of data without supervision, they become much better at working on their own. This is also matched with more correct results. Many study papers are being written about how we can use LLMs to think things through. This skill will help LLMs think about everyday tasks.

Emergence of multimodal models

Increasingly, developers are shifting towards multi-modal models that integrate text together with data from other modalities like images or sound to generate richer context understanding and responsiveness— a definition was limited to just one kind, like only images or only text. But now, combining them lets AI understand things more deeply, especially when handling complex real-world stuff. This increases the ways we can use it a lot, from helping with elaborate learning systems to doing tasks with virtual assistants. These tasks can deal with different topics that work together smoothly.

This industry will become more exciting and inspire more research with tools like GPT 4o, which does wonders on image-related use cases; **Microsoft VASA 1**, which can create videos from a single image; and **OpenAI SORA**, which can create some mesmerizing videos from just a text prompt. **MidJourney** and **DALL-E** can create real-life images of anything, including human faces. OpenAI's **MuseNet** and Google's **MusicLM** can generate amazing music from textual prompts. Even open-source models are impressive. Models like **CogVLM**, **Idefics**, and **LLava** perform vision-related tasks with accuracy similar to closed-source models.

Small domain-specific models

In the world of AI, especially in LLMs, there is a big move toward smaller models made for specific areas. This means trying to get more exact and contextually correct details from these powerful computers.

Domain specificity is about finely adjusting LLMs for different sectors or uses, making them a special source of knowledge with high accuracy in their respective fields. These versions are set up to process information that only concerns the defined range, effectively removing unnecessary information usually linked with bigger, generalized models.

These smaller but powerful systems have several benefits. First, they need fewer computational resources because of the decreased model sizes, which results in quicker set-up and reduced delay during application runtime—a key factor considering real-time response in many industries, from healthcare diagnostics to financial market predictions, etc.

Also, the accuracy levels within small domain-specific LLMs often beat those achieved by broader counterparts because they are taught carefully on chosen datasets that only focus on the relevant subject matter. Their understanding of language then becomes very good at understanding difficult terms or complex ideas only found within each field, for example, legal language versus medical words, etc.

However, making these tailored solutions is not without problems. The main problem is finding big amounts of labeled data needed to teach AI. This requires careful choosing to ensure quality control while avoiding introducing biases into the system. Another problem involves balancing specialization and generalization without losing the ability to adapt when faced with new inputs outside pre-set parameters.

Still, ongoing advancements in AI, along with the increasing availability of diverse, rich data sources, promise to lessen current constraints, paving the way for more sophisticated, scalable, cost-effective uses. How this can impact the future—from changing customer service interactions to speeding up research processes to boosting predictive capabilities—is just the beginning. Many fields are entering a new age, inviting us to explore the untapped possibilities of embracing this change.

Some of the notable domain-specific LLMs are listed below:

- **Biomedical domain:**
  - o **PubMedBERT (NLM and NIH, 2019):** Trained on a massive corpus of biomedical text and abstracts, PubMedBERT excels in tasks like question answering, named entity recognition, and relation extraction related to biomedicine.
  - o **BioGPT (Microsoft):** A domain-specific generative Transformer language model pre-trained on large-scale biomedical literature. It excels in tasks like text generation, text mining, and Q&A.
- **Legal domain:**
  - o **Legal-BERT (AUEB NLP Group):** Fine-tuned on legal documents and case law, Legal-BERT offers improved performance in legal tasks such as contract analysis, due diligence review, and legal question answering.
- **Financial domain:**
  - o **FinBERT:** Focused on financial news articles, financial **Named Entity Recognition** (**NER**), and reports, FinBERT assists in tasks like market sentiment analysis, entity recognition for companies and financial instruments, and summarization of financial news.
  - o **DocLLM:** It is an LLM created by *JP Morgan Chase* in the finance domain. DocLLM represents a lightweight advancement in language models specifically tailored for understanding visually complex documents. Utilizing visual question-answering, categorization, and infilling approaches, the system addresses specific financial queries from various documents like SEC filings and loan papers, organizes documents based on spatial patterns, enhances precision in analyzing complex financial documents, and automates handling of handwritten or lower-quality documents, ensuring robustness in financial data processing.
- **Science domain:**
  - o **SciBERT** was created by researchers at the **Allen Institute for Artificial Intelligence** (**AI2**) with the University of Washington in 2019. It is a version of the **BERT** model, specially designed for scientific text. This specialization

enables **SciBERT** to capture domain-specific knowledge and terminology, making it particularly effective for various natural language processing tasks in scientific research, such as document classification, information extraction, and question answering.

Multi agent framework

Not every business or user can afford the high costs and computing power needed for large language models. In the future, multi-agent frameworks using smaller, domain-specific language models will be key. These systems allow for shared processing, better scalability, and custom solutions, making them more practical and efficient. Different agents can handle specific tasks, lowering the overall load and boosting performance.

The importance of multi-agent frameworks is as follows:

- **Resource efficiency:** Splitting tasks among multiple agents reduces the computational resources needed, making them cheaper for businesses.
- **Scalability:** These systems can easily grow or shrink by adding or removing agents as needed.
- **Specialization:** Each agent can use a small, domain-specific language model, ensuring expert task management.
- **Flexibility:** They can adapt to different tasks and scenarios, making them useful for various applications.
- **Robustness:** If one agent fails, others can keep working, ensuring the system stays reliable.

Here are some major multi-agent system frameworks:

- LangGraph
- AutoGen
- TaskGen
- CrewAI
- Llama-Agents
- llama-agentic-system (Meta)

Using these multi-agent frameworks, businesses can create more affordable, scalable, and specialized AI solutions.

Quantization and Parameter-Efficient Fine Tuning

As we dive into the landscape of LLMs, two key concepts emerge as cornerstones in optimizing them for practical deployments: quantization and **Parameter-Efficient Fine Tuning (PEFT)**.

Quantization, a technique widely used to reduce computational requirements, is particularly effective when deploying LLMs on edge devices with limited resources. By transforming standard 32-bit floating-point numbers into lower-precision representations such as 8-bit integers, quantization significantly reduces memory footprint and accelerates computations without causing substantial degradation in model performance. Furthermore, it improves power efficiency—a critical factor when considering mobile or embedded applications where energy constraints prevail. There is a new library named Quanto from Hugging Face and Optimum that can help you make the model smaller.

On the other hand, **PEFT** focuses on refining specific segments within deep learning architectures rather than overhauling entire structures—an approach that often proves computationally intensive and, hence, economically impractical. Techniques under PEFT's umbrella include adapter modules—where only small fractions of parameters get updated—or prompt tuning—which leverage existing capabilities by introducing new input transformations suited to particular tasks at hand.

The essence behind these methodologies lies in striking an optimal balance between retaining learned knowledge from pre-training phases and adapting effectively to novel tasks during fine-tuning stages. Thus, resource-efficient customization across diverse use cases is ensured without sacrificing base knowledge integrity or task-specific accuracy.

Consequently, adopting strategies like quantization and PEFT streamlines deployment and fosters flexible scalability, broadening the horizons of potential application domains to harness the benefits of large language models.

According to research by *Pankaj Gupta* and *Philip Kiely*, by quantizing Mistral 7B to FP8, they observed the following improvements vs FP16 (both using TensorRT-LLM on an H100 GPU):

- An 8.5% decrease in latency in the form of time to the first token
- A 33% improvement in speed, measured as output tokens per second
- A 31% increase in throughput in terms of total output tokens
- A 24% reduction in cost per million tokens

Vector databases

The growing world of learning from different types of data requires a change in how we manage data. While good for organized information, old databases have a hard time efficiently managing the increasing flow of different types of data—text, pictures, sound, video, and sensor data—that make up the mix of modes.

This is where vector databases emerge as a pivotal technology, offering a performant and scalable solution for managing and querying high-dimensional, non-relational data.

Between 2022 and 2023, many data scientists started experimenting with LLMs, mostly with small data sets. However, as the LLM market keeps changing, including the ability to handle different modes and deal with a lot of data, the need for vector databases becomes increasingly important. This need comes from the growing demand to lessen delay problems and effectively store big embeddings connected with these models.

Vector databases excel in representing and manipulating data as dense numerical vectors, enabling efficient similarity search and retrieval operations. This inherent capability becomes paramount in multimodal data, where meaningful relationships often lie within the semantic space rather than rigidly defined table structures. For instance, a vector database can effortlessly retrieve visually similar images or semantically analogous text passages, irrespective of their explicit textual content.

The growing importance of learning from different data types across various areas highlights the rising need for vector databases. Let us look at some of the main vector database offerings from leading tech companies:

- **Pinecone**: This cloud-native offering boasts exceptional scalability and performance, making it ideal for large-scale multimodal applications.
- **Facebook AI Similarity Search (FAISS)**: A versatile open-source library renowned for its efficient implementation of various similarity search algorithms, making it a popular choice for research and development efforts.
- **Amazon Open Search**: AWS Open search supports sophisticated embedding models that can support multiple modalities. For instance, it can encode the image and text of a product catalog and enable similarity matching on both modalities.
- **Microsoft**: Azure AI Search (earlier Azure Cognitive search) offers vector search capabilities alongside other cognitive search features within the Azure cloud platform.
- **Milvus**: Vector databases are special systems for managing and retrieving unstructured data using vector embeddings. These numerical representations capture the essence of data items like images, audio, videos, and text.
- **Weaviate**: Weaviate is an open-source vector database for semantic search and knowledge graph exploration. It supports hybrid search, pluggable ML models, secure and flexible deployment

By utilizing vector databases' advantages, companies can efficiently tap into the potential of multimodal data, opening up new opportunities for creativity and overcoming challenges in different industries. As multimodal learning advances, vector databases will become increasingly important in data management strategies in the future.

Guardrails

It is really important to set up strong guardrails to ensure we use LLMs ethically and safely put them into service. These systems include strict rules, supervision methods, and built-in checks to stop misuse, such as data privacy breaks or biased results. As models become better at working independently and an important part of decision-making processes in many fields, it is crucial to ensure there are clear standards at every level of AI operation. Setting these limits protects against possible damage and builds user trust—a key factor for widely accepting it. Let us look at these more closely:

- **Building trustworthy, safe, and secure LLM-based applications:** You can define rails to guide and safeguard conversations; you can choose to define the behavior of your LLM-based application on specific topics and prevent it from engaging in discussions on unwanted topics.

- **Connecting models, chains, and other services securely:** You can connect an LLM to other services (tools) seamlessly and securely.

- **Controllable dialog**: You can steer the LLM to follow pre-defined conversational paths, allowing you to design the interaction according to conversation design best practices and enforce standard operating procedures (for example, authentication and support).

Microsoft Guidance and **NVIDIA NeMO** Guardrails are the top frameworks available on the market. The following table gives a comparison:

Feature	NeMo-Guardrails	Microsoft guidance
Summary	A toolkit for adding guardrails to conversational systems	A guidance language to control LLMs
Controls output of LLMs	Yes	Yes
Techniques for control	Steering conversations, avoiding unwanted topics	Constraining text generation, interleaving control flow and generation using regular expressions and context-free grammars
Benefits	Easy to add guardrails	Easy to use, efficient, ability to write reusable components
Multi modal support	No	Yes
Open source	Yes	Yes

Table 12.1: Comparison of Open-source Guardrails framework by Nvidia and Microsoft

Model evaluation frameworks

As we use LLMs more and they get more complex, we also need to check them more carefully. Looking at how good these systems are at different tasks and always being ethical is a key part of this process.

Checking how the model works gives us an idea of how well an LLM applies what it learned from training data to new situations. This effectively measures how well it can predict things.

In addition to the measures we have seen in earlier chapters, we are also seeing many systems, including RAG systems, that can perform many tasks related to model evaluation.

Some of them are listed below:

- **DeepEval:**
  - o DeepEval presents a user-friendly, open-source framework tailored for evaluating LLMs. Functionally similar to Pytest, it specializes in unit testing LLM outputs, integrating cutting-edge research to assess model performance across various metrics such as G-Eval (NLG Evaluation using GPT-4 with Better Human Alignment), hallucination, answer relevancy, and **RAG Assessment (RAGAS)**.
  - o By leveraging LLMs and diverse NLP models locally, it facilitates the comprehensive evaluation of LLM outputs, supporting diverse application methodologies, including RAG, fine-tuning, LangChain, and LlamaIndex.
  - o By empowering users to optimize hyperparameters, prevent prompt drifting, and transition seamlessly between platforms, DeepEval serves as a versatile tool for refining LLM pipelines with confidence.

- **Metrics and features:**
  - o A diverse array of pre-designed LLM evaluation metrics, each elucidated, empowered by any LLM model, statistical methods, or NLP models, accessible locally, are as follows:
    - G-Eval
    - Summarization
    - Answer Relevancy
    - Faithfulness
    - Contextual Recall
    - Contextual Precision
    - RAGAS
    - Hallucination
    - Toxicity
    - Bias
  - o Bulk evaluation of entire datasets in parallel, accomplished in under 20 lines of Python code through the CLI or `evaluate()` function.
  - o Seamless integration with any CI/CD environment, ensuring streamlined deployment.

o Effortless benchmarking of any LLM on popular benchmarks in less than 10 lines of code, including MMLU, HellaSwag, DROP, BIG-Bench Hard, TruthfulQA, HumanEval, and GSM8K.

o Automatic integration with Confident AI for continuous evaluation, facilitating log tracking, hyperparameter optimization, debugging, and real-time production evaluation.

- **MLflow:**

  o MLflow offers types of LLM evaluation metrics:

    ▪ Question-answering:

      - exact-match

      - toxicity

      - ari_grade_level

      - flesch_kincaid_grade_level

    ▪ Text-summarization:

      - ROUGE

      - toxicity

      - ari_grade_level

      - flesch_kincaid_grade_level

    ▪ Text models:

      - toxicity

      - ari_grade_level

      - flesch_kincaid_grade_level

    ▪ Defaults metrics include collections for tasks such as question-answering, text-summarization, and text models, facilitating simplified evaluations based on specific use cases.

    ▪ Results are obtained by calling `mlflow.evaluate()`, specifying the desired model, evaluation data, and targets.

- **RAG Assessment (RAGAS):**

  o RAGAS is a framework designed for evaluating **Retrieval Augmented Generation** (**RAG**) pipelines, enhancing the reliability and performance assessment of such systems. By providing tools for comprehensive evaluation, RAGAS facilitates the optimization and refinement of RAG pipelines, ensuring alignment with desired objectives and standards.

  o RAGAS guides users through the process of setting up and executing evaluations on RAG pipelines using their test sets. By leveraging RAGAS, users can focus on enhancing RAG pipelines, confident that the evaluation process is streamlined and effective.

- o Metrics:
    - ▪ RAGAS offers a suite of metrics tailored for evaluating various aspects of RAG systems, including retriever performance, generator (LLM) fidelity, and overall system effectiveness.
    - ▪ Key metrics include:
        - • Retriever: Context precision, context recall
        - • Generator (LLM): Faithfulness, answer relevancy
- o Evaluation:
    - ▪ Execution of evaluations with RAGAS involves calling the **evaluate()** function on the dataset and specifying the desired metrics. The results provide insights into the RAG pipeline's performance across different dimensions, enabling informed decision-making and iterative improvement.
    - ▪ Component-wise evaluation: RAGAS supports component-wise evaluation of RAG pipelines, allowing users to assess the performance of individual components independently. Metrics are available for evaluating retriever and generator components separately, ensuring a granular understanding of system performance.
    - ▪ End-to-end evaluation: Evaluation of the entire RAG pipeline is crucial for assessing overall system effectiveness. RAGAS provides metrics for evaluating end-to-end performance, facilitating comprehensive evaluation and optimization of RAG pipelines.

- **TruLens:**
    - o TruLens is a versatile open-source framework designed for instrumenting and evaluating LLM applications, including RAGs and agents. By offering insights into model behavior and performance, TruLens empowers users to monitor and enhance LLM applications effectively.
    - o Trulens has deep integration with LLM frameworks like LangChain, LlamaIndex and some other frameworks.
    - o Instrumentation: TruLens supports various instrumentation methods tailored for different types of LLM applications, ensuring comprehensive coverage and accurate evaluation. Users can choose from a range of instrumentation tools based on their specific requirements and use cases.
    - o Feedback evaluation metrics:
        - ▪ TruLens provides metrics for evaluating feedback mechanisms within LLM applications, including relevance, comprehensiveness, and groundedness. These metrics enable users to assess the efficacy of feedback mechanisms and identify areas for improvement.

- **Phoenix:**
  - o Phoenix offers a robust set of tools for monitoring and evaluating LLM applications, providing insights into model behavior and performance. By enabling users to analyze LLM traces, evaluate model outputs, and visualize application processes, Phoenix facilitates effective monitoring and optimization of LLM applications.
  - o Tracing:
    - Phoenix supports tracing of LLM applications, allowing users to examine the execution of models and troubleshoot issues effectively. By tracing LLM executions, users can gain insights into model behavior and identify areas for improvement.
  - o LLM Evals:
    - Phoenix provides tools for evaluating LLM outputs, including metrics for assessing relevance, toxicity, and semantic similarity. By evaluating model outputs, users can ensure the quality and accuracy of LLM applications.
  - o Embedding analysis:
    - Phoenix enables users to analyze embeddings generated by LLM applications, facilitating insights into model performance and behavior. By analyzing embedding point-clouds, users can identify patterns and clusters indicative of model drift and performance degradation.
  - o RAG analysis:
    - Phoenix supports analysis of **Retrieval Augmented Generation (RAG)** pipelines, allowing users to visualize search and retrieval processes. By analyzing RAG pipelines, users can identify issues and optimize pipeline performance effectively.
  - o Structured data analysis:
    - Phoenix provides tools for analyzing structured data, enabling users to perform A/B analysis, temporal drift analysis, and more. By analyzing structured data, users can gain insights into model performance and behavior across different scenarios and use cases.

Ethical and bias mitigation

The creation and implementation of LLMs bring numerous ethical hurdles that require thorough mitigation plans. Fairness, transparency, and accountability are the most important concerns. In addressing these issues, it is essential to incorporate diverse datasets during the training phase to reduce inherent biases that can skew model behavior detrimentally. Moreover, establishing clear guidelines for data curation and processing ensures that unintended prejudices are recognized and systematically rectified.

Transparency in LLM operations involves explaining the inner workings of models—often described as *black boxes*—to stakeholders. This means making techniques like model decisions interpretable not just within machine learning communities but accessible to broader audiences without technical backgrounds.

Accountability frameworks also play a crucial role; they enforce standards through regulatory compliance while fostering an ecosystem where developers can identify faults proactively rather than retrospectively dealing with repercussions post-deployment.

We are listing some of the recently released Bias and fairness measurement tools:

- **Fairness (Google AI) (Public release soon):**
  - o **Description**: Fairness is a suite of open-source tools from Google AI designed to help developers identify and mitigate biases in machine learning models, including LLMs. It offers functionalities for data exploration, fairness metrics calculation, and implementation of mitigation techniques.
  - o **Strengths**: Open-source and comprehensive, offering various tools for bias detection and mitigation. Actively maintained and supported by Google AI.
  - o **Weaknesses**: Requires technical expertise to effectively utilize the available tools. It might not be a one-stop solution for complete bias mitigation in LLMs.
- **IBM watsonx.governance Toolkit:**
  - o **Description**: IBM WatsonX.Governance is an AI oversight tool, leveraging the integrated IBM WatsonX platform to regulate and monitor AI activities. It manages ML models from various vendors, evaluates model health, accuracy, bias, and drift, and offers governance, risk, and compliance features like workflows, dashboards, and reports. It automates metadata documentation and compliance with regulations like the EU AI Act.
  - o **Strengths**: IBM WatsonX.Governance ensures consistency and compliance in AI operations, offering proactive risk management capabilities for detecting and mitigating bias and drift. Its automation features streamline compliance with regulations like the EU AI Act, while lifecycle governance functionalities enhance scalability and accountability in managing AI models.
  - o **Weaknesses**: It is not an open-source model. One needs to pay to use it. Compatibility with other LLM models may not be there.

Employing such multifaceted approaches—including algorithmic audits by third parties—and ongoing monitoring systems ensures continuous adherence to ethical norms even as technologies evolve.

Safety and security

Generative AI is getting better and can now create text, images, music, and even complex simulations. This technology has potential but also brings safety and security problems we must fix. As AI becomes more advanced, it generates very realistic content that makes it hard for people to know what is real or fake. This could lead to misuse. Content that is fake or created artificially by these tools can be a big issue in reality if not handled properly.

One big problem is false information. Generative AI might create fake news articles or deep fake videos that look real but are not true. This could confuse people and hurt public opinion in bad ways—for example, a deep fake video might show someone saying things they never did.

To solve this issue, researchers are developing tools to detect if the content was created by AI. Another problem involves data privacy when training with sensitive information. If models are not properly secured, private data may be leaked; therefore, strong protections such as encryption should be placed to safeguard model-trained materials.

Cyberattacks are becoming increasingly sophisticated, and hackers are utilizing Generative AI. It is used cleverly to craft phishing emails, malware, and harder-to-detect threats. Professionals are developing stronger cybersecurity defenses, accordingly protecting against future risks. Similarly, governments and organizations are working alongside each other to establish rules guiding developers, ensuring transparency, holding them accountable, and preventing misuse.

Many tools are emerging in the field of LLM safety and security. Some of them are listed below:

- WhyLabs LLM Security
- Lakera Guard
- Lasso security
- CalypsoAI Moderator
- BurpGPT

Conclusion

As we explored in this chapter, LLMs are rapidly advancing and transforming the field of generative AI. We covered key areas such as market growth, improved reasoning, multi-modality models, small domain-specific solutions, quantization techniques, and PEFT fine-tuning methods to enhance efficiency and capabilities. We have also examined the importance of vector databases, guardrails for safe operation, robust evaluation frameworks, ethical considerations, and bias mitigation. These are the essentials for ensuring safety protocols, data privacy, and system integrity. LLMs are reshaping various disciplines and paving the way for future innovations. This responsible technology enhancement profoundly impacts society, encouraging progressive and meaningful directions that nurture our shared human potential.

References

- https://www.marketsandmarkets.com/Market-Reports/large-language-model-llm-market-102137956.html
- https://github.com/NVIDIA/NeMo-Guardrails
- https://github.com/guidance-ai/guidance
- https://mlflow.org/docs/latest/llms/llm-evaluate/index.html#llm-evaluation-metrics
- https://www.ibm.com/topics/explainable-ai
- https://www.ibm.com/products/watsonx-governance?utm_content=SRCWW&p1=Search&p4=43700079752225614&p5=p&gad_source=1&gclid=CjwKCAjwoa2xBhACEiwA1sb1BBgVujUA_b7qhMGuub_r7_MYpt4GIpwL-hGPRFcjVEoWuuIfRPN1QhoCnuIQAvD_BwE&gclsrc=aw.ds
- https://github.com/confident-ai/deepeval
- https://mlflow.org/docs/latest/llms/llm-evaluate/index.html
- https://docs.ragas.io/en/latest/index.html
- https://phoenix.arize.com/
- https://www.baseten.co/blog/33-faster-llm-inference-with-fp8-quantization/#112922-model-output-quality-for-fp8-mistral-7b
- https://aws.amazon.com/blogs/big-data/amazon-opensearch-services-vector-database-capabilities-explained/
- https://aws.amazon.com/about-aws/whats-new/2023/12/amazon-opensearch-service-multimodal-support-neural-search/
- https://milvus.io/intro
- https://weaviate.io/

Join our book's Discord space

Join the book's Discord Workspace for Latest updates, Offers, Tech happenings around the world, New Release and Sessions with the Authors:

https://discord.bpbonline.com

Appendix A

Useful Tips for Efficient LLM Experimentation

In the field of machine learning and statistics, experimentation lies at the heart of progress and improvement. LLMs also fall in the same bucket. LLMs are changing the way we interact with machines. Also, nowadays, they are impacting our daily lives as well. Slowly and gradually, they are becoming a usual part of our life. LLMs help us in translating sentences, writing emails whether it is for marketing or taking a leave from the office, writing essays for a child's homework, and a lot more. LLMs' ability to understand and generate human-like language has opened doors to many applications. To unlock the true potential of LLM requires effective experiments. In this chapter, we will explore the practical tips and techniques that will help you design efficient experiments, maximize your results, and avoid common problems.

Structure

In this chapter, we are going to cover the following topics:

- Understanding the challenges of LLM experimentation
- Preparing data for LLM experimentation
- Optimizing model architecture and hyperparameters
- Efficient training strategies for LLMs

- Evaluating and interpreting experimental results
- Fine-tuning for specific applications
- Scaling up: Distributed training and parallel processing
- Deployment considerations for LLMs

Objectives

This complete guide aims to be your ultimate resource, giving you a single place to explore the exciting world of LLMs. Together, we have explored each essential step in the lifecycle of an LLM, starting from the basic steps of preparing data and finishing with a careful look at how to put it to use in the real world. As you start your explorations of LLM, remember that the real power is in never stopping learning and always pushing the limits of what can be done. Let this guide be your jumping-off point for your work with LLM, and together, let us unlock the amazing potential of these models.

Understanding the challenges of LLM experimentation

LLM experimentation poses unique challenges, including data preprocessing complexities, resource-intensive training requirements, and model evaluation intricacies. Understanding these challenges is crucial for developing effective experimentation strategies. While LLMs offer immense potential, effectively experimenting with them presents unique challenges. Here, we will delve into some of the key hurdles researchers and users face in the LLM experimentation landscape:

- **Non-deterministic outputs**: Traditionally, the running of computer programs follows deterministic behavior. On the other hand, language models do not behave deterministically. LLMs can be given the same prompt, but their output could be different based on usage. Hence, the phenomenon is called non-deterministic. The reason behind it is that the language model is inherently statistical and hence its behavior depends on internal statistical processes. This makes arguments like the replicability of results or the making of definitive conclusions from the experiments hard to win.

- **Black box nature**: LLMs are often like black box systems, meaning you cannot understand the internal behavior of a model and how things are constructed there. This loss of interpretability affects the debugging process and restricts the disclosure of language generation biases and errors.

- **Data bias**: LLMs learn from huge datasets, which can have biases. These biases can affect the LLM's answers, showing up as wrong facts, unfair language, or repeating stereotypes. Mitigating data bias requires careful selection of training data and vigilant evaluation of outputs. One golden quote is: Humans are biased, so machines will be biased, too, because humans create the prompts.

- **Factual accuracy and hallucination**: LLMs can sometimes generate text that appears plausible but lacks factual grounding. This phenomenon, hallucination, can lead researchers and users astray if factual accuracy is paramount in the experiment. Techniques like RAG Evaluation and human verification will help in this case.

- **Example of hallucination**

  a. Question: "Who won the Nobel Prize in Literature in 2023?"

  b. Hallucinated response by LLM: "The Nobel Prize in Literature in 2023 was awarded to the renowned African author *Fatima Bianco* for her novel *Echoes of the Forgotten*.

  From the above response, we can see LLM made a mistake because of its limited knowledge. There is no record of a person named Fatima Bianco winning the Nobel Prize in Literature in 2023 or even existing as a prominent author. The novel Echoes of the Forgotten is also a fabrication.

- **Evaluating creativity and originality**: The creativity and originality of LLM outputs, particularly in creative tasks like writing poems or code, can be subjective. Defining clear evaluation metrics for these tasks is an ongoing challenge, and human judgment often plays a significant role.

- **Resource constraints**: Training and running LLMs can be computationally expensive, requiring significant computing power and resources. This can limit access to experimentation for smaller research groups or individuals.

- **Safety and security concerns**: Safety and security concerns: As LLMs become more advanced, worries arise about their misuse. They might create harmful content or leak personal data like names or health info like leakage of **Personally Identifiable Information (PII)** or **Protected Health Information (PHI)** data. It's important to have rules and protections to reduce these risks.

- **Evolving technology**: The field of LLM development undergoes constant evolution, with new models and architectures emerging rapidly. Keeping up with these advancements and changing experimental techniques is a tough job.

- **Legal and ethical considerations**: Using LLMs raises legal and ethical questions. These include copyright issues, plagiarism, deep fakes, hallucination, fake news, and possible misuse. Clear rules for using LLMs responsibly are very important.

- **Human oversight and collaboration**: While LLMs offer powerful capabilities, human oversight and collaboration remain crucial. Researchers and users need to evaluate LLM outputs critically, guide through prompts, and ensure that LLMs are used for beneficial purposes.

Preparing data for LLM experimentation

Data preprocessing plays a critical role in LLM experimentation. This section explores techniques for data cleaning, tokenization, and augmentation to improve model performance and efficiency. Effective LLM experimentation hinges on high-quality data. Like building a strong foundation for a house, well-prepared data sets the stage for successful LLM interactions. Here are essential tips to ensure your data is primed for optimal LLM experimentation:

- **Data selection and curation**:
  - o **Task relevance**: When considering task relevance, the selection of data must precisely match the intended function of the LLM. For example, when training an LLM for code generation, utilizing data centered around code becomes imperative. Conversely, a varied and extensive literary collection would serve better for endeavors in creative writing.

  - o **Quality control**: A meticulous data assessment is essential to detect errors, disparities, and omissions. Ensuring the data maintains proper formatting and follows a coherent structure is paramount. Employing tools designed for data cleansing and pre-processing can immensely benefit this aspect.

  - o **Diversity and balance**: Strive for a diverse dataset that reflects the real-world complexities of the task. This helps the LLM avoid biases present in skewed data. If your initial data lacks diversity, consider techniques like data augmentation to artificially create a more balanced dataset.

- **Data preprocessing techniques**:
  - o **Text cleaning**: Remove irrelevant information like punctuation, special characters, HTML tags for text-based data etc. Normalization techniques like lowercasing or stemming words should be considered to improve consistency.

  - o **Tokenization**: Break down text data into smaller units like words or sub-words (tokens) that the LLM can understand and process effectively. **https://platform. openai.com/tokenizer** is a good website to visualize how tokenization works.

  - o **Text encoding**: Text encoding involves converting textual tokens into numerical representations to facilitate efficient processing by LLMs. Techniques such as word embedding or one-hot encoding can be utilized.

  - o **Data augmentation**: Data augmentation becomes necessary when dealing with a limited dataset. You can artificially expand the dataset's size and diversity by employing augmentation techniques. This can entail methods like synonym replacement, back-translation, or random shuffling.

- **Additional considerations**:
  - o **Data labeling (if applicable):** For tasks requiring labeled data (for example, sentiment analysis), ensure the labels are accurate and consistent. Consider employing multiple annotators to mitigate bias in labeling.

- o **Data splitting**: Segment your prepared data into three subsets: training, validation, and testing. The training subset educates the LLM, while the validation subset aids in refining hyperparameters. Lastly, the testing subset assesses the LLM's ultimate efficacy. A common way to split data is to use 80% for training, 10% for validation, and 10% for testing.

- o **Data versioning**: Carefully keep track of changes to your data so you can return to earlier versions if needed. This helps ensure your work can be repeated and makes fixing problems easier.

- **Tools and resources**:

  - o Numerous open-source libraries and tools exist to facilitate data preprocessing for LLMs. Popular options include unstructured, **Natural Language Toolkit (NLTK)**, and spaCy for Python.

  - o Consider cloud-based platforms offering data preprocessing and management services for LLMs, especially if dealing with large datasets.

By meticulously preparing your data using these tips, you will equip your LLM with the foundation it needs to learn effectively, generate accurate outputs, and, ultimately, unlock its full potential in your experiments. Remember, high-quality data is the cornerstone of successful LLM experimentation.

Optimizing model architecture and hyperparameters

Choosing the appropriate model structure and adjusting hyperparameters are pivotal to attaining peak performance. This section delves into tips for selecting architecture, fine-tuning hyperparameters, and capitalizing on preexisting models. Let us take a look at them:

- **Understanding model architecture**:

  - o **Model framework:** This outlines the blueprint of the LLM, including the type of neural network used (like Transformer, Recurrent Neural Network), the number of layers, and connections between layers. Different architectures all have their strengths and weaknesses across many tasks.

  - o **Performance implication:** The selected architecture profoundly influences the LLM's capacity to grasp intricate data relationships and produce precise outcomes.

- **Optimizing model architecture**:

  - o **Start with established architectures:** Initiate the quest by examining renowned LLM frameworks like Transformer models, renowned for their versatility across assorted tasks. These pre-trained models furnish a robust groundwork for customization.

o **Consider task-specific architectures:** Frameworks: If your task needs special features, look into designs made for that purpose. For example, convolutional layers can be helpful for jobs involving image understanding

o **Experiment with variations:** Once comfortable, experiment with architectural variations. This could involve adjusting the number of layers, units per layer, or connection patterns. However, tracking changes and evaluating their impact on performance is crucial.

- **Hyperparameter tuning - The fine-tuning process:**

    o **Hyperparameters:** These constitute configurations within the model framework governing the learning procedure, yet they are not directly acquired from the data. Instances encompass learning rate, optimizer selection, and batch size.

    o **Impact on learning:** Hyperparameters significantly influence how effectively the LLM learns from the data. Tuning them can optimize the learning process and improve the model's performance.

- **Hyperparameter tuning techniques:**

    o **Grid search:** This methodical strategy assesses every conceivable combination of hyperparameter values within a predetermined scope. Nevertheless, it can entail substantial computational resources, particularly when dealing with many hyperparameters.

    o **Random search:** This method randomly samples hyperparameter values from a defined range. It can be more efficient for large search spaces but might miss optimal combinations.

    o **Bayesian optimization:** This advanced technique uses past evaluations to guide the search for promising hyperparameter combinations. It can be a good option for complex models with many hyperparameters.

- **Additional considerations:**

    o **Hardware constraints:** Consider your computational resources when choosing architecture and tuning hyperparameters. More complex architectures require significant computing power.

    o **Evaluation metrics:** Define clear metrics to evaluate the LLM's performance after each hyperparameter adjustment. This could involve accuracy, fluency, or task-specific metrics relevant to your application.

- **Collaboration and open-source resources:**

    o **Community collaboration:** Engage with the vibrant and cooperative LLM research community through online forums and scholarly articles to glean insights from others' encounters with model design and hyperparameter adjustment.

    o **Open-source tools:** Delve into open-source repositories and platforms such as TensorFlow or PyTorch, which furnish utilities and features for constructing and refining LLMs.

Through strategic refinement of model structure and meticulous hyperparameter tuning, you can unleash the full capabilities of your LLM. Remember that this journey is iterative, demanding experimentation, assessment, and enhancement. Embrace the spirit of exploration and contribute to the continual evolution of LLM research.

Efficient training strategies for LLMs

Training LLMs can be computationally expensive. This section explores techniques such as gradient accumulation, mixed-precision, and distributed training to accelerate training and reduce resource requirements. Here, we will explore efficient training strategies to maximize learning outcomes while minimizing resource consumption:

- **Data-centric strategies**:
  - o **Data curation and augmentation:** High-quality and diverse data are very important. Use data cleaning methods and think about data augmentation to improve your dataset and reduce biases. This can help improve learning efficiency.
  - o **Active learning:** Prioritize training on the most informative data points. Active learning techniques identify these points, allowing the LLM to focus its learning efforts on the data that will yield the most significant improvement.
  - o **Curriculum learning:** Introduce the LLM to concepts gradually, starting with simpler tasks and progressing to more complex ones. This structured approach allows for more efficient learning than throwing the LLM into the deep end with complex tasks from the outset.
- **Model-centric strategies**:
  - o **Transfer learning and fine-tuning:** Leverage pre-trained LLMs as a foundation. These models have already learned a vast amount of information from massive datasets. Fine-tuning a pre-trained LLM on your specific task can significantly reduce training time and improve performance compared to training from scratch.
  - o **Efficient model architectures:** Investigate model architectures tailored for efficiency. Approaches such as knowledge distillation entail condensing insights from a vast, pre-trained model into a more compact, resource-efficient model.
  - o **Gradient accumulation and early stopping:** Gradient accumulation facilitates training with extensive data batches, enhancing efficiency. Premature termination monitors the LLM's progress and halts training when marginal gains diminish, averting resource squandering.
- **Training optimization strategies**:
  - o **Gradient clipping:** This technique prevents exploding gradients, which can hinder training progress. It limits the magnitude of updates applied to the

model's weights, promoting stability and potentially improving training efficiency.

o **Mixed precision training:** Utilize mixed precision training techniques that leverage a combination of data types (for example, float16 and float32) during training. This can significantly reduce memory usage and potentially accelerate training speed on compatible hardware. Major libraries like Tensorflow, HuggingFace, etc. allow mixed precision training.

o **Parallelization and distributed training:** Distribute the training process across multiple GPUs or machines for massive datasets and complex models. This allows for parallel processing and significantly reduces training time. This approach requires expertise in distributed computing frameworks.

- **Crafting effective prompts:**

  o The prompt bridges you and the LLM, guiding it towards the desired outcome. Here is how to craft effective prompts in general as well as while using LangChain:

  o **Clarity and specificity:** Clearly articulate your goal. Instead of a vague prompt like "Write a poem," specify the poem's theme (for example, "Write a poem about nature's beauty").

  o **Context provision:** Provide relevant background information to contextualize the LLM's response. For instance, provide details about characters, setting, or plot if prompted for creative writing.

  o **Instruction tuning:** Use clear instructions that guide the LLM's response format. Examples include "Write a news article in a formal style" or "Generate a list of bullet points summarizing this topic."

  o **Example inspiration:** If applicable, provide examples to illustrate the desired response style or tone. This can be particularly helpful for creative tasks.

  o **Length and complexity:** Consider the LLM's capabilities and tailor the prompt length and complexity accordingly. Start with concise prompts and gradually increase complexity as you gain experience.

  o **Test and iterate:** Experiment with different prompts and iterate based on the model's responses to find the most effective prompt.

Evaluating and interpreting experimental results

Effectively evaluating and interpreting experimental results is crucial for deriving meaningful insights. This section discusses metrics for evaluating LLM performance and techniques for result interpretation. This section delves into strategies for assessing LLM performance and extracting meaningful knowledge from your experiments:

- **Defining success metrics**:
  - o **Task-specific measures:** Match your evaluation criteria to the specific task. For example, in question answering, it is very important to get the right information. Being smooth, creative, and true to the prompt matters most in creative writing.
  - o **Human evaluation:** Recognize the power of human judgment. Use human evaluators to check factual accuracy, coherence, and overall quality. These are areas where automated metrics might struggle.
  - o **Comparative analysis:** Where applicable, juxtapose the LLM's performance against a benchmark model or human proficiency in the identical task. This furnishes a valuable benchmark for appraising the LLM's efficacy.
- **Evaluating outputs for quality**:
  - o **Factual accuracy:** Verify the factual grounding of the generated text, especially for tasks involving information retrieval or question answering. Use credible sources to confirm the information presented by the LLM.
  - o **Internal consistency:** The LLM's output should be internally consistent, avoiding logical contradictions or factual inconsistencies within the generated text. Scrutinize the output for any illogical elements.
  - o **Coherence and cohesion:** Assess the overall flow and structure of the generated text. Does it present a clear and cohesive narrative or argument? Ensure the ideas flow logically and seamlessly.
  - o **Creativity and originality (if applicable):** For creative tasks, evaluate the LLM's ability to generate unique and engaging content that adheres to the prompt's style and tone. Look for fresh perspectives and unexpected ideas.
- **Interpreting results with caution**:
  - o **Understanding limitations:** LLMs are still under development and prone to biases and errors. Do not over-interpret results or treat them as absolute truths.
  - o **Identifying biases:** Be mindful of potential biases present in the data used to train the LLM or within the prompt itself. Evaluate the outputs for signs of bias and adjust your interpretation accordingly.
  - o **Contextualization:** Consider the context in which the LLM generated the output. The prompt, available information, and task all play a role in shaping the results. Interpret the outputs within this context.
- **Visualization techniques**:
  - o **Attention visualization:** If your LLM supports attention mechanisms, utilize visualization tools to understand which parts of the input data the LLM focused on when generating the output. This can provide insights into the LLM's reasoning process.

      o **Error analysis:** Closely examine cases where the LLM performed poorly. Identify the reasons for these errors (for example, factual inaccuracy, lack of coherence). This analysis can guide future experiment design and prompt refinement.

- **Sharing and collaboration**:
  - o **Reproducibility:** Make sure your experiments are clearly written down and can be repeated. This helps others check your results and use your work to make new discoveries.

  - o **Open-source tools:** Utilize and contribute to open-source libraries and tools designed for LLM evaluation and interpretation. This fosters collaboration and accelerates progress in the field.

By employing these evaluation and interpretation strategies, you can transform the raw outputs of your LLM experiments into valuable insights. Remember, effective LLM experimentation is an ongoing learning process. Embrace the iterative nature of evaluation, refine your techniques, and contribute to the ever-evolving field of LLM research.

Fine-tuning for specific applications

Fine-tuning LLMs for specific applications requires careful consideration of domain-specific data and objectives. This section provides tips for effective fine-tuning and transfer learning:

- **Understanding fine-tuning**:
  - o **Pre-trained foundation:** Fine-tuning leverages a pre-trained LLM as a foundation. These models, trained on massive datasets, possess a wealth of general language knowledge.

  - o **Targeted specialization or industry specific fine tuning:** Fine-tuning entails further training the LLM on a dataset tailored to your application's domain. This dataset hones the LLM's comprehension of the subject matter, its lexicon, and its capability to tackle tasks pertinent to that domain.

- **Benefits of fine-tuning**:
  - o **Enhanced performance:** A fine-tuned LLM often surpasses a generic pre-trained model for a specific application. Tailored training enables specialization in the designated task, resulting in heightened accuracy, improved task completion rates, and overall enhanced effectiveness.

  - o **Reduced training time:** Fine-tuning capitalizes on pre-existing knowledge, markedly diminishing the training period in contrast to training a model from scratch on your unique dataset. This facilitates expedited development cycles and swifter deployment of LLM-powered solutions.

  - o **Flexibility and adaptability:** The fine-tuning methodology permits adaptation to diverse applications. With varied datasets, you can fine-tune the same LLM for multiple tasks, maximizing the utility extracted from a single pre-trained model.

- **Examples of fine-tuning in action**:
  - **Machine translation:** An LLM can be fine-tuned on a dataset of translated documents for a specific language pair. This enhances its ability to translate text accurately and idiomatically within that specific context.

  - **Text summarization:** Fine-tuning a corpus of news articles or scientific papers allows the LLM to hold onto the nuances of different writing styles and generate concise summaries tailored to the type of text encountered.

  - **Code generation:** By fine-tuning a repository of code samples for a particular programming language, the LLM can adeptly generate code snippets based on natural language descriptions, substantially augmenting developer efficiency.

  - **Chatbots and virtual assistants:** LLMs fine-tuned on customer service conversations can power chatbots that understand user queries, respond appropriately, and provide helpful information or complete tasks.

- **Approaches to fine-tuning**:
  - **Data selection and preparation:** Data selection and preparation are crucial for successful fine-tuning. Start by gathering a high-quality, diverse dataset that fits your application's needs. Make sure the data is well-organized, possibly labeled, and free from biases that could harm the fine-tuned LLM's performance.

  - **Prompt engineering:** Creating clear prompts that clearly explain the task and desired output style greatly impacts how well a fine-tuned LLM works. Try different prompt formats to find the best one.

  - **Fine-tuning techniques:** Tailored to the task's complexity and dataset size, various fine-tuning methodologies can be employed. These techniques may encompass fine-tuning specific layers of the pre-trained model or retraining the entire model with a diminished learning rate.

Fine-tuning represents a potent tool for unlocking the genuine potential of LLMs in real-world scenarios. As LLM technology progresses, pre-trained models will exhibit greater versatility, and fine-tuning methodologies will continue to evolve. This progression will empower us to harness LLMs across an even broader spectrum of applications, pushing the boundaries of possibility across various domains.

Scaling up: Distributed training and parallel processing

Scaling LLM experimentation to large datasets and models often requires distributed training and parallel processing. Strategies for distributed training, model parallelism, and data parallelism are explored in this section. Let us take a look at them:

- **Understanding the bottlenecks**:
  - o **Massive datasets:** LLMs often require massive datasets for effective training. These datasets can strain the storage capacity of a single machine.
  - o **Complex model architectures:** Modern LLM architectures can have millions or even billions of parameters. Training such models on a single machine can be incredibly slow, taking days or even weeks.
  - o **Limited memory resources:** A single machine's memory might not be sufficient to store and process the intermediate calculations involved in training a large LLM.

- **Power of distributed training**:
  - o **Workload distribution:** Distributed training solves these problems by spreading the training process across many machines (nodes) working together. This helps manage large datasets and complex models by sharing the work among available resources.
  - o **Reduced training time:** By leveraging the combined processing power of multiple machines, distributed training significantly reduces the overall training time for LLMs. This translates to faster experimentation cycles and quicker deployments of LLM-powered solutions.
  - o **Scalability:** Distributed training offers remarkable scalability, allowing effortless addition or removal of nodes within the training cluster. This flexibility enables the scaling of the training process in accordance with the LLM's complexity and the dataset's magnitude.

- **Parallel processing techniques**:
  - o **Data parallelism:** This method partitions the training dataset into smaller segments and disperses them across distinct nodes. Each node trains the LLM on its allocated data segment, and subsequent results are amalgamated to update the global model parameters. Data parallelism stands as a prevalent and efficient technique for distributed training.
  - o **Model parallelism:** In this approach, the LLM model is fragmented into sub-components, with each sub-component assigned to a separate node. These nodes collaborate to concurrently train the complete model. Model parallelism proves particularly advantageous for exceedingly large models that surpass the memory capacity of a single machine.

- **Emerging techniques and future trends**:
  - o **Cloud-based training platforms:** Cloud platforms like Google Cloud TPUs, Anyscale or Amazon SageMaker offer readily available, scalable infrastructure for distributed LLM training. These platforms simplify the process and reduce the need for in-house cluster management.
  - o **Specialized hardware:** Hardware advancements like specialized AI accelerators and high-bandwidth networking solutions are constantly

improving, pushing the boundaries of what's possible in distributed LLM training. Nvidia is leading the race for deep learning and LLM related hardware solutions, holding a significant market share. As of June 2024, Nvidia held over 88% of the market share in the GPU segment [source **Jon Peddie Research (JPR)**], which is crucial for deep learning computations.

Distributed training and parallel processing techniques are essential tools for scaling up LLM training and unlocking their full potential. By leveraging these techniques, you can train complex models on massive datasets in a reasonable timeframe.

Deployment considerations for LLMs

Deploying LLMs in production environments necessitates meticulous attention to factors such as inference speed, model size, and hardware limitations. This segment delves into deployment strategies and optimization methodologies for achieving streamlined inference. Let us explore pivotal deployment considerations to ensure a seamless and triumphant LLM deployment:

- **Infrastructure and hardware**:
    - **Computational resources:** LLMs often impose substantial computational demands. When selecting deployment hardware, contemplate factors such as the LLM's size, anticipated user traffic, and latency requisites. Explore alternatives like GPUs, **Tensor Processing Units (TPUs)**, or cloud-based platforms offering scalable infrastructure.
    - **Storage needs:** Evaluate and assess the storage prerequisites for both the LLM model and any ancillary data essential for inference (generating predictions). Implement efficient storage solutions such as distributed file systems or cloud-based storage services.
    - **Monitoring and observability:** Deploy robust monitoring tools to track the LLM's performance in production. Monitor metrics like latency, accuracy, resource utilization, and potential errors. This allows for proactive identification and resolution of issues. Libraries like **Weights and biases (W&B)**, **Comet**, **MLFlow** etc. helps us to do the monitoring and observability of the LLM model.
- **Serving and inference**:
    - **Model optimization:** When preparing for production deployment, explore methods to streamline the LLM model for enhanced efficiency. This may entail employing techniques such as model pruning, quantization, or knowledge distillation to curtail the model size and bolster inference speed while upholding accuracy.
    - **Application Programming Interface (API) design:** Construct a meticulously crafted API facilitating seamless interaction with the LLM in a lucid and standardized manner. The API should proficiently manage inputs, outputs,

error handling, and requisite authentication mechanisms to ensure a smooth user experience.

o **Load balancing and scalability:** Design your deployment architecture to handle varying user loads. Implement load balancing techniques to distribute requests across multiple LLM instances if necessary. This ensures smooth operation even during peak traffic periods.

- **Security and privacy:**

    o **Data security:** Given the extensive data LLMs are typically trained on, prioritize robust security protocols to safeguard user data and thwart unauthorized access. Employ encryption methodologies and enforce stringent access controls to fortify sensitive data against breaches.

    o **Privacy considerations:** Exercise caution regarding potential privacy implications when deploying LLMs. When dealing with user data, follow relevant privacy rules. Use methods like anonymization or differential privacy to reduce privacy risks and protect user confidentiality.

    o **Bias and fairness:** As we quoted earlier, Humans are biased; hence, machines are going to be biased. Having said that, LLMs are susceptible to inheriting biases from their training data. Vigilantly monitor the LLM's outputs for signs of bias and adopt fairness mitigation measures when warranted. This may entail deploying debiasing techniques or retraining the LLM on more balanced datasets to promote equitable outcomes.

- **Monitoring and maintenance:**

    o **Performance monitoring:** Continuously monitor the LLM's performance in production. Track metrics like accuracy, latency, and resource usage to identify any performance degradation or potential issues.

    o **Model updates and refresher training:** As new data becomes available or the application requirements evolve, consider retraining or fine-tuning the LLM to maintain optimal performance. This ensures the LLM stays up-to-date and adapts to changing needs.

- **Version control and rollbacks:** Implement a version control system for your LLM deployments. This will allow you to track changes, revert to previous versions if necessary, and effectively manage rollouts of updated models.

By carefully considering these deployment factors, you can ensure a smooth transition for your LLM from the research environment to the real world. Remember, successful LLM deployment is an ongoing process that requires continuous monitoring, adaptation, and improvement.

Conclusion

In conclusion, this chapter has presented valuable tips and strategies for streamlining LLM experimentation. By implementing these methodologies, users can expedite their experimentation processes and endeavor to unlock the full capabilities of LLMs in natural language processing applications.

LLMs hold tremendous promise for reshaping various domains. By capitalizing on the strategies delineated in this guide, you can effectively harness their potential. From efficiently preparing data for experimentation to tactically deploying the LLM in real-world scenarios, each step contributes significantly to unleashing the genuine potential of these transformative models.

It is essential to remember that the landscape of Generative AI is continuously evolving, with new techniques and advancements emerging more rapidly than we ever thought possible. To remain at the forefront of this dynamic and exciting field, embrace a mindset of perpetual learning and exploration.

References

- https://www.techradar.com/computing/gpu/nvidia-now-owns-88-of-the-gpu-market-but-that-might-not-be-a-bad-thing-yet

Join our book's Discord space

Join the book's Discord Workspace for Latest updates, Offers, Tech happenings around the world, New Release and Sessions with the Authors:

https://discord.bpbonline.com

APPENDIX B

Resources and References

Introduction

This chapter is an appendix. It is a valuable resource to the main text. It contains a list of resource links. These resources will help you understand the book's topics even more. These materials are carefully curated. They are here to help you dive deeper into the concepts the book introduces. They will also help you see the big picture. Plus, they will make your own research easier. Ready to explore these resources and dive deeper into learning?

Books and articles

- "Natural Language Processing with Transformers" by *Lewis Tunstall, Leandro von Werra*, and *Thomas Wolf*.

  o An in-depth exploration of using transformer models, specifically those provided by Hugging Face, for various NLP tasks.

  o Link to the book- **https://www.oreilly.com/library/view/natural-language-processing/9781098136789/**

- "Deep Learning for Natural Language Processing" by *Jason Brownlee*

  o A practical book that covers deep learning techniques for NLP, providing foundational knowledge that complements the use of LangChain and Hugging Face tools.

o Link to the book: **https://books.google.co.in/books?id=_ pmoDwAAQBAJ&printsec=copyright&redir_ esc=y#v=onepage&q&f=false**

- "Transformers for Natural Language Processing" by *Denis Rothman*
  - o Focuses on transformer architectures and their applications in NLP, providing insights into building effective models with Hugging Face.
  - o Link to the book:- **https://www.amazon.in/Transformers-Natural-Language-Processing-architectures-ebook/dp/B08S977X8K**

Research papers

- "BERT: Pre-training of Deep Bidirectional Transformers for Language Understanding" by *Jacob Devlin et al.*
  - o The foundational paper on BERT, which underpins many models available through Hugging Face.
- "Attention is All You Need" by *Ashish Vaswani et al.*
  - o Introduces the transformer model architecture, which is fundamental to understanding modern NLP models.
- "GPT-3: Language Models are Few-Shot Learners" by *Tom B. Brown et al.*
  - o Discusses the architecture and capabilities of GPT-3, a model accessible via Hugging Face.
- "RoBERTa: A Robustly Optimized BERT Pretraining Approach" by *Yinhan Liu et al.*
  - o Explores improvements over the original BERT model, leading to more robust and efficient NLP applications.
- "XLNet: Generalized Autoregressive Pretraining for Language Understanding" by *Zhilin Yang et al.*
  - o Presents an alternative to BERT with improved performance on various NLP benchmarks.
- "Retrieval-Augmented Generation for Knowledge-Intensive NLP Tasks" by *Patrick Lewis et al.* (**https://arxiv.org/abs/2005.11401v4**)
  - o Advanced large language models can store and use facts to perform language tasks well, but struggle with detailed knowledge tasks. By merging these models with a system that can retrieve information from sources like Wikipedia, they perform better on complex tasks and produce more accurate, varied language.
- "Merging Mixture of Experts and Retrieval Augmented Generation for Enhanced Information Retrieval and Reasoning" by *Xiong, Xingyu & Zheng, Mingliang.* (2024). Merging Mixture of Experts and Retrieval Augmented Generation for Enhanced Information Retrieval and Reasoning. 10.21203/rs.3.rs-3978298/v1

o This study integrates **Retrieval Augmented Generation (RAG)** into the Mistral 8x7B LLM with **Mixture of Experts (MoE)**, resulting in significant improvements in complex information retrieval and reasoning tasks, as demonstrated by enhanced metrics on the Google BIG-Bench dataset. The findings highlight a pivotal advancement in AI research, showcasing the potential for more adaptable and intelligent AI systems, while acknowledging dataset scope and computational limitations.

LangChain resources

- **LangChain documentation:**
  o **https://python.langchain.com/v0.2/docs/introduction/**
  o The official LangChain documentation provides a comprehensive guide to installation, core concepts, and how to use LangChain for various tasks.
- **LangChain tutorials:**
  o **https://python.langchain.com/v0.2/docs/tutorials/**
  o Dive deeper with LangChain tutorials covering specific use cases and applications.
- **LangChain: Building Autonomous Agents with LangChain:**
  o **https://js.langchain.com/v0.1/docs/use_cases/autonomous_agents/**
  o Guide and insights on building autonomous agents using LangChain.
- **Advanced RAG-based chatbot using LangChain:**
  o **https://huggingface.co/learn/cookbook/en/advanced_rag**
  o Advanced RAG with Vector database using LangChain.

Hugging Face resources

- **Hugging Face Transformers library:**
  o **https://huggingface.co/docs/transformers/en/index**
  o The Hugging Face Transformers library is a fundamental resource for working with LLMs. It provides pre-trained models, training tools, and functionalities for various NLP tasks.
- **Hugging Face Model Hub:**
  o **https://huggingface.co/docs/hub/en/index**
  o Discover and explore a vast collection of pre-trained LLM models for numerous languages and tasks.
- **Hugging Face Tutorials:**
  o **https://huggingface.co/learn/nlp-course/chapter1/1**

- o Broaden your knowledge with Hugging Face's collection of tutorials on various NLP concepts and applications using Transformers.
- **Hugging Face Datasets:**
  - o https://huggingface.co/datasets
  - o It provides links of datasets which are available for free to use by the AI ML researcher's community.
- **Hugging Face Course:**
  - o https://huggingface.co/course/chapter1
  - o This course will teach you about **natural language processing (NLP)** using libraries from the Hugging Face ecosystem, including Transformers, Datasets, Tokenizers, and Accelerate, as well as the Hugging Face Hub. It's completely free and has no ads.
- **Transformers Introduction**:
  - o **Quickstart — transformers 2.9.1 documentation (huggingface.co)**
  - o QuickStart guide for setting up and using Hugging Face Transformers.
- **Fine-tuning a Transformer Model**:
  - o https://huggingface.co/transformers/training.html
  - o Detailed instructions on how to fine-tune Transformer models on customized datasets.
- **Hugging Face Example Notebooks**:
  - o https://github.com/huggingface/notebooks
  - o Example Jupyter notebooks covering various NLP tasks using Hugging Face Transformers.

Alternative resources to LangChain

- **Haystack:**
  - o **Haystack documentation:**
    - ▪ **https://haystack.deepset.ai/**
    - ▪ The official documentation for the Haystack framework, covering setup, usage, and advanced features.
  - o **GitHub repository for Haystack:**
    - ▪ **https://github.com/deepset-ai/haystack**
    - ▪ The public GitHub repository for Haystack, providing source code, examples, and contribution guidelines.
  - o **Integrating RAG with Haystack:**
    - ▪ **https://haystack.deepset.ai/tutorials/27_first_rag_pipeline**
    - ▪ Tutorial explaining how to set up and use RAG within the Haystack framework.

- o **Haystack blog:**
  - **https://haystack.deepset.ai/blog/tags/retrieval**
  - Advances in Retrieval-Augmented Generation - Blog post discussing recent advancements in Retrieval-Augmented Generation using Haystack.
- o **Haystack tutorials and examples:**
  - **https://haystack.deepset.ai/tutorials**
  - A collection of tutorials and example projects demonstrating various use cases of Haystack.
- o **Building QA systems with Haystack:**
  - **https://haystack.deepset.ai/tutorials/01_basic_qa_pipeline**
  - Comprehensive guide on building question-answering systems using Haystack.
- o **Haystack Slack community**:
  - **https://slack.com/apps/ASQ2GCA77-haystack**
  - Join the Haystack community on Slack to discuss issues, ask questions, and share knowledge.
- o **Haystack GitHub discussions:**
  - **https://github.com/deepset-ai/haystack/discussions**
  - A place to discuss future versions and issues related to Haystack on GitHub.
- **LlamaIndex:**
  - o **LlamaIndex documentation:**
    - **https://docs.llamaindex.ai/en/latest/module_guides/loading/documents_and_nodes/**
    - Comprehensive guide on using LlamaIndex for various applications, including detailed instructions and examples.
  - o **GitHub repository for LlamaIndex:**
    - **https://github.com/run-llama/llama_index**
    - Access the source code, contribute to development, and find detailed usage examples for LlamaIndex.
  - o **LlamaIndex tutorial:**
    - **https://docs.llamaindex.ai/en/stable/getting_started/starter_example/**
    - **https://www.llamaindex.ai/blog/introducing-llama-agents-a-powerful-framework-for-building-production-multi-agent-ai-systems** Getting Started - Step-by-step tutorial for beginners to set up and start using LlamaIndex effectively and how to use LLaMA index Agent system. **Using LlamaIndex with Hugging Face transformers:**

- https://docs.llamaindex.ai/en/stable/examples/llm/huggingface/
- Guide on integrating LlamaIndex with Hugging Face Transformers for enhanced NLP tasks.

o **Blog:**
  - https://docs.llamaindex.ai/en/latest/getting_started/concepts/
  - LlamaIndex for Retrieval-Augmented Generation - Blog post covering the application of LlamaIndex in RAG tasks, highlighting its features and benefits.

o **LlamaIndex model card:**
  - Detailed model card providing specifications, intended uses, limitations, and ethical considerations for LlamaIndex. LlamaIndex Model Card.

Community and support

- **Forums and discussion boards:**
  - o Hugging Face Forums: Community forum for discussing Hugging Face's tools and asking questions. **https://discuss.huggingface.co/**
  - o LangChain GitHub Discussions: Platform for engaging with the LangChain community and developers. **https://github.com/hwchase17/langchain/discussions**
- **Social media and blogs:**
  - o Hugging Face on Twitter: **https://twitter.com/huggingface**
  - o Hugging Face Blog: Blog featuring articles, tutorials, and announcements related to Hugging Face. **https://huggingface.co/blog/**
  - o LangChain Blog Posts on Medium: A collection of blog posts discussing LangChain's latest developments and use cases., **https://medium.com/@langchain/**

Other important resources

- **Official MLflow documentation:** Comprehensive guide on managing the ML life cycle with MLflow, including experiment tracking and model deployment of LLM models. **https://mlflow.org/docs/latest/llms/index.html**
- RAGAS a framework to evaluate RAG pipelines **https://docs.ragas.io/en/stable/**

Conclusion

We trust you have found this book both enlightening and enjoyable as we navigated the theoretical and practical realms of constructing a RAG-based chatbot using Hugging Face and LangChain. We hope you find value in this resource, and we kindly encourage you to share it with your peers, helping us extend its reach and success.

Index

Made in United States
Troutdale, OR
12/05/2024

25898687R00210